Changing the Rules of the Game

Changing the Rules of the Game

Economic, Management and Emerging Issues in the Computer Games Industry

Edited by

Sabine Hotho
Dundee Business School, University of Abertay Dundee, UK

and

Neil McGregor
Dundee Business School, University of Abertay Dundee, UK

First published 2013 by
PALGRAVE MACMILLAN

Palgrave Macmillan in the UK is an imprint of Macmillan Publishers Limited,
registered in England, company number 785998, of Houndmills, Basingstoke,
Hampshire RG21 6XS.

Palgrave Macmillan in the US is a division of St Martin's Press LLC,
175 Fifth Avenue, New York, NY 10010.

Palgrave Macmillan is the global academic imprint of the above companies
and has companies and representatives throughout the world.

Palgrave® and Macmillan® are registered trademarks in the United States,
the United Kingdom, Europe and other countries.

ISBN 978-1-349-33819-1   ISBN 978-1-137-31841-1 (eBook)
DOI 10.1057/9781137318411

This book is printed on paper suitable for recycling and made from fully
managed and sustained forest sources. Logging, pulping and manufacturing
processes are expected to conform to the environmental regulations of the
country of origin.

A catalogue record for this book is available from the British Library.

A catalog record for this book is available from the Library of Congress.

Typeset by MPS Limited, Chennai, India.

Contents

List of Figures and Tables

Figures

Tables

Notes on Contributors

Katherine Champion is Research Associate at the Centre for Cultural Policy Research, University of Glasgow on an ESRC-funded project 'Multi-platform Media and the Digital Challenge: Strategy, Distribution and Policy'. Her research interests include the spatial organization of creative and digital media industries, creative industries policy and creative cities and multi-platform media strategy. She holds a PhD from the Department of Urban Studies, University of Glasgow.

Jordi Comas is Assistant Professor at Bucknell University and specializes in networks, institutions and organization theory. He holds an MA in Sociology from the University of Virginia and a PhD in Management from IESE/Universidad de Navarra. He likes to apply his theoretical 'toolkit' to areas as varied as virtual worlds, nation-building in the Balkans and student-run companies.

Gill Homan is Associate Lecturer (formerly Principal Lecturer) at Manchester Metropolitan University and freelance consultant specializing in individual and group development and reward systems development. She is currently involved in the development of an online business game linking HR decisions with business strategy.

Sabine Hotho is Professor in Strategic and Change Management and Head of the Dundee Business School at the University of Abertay Dundee. She has published in the fields of critical management, public sector management and change management. Her current research addresses the organizational and management practices in the digital games industry.

Neil McGregor is Division Leader of the Accounting, Finance and Economics Division at the University of Abertay Dundee, and Lecturer in Economics and Finance. His interests include energy investment and risk management, local economic development and high-tech cluster development (e.g. computer games industry and links to higher education and the role and impact of higher education in economic development) and labour market and skills analysis.

Wallace McNeish is Division Leader of the Sociology Division at the University of Abertay Dundee. In the past he has researched and published on social movements and political protest, and on young people, education and labour market transitions. His current research interests include the creative industries, digital cultures and contemporary apocalypticism.

Joe Nandhakumar is Professor of Information Systems at Warwick Business School, University of Warwick. He has a PhD in Management Information Systems from the University of Cambridge. His primary research interest focuses on the interrelationship between people in organizations and information technology, and its implications for the nature of work and the design and use of information systems.

Nicola Searle specializes in intellectual property and the creative industries and is an economic advisor in the UK Intellectual Property Office. Prior to joining the Government Economic Service, she was a researcher at the Institute for Arts, Media & Computer Games at the University of Abertay Dundee where she analyzed business models and digital media. In addition, she researched film distribution and intellectual property in the Scottish creative industries at the Institute for Capitalizing on Creativity, University of St Andrews. She holds an MSc in International Strategy and Economies and a PhD in Economics from the University of St Andrews.

Sue Shaw is Head of the Department of Management and Associate Dean, Learning and Teaching at Manchester Metropolitan University Business School. Her teaching and research interests are in international HRM/HRD, individual performance and women in management, and she is currently researching the development experiences of women expatriates.

Patrick Stacey is Lecturer in Information Systems and a Co-Director of the HighWire doctoral programme at Lancaster University. He is also Chapter convener of TIGA at Lancaster University. His general research focus is on the socio-technical dynamics of IS development in computer game contexts. He is currently investigating creative well-being in a national study of UK computer game studios.

David Thomas is undertaking a PhD on Lancaster University's HighWire doctoral programme. In the past his research has focused on workplace well-being and game development. He is currently investigating the information ecologies that arise following natural disasters, with a particular focus on communities affected by regional flooding in the United Kingdom.

Feichin (Ted) Tschang is Associate Professor of Strategic Management at Singapore Management University. His research focuses on product development in the video games industry and in particular on theories of creativity and design. He also studies the design and organizational practices of communities of practice in virtual world environments based on user-generated content.

Gregor White is Director of Academic Enterprise in the Institute of Arts, Media and Computer Games at the University of Abertay Dundee. His work includes research and development with games companies and broadcast organizations in relation to user engagement and audience innovation. He currently leads a project aimed at developing audience engagement strategies through the co-creation of content with creative media companies.

Timothy L. Wilson is Adjunct Professor of Marketing and Management at the Umeå School of Business and Economics (USBE), Sweden. He was previously Professor of Marketing at Clarion University, Clarion, PA, USA. His research interests are in the general areas of business services, project organizations and management, international business and regional development. On an annual basis he offers a PhD course in academic writing and works with faculty and staff at USBE on their writing and publication efforts.

Peter Zackariasson is Associate Professor of Marketing at University of Gothenburg, School of Business, Economics and Law. Since 2001 he has studied the video games industry and published articles and books on leadership, creativity and marketing. His current research interests focus on marketing practices in the cultural industries and sponsorship practices in motorsports.

Introduction: Emerging Perspectives on an Emerging Industry

Sabine Hotho and Neil McGregor

Introduction

Few industries fit the description of high turbulence and high velocity (Eisenhardt, 1989) better than the computer games industry. It is relatively young, rapidly evolving and frequently experiencing disruptive innovation. These disruptions create new opportunities as they lower entry barriers and reduce the cost of distribution and production. The pace of technological change and the options it affords have generated a spate of business model innovations as gamers embrace freemium, Free2Play, virtual currencies and micro-transactions to participate in online and social network games. And with open innovation and crowd funding becoming regular means of generating and extending products or accessing finance, the potential for growth and business opportunities seems barely exhausted.

Prospects for computer games look promising indeed. The industry's growth trajectory remains exceptional as technological advances relating to platforms, their capacities and functionalities, and their potential for compatibility are unpredictable. Indeed, throughout the current economic crisis, the global games industry has grown by nearly 23 per cent, with different segments growing at different rates (TIGA, 2012). The Institute of Audiovisual Affairs and Telecommunications in Europe (IDATE – Institut de l'Audiovisuel et des Télécommunications en Europe) has predicted double-digit growth by 2015 in digital games and, significantly, in the serious games market (Michaud, 2012). Online and wireless games have seen undiminished growth in demand and are predicted to be 36 per cent larger by 2016 than the video games segment (PricewaterhouseCoopers, 2011), but confidence remains that new generations of consoles will allow that sector, too, to rebound with refreshed energy.

1

Dematerialization of development and distribution have enabled developers to move into emerging markets where hand-held devices are the platform of choice, thus opening the space for a new generation of business that is independent of conventional channels. This combines with the generation shift in established markets where the first generation of gamers and game developers has matured, thus extending the potential market for games across at least three generations. Commitment to substantial tax breaks in, for instance, Canada, France, Singapore, the United States and, since spring 2012, the United Kingdom recognize the economic contribution and significance of the digital games industry for purposes of regional and national economic growth, high value-adding employment creation and talent retention. Business birth rates reflect the undiminished vitality of an opportunity-rich industry, reported on in digitally distributed *fora* such as *GamesIndustryInternational,* and on an almost daily basis.

Projected growth rates confirm the significance of the digital games industry as a key contributor to the economy, regionally and globally. Value loss in segments such as video games will be compensated for by the seemingly unstoppable value creation in the online games market (Michaud, 2012). But that applies only, of course, if value creation is defined by global spent and other measures of market size and share. Put differently, such global optimism hides much variation in company fate and fortune that is often overlooked. The business growth rate of games developers, for instance, remains of concern to policy makers, and the industry is overpopulated with micro-enterprises. The verdict on business success is mixed. Some report below-average business survival rates for the industry (Reid *et al.,* 2010) or an equal balance of business birth and business death rates, and hence only limited replenishment of the sector (TIGA, 2012). Industry *fora* report steadily on both new ventures and business exits, and so far the cost of this churn has not been established. The pace of technology changes and ever new route-to-market opportunities will ensure that overall value generation can be sustained. But the same opportunities also create an adapt-or-perish imperative for all actors in the industry. At times it seems that value generation follows a revolving-door principle as current players exit and new players – or new reconfigurations of existing players – enter (or re-enter) the industry. At what cost is not known.

Increased competition is indeed a main issue for this highly polarized yet increasingly crowded industry (Kerr, 2006). Large studios can use their intellectual property (IP) to build and extend their brand and invest in risky new ventures. Scale allows efficiencies, and production costs can be reduced by revisiting classics rather than developing new IP. Whether larger players can build future growth on this model is, however, increasingly questioned by insider experts. The spiralling cost of games development may well herald the end of the blockbuster game and the focus on much hyped launches and speed up the search for faster, quicker and more provisional forms of game development and gaming. Companies such as Zynga, Playfish or Mind Candy have introduced an entirely different approach to gaming that positively eliminates the boundaries between game development and finished game (Lovell, 2010). Open innovation and coproduction help smaller developers to engage directly with their current and future customers, and through building their feedback directly into the development process a new form of game ownership can be developed. The future, as Lovell (2010) assures us, is 'very very bright'. But it is not equally bright for all. Small developers will remain vulnerable and competition from micro-firms exploiting the lowered entry barriers afforded by new platforms and direct routes to market will grow. We need look no further than the AppStore where up to 300 apps are released every day. Of these, 75 per cent make less than $18,000, and of these 2 per cent make less than $120 (Rawlings, 2012). Whether this affords a basis for sustained business remains to be seen. It will certainly be the basis for ever new business creation.

In the current economic climate, the games industry thus remains a promising but increasingly more difficult entrepreneurial space to be in. Rich in entrepreneurial opportunity, it is a challenging space to survive in. It is perhaps time to move towards an analytical space where we combine the examination of trends, innovations and business opportunities with an examination of business, organizational and societal challenges. Michaud (2012) rightly suggests that success in the games industry depends on four elements: business model, content, marketing and communications, and technical services. These tasks are often underestimated in the day-to-day work of development studios. And this shifts the focus away from the market and the firms that populate it to the games studio as a commercial organization, to its management capacity and capabilities and the ways in which management practices interact with industry, consumer and societal trends, on the one hand, and the needs and aspirations of those working in games development and production, on the other.

A broader perspective on the computer games industry is required, and recent examples of changing company fate and fortune confirm this. When Dundee-based Realtime Worlds collapsed spectacularly in 2010 (see also McGregor, this volume), its failure was quickly attributed to spiralling production costs and technical delays that had been hampering the development of APB, the company's much talked about new game. But within days the blogger scene exposed management blind spots, poor project controls and internal tensions as indicative of a business struggling to survive. This suggests a need to debate the contingencies and challenges of management practice in this fast-moving industry and to address the concerns expressed with regard to the homogeneous nature of the workforce, pressurized work practices, project work and other aspects of internal organization. The question arises whether the games industry faces distinct business and management challenges or whether these are the same as those faced by other industries, albeit at a faster pace, or in more exacerbated forms.

It is not possible to write a definitive account of the games industry, nor should this be attempted. But as the industry matures, such debates are expanding and highlighting the many different strands of research that require to be integrated in this context. In this introduction, we have briefly mentioned some of the challenges and polarities that characterize the games industry. We have considered business trends and have pointed towards the need to consider the managerial and organizational aspects of the industry. And we argue that no discussion of the computer games industry should leave out a consideration of its wider and societal impact, its production processes, or the pervasiveness of its products and the nature of their consumption. Few industries if any have been so forcefully accompanied by a simultaneous self-produced and self-published discourse. Online *fora,* networks, blogs and consultancies accompany the ups, downs and sideways moves of games developers, technologies and products. The discourse is self-reflexive, predictive, prescriptive as well as celebratory, with speculation about future opportunities endemic. It fundamentally contributes to the confident (self)-construction of the industry, the identity of its actors and its consumers. To further our understanding of the industry, we should thus combine the robust analysis of business intelligence, industry trends, management and organizational dimensions, and a critical perspective that enables an additional and deeper layer of insight. The games industry is as much a concrete phenomenon arising from economic and technological opportunities, generating value, wealth and employment, as a self-constituting institutionalizing phenomenon, and a cultural phenomenon that shapes and is shaped by the behaviours of those who make and play the games and those who try to escape them.

This volume aims to make a contribution to this emerging debate. We set out by defining and commissioning chapters to capture the width of issues that need to be addressed. Within their wider brief, authors were encouraged to shape their perspectives and to formulate their own standpoints. The end result is a set of contributions that are as diverse as the subject they are tasked to cover. Throughout the volume enthusiasm for the industry and confidence in its prospects is expressed, but no chapter expresses merely unbridled optimism. A need for critical reflection, the awareness of a significant and potentially constraining self-construction effort, reflections on business and management capability and short-comings are similarly present, at times explicit, at times as an undercurrent. That, precisely, is what we had hoped to achieve. The chapters, while not explicitly linked, present a narrative of the games industry as an emerging industry but also one poised to step beyond the sphere of gaming.

In Chapter 1 Katherine Champion situates the computer games industry within the broader creative industries sector to explore whether the same spatial logic applies to both narrower and broader categories. In the absence of detailed research, Champion suggests that the spatial logic of the games sector is more distinct from established patterns of the wider creative sector than is assumed, with location patterns being determined at times more by rationalizations or acquisitions than by cluster factors such as networks and sharing of ideas. Pointing out social (and self-)construction efforts evident in the sector, she concludes that while aggregating industry sectors under the wide creative industries sector might serve politics, a more differentiating understanding of the spatial logic of the games sector might yield better policy.

Policy makers recognize the role of the games industry in the context of regional economic growth. But recognition and exploitation of growth potential comes from within. Gregor White and Nicola Searle, in Chapter 2, relate the games industry and its potential for growth and the wide-ranging and technology-facilitated opportunities for business model innovation. User-generated content and modding, for instance, are binding the consumer-gamer as a co-producer into the games value chain, and this requires the games industry to opt for flexible and changeable business models that are reflective of changing user demographics and the consequences of disruptive technologies. These in particular challenge conventional fee or subscription models and non-responsive pricing strategies and will continue to require continued adaptation as the games industry continues to evolve.

In Chapter 3, Peter Zackariasson and Timothy L. Wilson expand further on the evolving and distinct relationship (and interdependence) between consumer, technology and developer/producer. Similarly to

White and Searle, they locate the consumer as co-producer at the heart of the games value chain, and trace the significant shift from consumer as recipient of products to consumer as co-producer. Combined with the argument that the games industry might be appropriately defined as a service industry that shares features with the tourism industry, they develop a strong case for the adoption of a marketing rather than production logic if businesses are to sustain their marketplace.

While the early chapters address the business opportunities in the computer games industry, Neil McGregor, in Chapter 4, adopts an opposite perspective. Using recent case studies of business failure and success, and general risk management literature, McGregor reminds us that businesses in the games industry, however distinct, share features and commonalities with businesses in any other sector.

In Chapter 5, Sabine Hotho combines internal and external business and organizational perspectives to address the issue of business sustainability. Hotho uses a social constructivist approach to debate to what extent managers' sense making produces and shapes the way games developers frame and respond to market opportunities as well as management challenges. Her case study provides insight into organizational reality where conflicting interests between commercial and proprietary work, creative freedom and managerial control need to be kept in an ever provisional balance.

Peter Zackariasson extends the focus on intraorganizational dimensions further in Chapter 6 and provides a discussion of creativity as the central ingredient of computer games development. He takes issue with a definition of creativity that presents production processes in the creative industries as distinct from other fields and argues that creativity can reside in all parts of a value chain. The chapter highlights the tension between experimental and institutionalized patterns of behaviour as much as the tensions between artistic and commercial interests. Drawing on Bourdieu's notions of habitus and field, Zackariasson offers an alternative framework for understanding the concept of creativity in the games industry.

Chapters 7 and 8 discuss the contingencies of human resource and people management and of working conditions in the industry. Sue Shaw and Gill Homan, in Chapter 7, discuss the emerging human resource issues and practices in an industry that is highly genderized, has a relatively young, well-educated and mobile workforce, and is fuelled by fast-paced change. Given the relative use of companies and their small size, HR professionals are still rare in the industry; yet challenges such as performance management, motivation and reward, employee and career development all need to be addressed. Shaw and Homan conclude that merely considering the industry as distinct might be as inadequate as the assumption that well-established HR practices can simply be incorporated into the routines of studio management. In Chapter 8, Patrick Stacey, David Thomas and Joe Nandhakumar use empirical data from two case studies to discuss the links between violent games content and worker well-being. The impact of violent games on users/players and their social behaviours has indeed been discussed widely. But how does the production of violent games affect those developing these? Using an interpretive model comprising social, psychological and physical dimensions of subjective well-being, the authors explore how studio workers make sense of, rationalize or otherwise legitimize the violence they build into a game, thus enabling the co-existence of violence and well-being.

Wallace McNeish, in Chapter 9, adds a critical sociological perspective. He addresses the industry's undiminishing efforts to construct itself in economic, cultural and socio-political terms as democratic, playful and as a progressive provider of social spaces, leisure, and cultural and educational services that can legitimately request continued policy support. Drawing on Bourdieu's notion of the charismatic ideology of creativity and Marx's notion of the fetish of commodity, and its distraction from the real social relations of production, McNeish arrives at a sophisticated critique. Computer games, defined as a phantasmagoric commodity, obscure their true nature as mass commodities produced by a powerful multinational industry. While they create near-transcendent experiences among their players, they are *also* the product of a discourse that uses creativity and culture as legitimizing brackets.

The final Chapter 10 extends the boundaries of the computer games phenomenon. Technology enables virtual social existence and a virtual space where true and imagined (playful) social encounters and economic activities can take place and avatars can assume the role of a forever evasive *doppelgänger*. Jordi Comas and Feichin Tschang trace the emergence of virtual worlds as synthetic and fabricated yet potentially real, and spaces where the boundaries between playful and real, fictional and factual realities blur. While intangible, virtual worlds, as the authors conclude, have histories of their own, and seemingly playful cyberspaces might assume a reality as real as the physical world.

References

Eisenhardt, K. (1989) Making fast strategic decisions in high-velocity environments, *Academy of Management Journal*, 32(3): 543–76.

Kerr, A. (2006) *The Business and Culture of Digital Games: Gamework/Gameplay*, London: Sage.

Lovell, N. (2010) The future of the games industry? It's in three parts, *GAMESbrief*, 13 October, http://www.gamesbrief.com/2010/10/the-future-of-the-games-industry-its-in-three-parts/.

Michaud, L. (2012) Crises and rebounds in the games industry, *Digiworld by Idate*, http://www.idate.org/en/News/Crises-and-rebounds-in-the-games-industry-_773.html.

PricewaterhouseCoopers (2011) *Global Entertainment and Media Outlook 2011– 2015: Events and Trends*, ed. by D. Gilhawley, http://www.pwc.com/gx/en/entertainment-media/index.jhtml.

Rawlings, T. (2012) From paper to digital: The Cthulhu strategy of games development, *gamesindustry International*, http://www.gamesindustry.biz/articles/2012-05-04-from-paper-to-digital-the-cthulhu-strategy-of-games-development.

Reid, R., Morrow, T., Kelly, B. and McCartan, P. (2002) People management in SMEs: An analysis of human resource strategies in family and non-family businesses, *Journal of Small Business and Enterprise Development*, 9(3): 245–59.

TIGA (2012) TIGA promises successful future for UK games studios with targeted games tax relief, http://www.tiga.org/news/press-releases/tiga-promisessuccessful-future-for-uk-games-studios-with-targeted-games-tax-relief, 16 February 2012.

1
Problematizing a Homogeneous Spatial Logic for the Creative Industries: The Case of the Digital Games Industry

Katherine Champion

Introduction

The computer games industry can be regarded, in many ways, as a paradigmatic sector of the creative economy. It has been firmly on the policy agenda in the United Kingdom since New Labour's election in 1997 and, in particular, since 1998 with the inclusion of digital games as a sub-sector of creative industries as defined by the Creative Industries Task Force. Its high public profile has been justified by claims of economic weight and potential externalities (DCMS, 2012a; TIGA, 2012). As well as a belief that the sector can provide direct benefits to the economy, it is suggested that it also provides additional advantages through a multiplier effect and can even ameliorate the impact of the recent recession. In terms of policy interventions aimed at fostering growth within the computer games industry, many efforts have taken a spatially targeted focus including the funding and development of hubs and clusters. The rationale for this attention rests on a belief that the sector has a particular spatial logic in common with the wider creative industries, which preferences proximity and is subject to advantages of agglomeration. Despite a paucity of empirical research specifically reviewing the spatial rationale of the computer games sector, significant work has been undertaken to identify the location patterns within the wider creative economy. The existing research suggests that the creative industries have a dominant spatial rationale which tends to favour co-location, and that large metropolitan centres act as natural hubs of activity, but there remain gaps in the evidence base.

This chapter explores the emergence of the creative industries sector as a policy priority and then reviews the existing evidence of a common spatial rationale. The key attributes of the computer games industry are compared to those of the wider creative industries sector to determine if the former reflects the key characteristics seen to define the latter. Next, the existing empirical evidence regarding the spatial organization of the games sector is examined to determine convergence or deviation from the accepted creative industries logic. A scarcity of robust evidence is highlighted alongside an examination of some of the key challenges of researching the computer games industry and the wider creative industries sector. Finally, it is argued that a tendency towards the social construction of the sector as a discrete industry can do more to obscure than reveal trends, especially in a time of increasing convergence and digitization affecting the economy as a whole.

The development of the creative industries as a policy priority

The historiography of the current term creative industries began with Max Horkheimer's and Theodor Adorno's definition of the cultural industries (1944), which focused on industrially produced commercial entertainment as distinct from the subsidized arts sector. The term was deployed in an ironic fashion to demonstrate what they saw as the absorption of the arts within capitalist industry (Flew, 2002). Culture and industry were argued to be opposites and the term was used to express dissatisfaction with popular forms of culture such as magazines and films (UNCTAD, 2008). Similarly, and much later, the Greater London Council used the term cultural industries during the 1980s to emphasize the mass consumption and wealth creation of the cultural goods of the non-subsidized part of the sector (O'Connor, 2000).

The term creative industries first appeared in Australia in 1994 when *Creative Nation* was published, a report in which an Australian federal government developed, for the first time, a comprehensive cultural policy (UNCTAD, 2008); the term reached the United Kingdom in 1997, shortly after the election of New Labour, when the Department of Culture, Media and Sport (DCMS) was set up. The DCMS created the Creative Industries Task Force, which was mandated to define, map and measure the creative industries. Two mapping documents were published in 1998 and 2001 and significantly raised the profile of the sector (Oakley, 2004). These documents highlighted the economic weight and regenerative possibilities of the sector.

Britain's Creative Industries Task Force defined the creative industries as 'those activities which have their origin in individual creativity, skill and talent and which have a potential for wealth and job creation through the generation and exploitation of intellectual property' (DCMS, 2001: 3; 2011). This definition identifies the central role of intellectual property rights as the criterion for inclusion (Taylor, 2006). Though not universally accepted, this definition is commonly deployed in UK policy and academic discussion. It has been argued that the change in terminology from 'cultural' to 'creative' represented a repositioning towards the more universal and democratic connotations of creativity (Matarasso and Landry, 1999; O'Connor, 2000). It represents a move away from the traditional connotations of culture, which can be 'seen to reflect a top-down dispensation of elitist cultural values developed in the context of time and class, and which neglected or dismissed many forms of cultural expression and identity' (Matarasso and Landry, 1999: 13).

The sector has risen substantially in profile in the United Kingdom since 1997 and there are features of it which are regarded as providing particular opportunities and advantages. The statistics tell an impressive story. The creative industries accounted for 10.6 per cent of the United Kingdom's exports in 2009 and, in the same year, the sector contributed £36.3 billion in gross value-added (GVA) to the United Kingdom, 2.89 per of total UK GVA (DCMS, 2011). Overall there are calculated to be 1.5 million people employed in the creative industries themselves or in a creative role in other industrial sectors, constituting 5.14 per cent of UK employment (DCMS, 2011). For these workers incomes are generally higher than average, particularly for those employed in the software, computer games and electronic publishing sectors. In 2006 incomes were 36 per cent higher than the UK average, although since then there has been some slowdown. Creative occupations generated over £40 billion in salaries and wages in 2006, while support staff in creative industries earned an additional £16.8 billion. Overall, the creative industries workforce earned 9.6 per cent of all UK earnings (Higgs *et al.*, 2008).

The benefits associated with developing the sector have led to its identification by the UK government as a key area for employment growth, with a raft of policy interventions aimed at cultivating jobs in the sector. Beyond pointing to the growing economic weight of the creative industries, advocates also stress their potential for regeneration. As Hutton (2009: 987) describes, the sector 'can be seen as phoenix rising from the ashes of traditional manufacturing, light industry and engineering sectors'. These proposed spillover effects are often associated with city renaissance and linked to prospects for increased liveability and quality-of-life advantages (Landry, 2000; Florida, 2002; Champion, 2008).

In particular, there has been a significant policy thrust from former industrial cities to build a share in this sector, often touted as a panacea for urban decline, although critical evidence regarding the possibilities for this is hard to find. Many of these policies are spatially targeted and focus on hubs and clusters of activity which have either emerged organically or have been state-led. This place-based focus for policy assumes a spatial rationale which favours proximity and co-location. The next section explores the commonly identified spatial characteristics of the creative industries sector from which this picture stems.

Spatial logic of the creative industries

Particular spatial and place-based factors are argued to be central to the development and organization of creative industries. The need for proximity is commonly identified as a priority in this sector to allow flexibility, develop networks and offset risk (Banks *et al.*, 2000; Scott, 2001). Creative businesses are also said to 'thrive in milieus, networks, clusters, embedded knowledge and informal infrastructures of the city' (Banks *et al.*, 2000: 454). Other place-based factors relating to the built environment, existence of cheap space, public sector support framework, connectivity, local identity, institutional environment and availability of amenities are also drawn upon as possible influences on the locational choices of creative industry firms (see, for instance, Helbrecht, 1998; Leadbeater and Oakley 2001; Drake, 2003; Hutton, 2004; Markusen, 2006; Champion, 2010).

Research suggests that co-location is an ideal environment for creative industries to operate within. Commonly drawn upon as one of the most crucial factors in creative industry success is the presence of human capital. Mommaas (2004) draws on three factors which demonstrate the importance of clustering in the creative industries. He asserts that clusters are expected to create a local climate favourable for creative workers to be active in. There is also thought to be a wider symbolic and infrastructural spinoff, which is likely to attract more workers. Finally, clusters are expected to function as a context for trust, socialization, knowledge, inspiration, exchange and innovation in a product and service environment characterized by high risk. Geographically clustered networks of resources, including human capital, are very important to the creative industries and are often considered the key to successful project work. Deep local pools of creative and skilled labour are advantageous both to firms and employees (Reimer *et al.*, 2008). The literature suggests that the geographic proximity of individuals possessing human capital, skills, expertise or creative capabilities enables interactions which result in the spillovers that are crucial for innovation (Stolarick and Florida, 2006). This appears to be true, for example, in the film industry where access to networks is crucial both in the United States (Hollywood) and the United Kingdom (London) (Ekinsmyth, 2002). Further to this, there may be an atelier effect where the number of skilled individuals exceeds the labour demand, paving the way for new entrepreneurial activities (Santagata, 2002). In Cook and Pandit's (2007) study comparing the broadcasting industry in three city-regions, London was found to be advantaged by several factors relating to the possibility for knowledge spillovers. The labour market in London offers a pool of talent unrivalled in the United Kingdom. The highest financial rewards and the most prestigious projects are located there. Moreover, as a deep labour pool is necessary for the security of employees, skilled workers are likely to be encouraged to settle in a large urban centre offering a range of employment opportunities.

The industrial structure of the creative industries sector tends to make clustering even more advantageous than in the wider knowledge economy. The sector contains large numbers of very small firms. This allows them to be flexible but poses certain problems that can be somewhat offset by co-location. The problems associated with small firm size include low access to technological information, restricted resources and high training costs. Clustering is beneficial in this regard, as it 'can derive competitive advantage by obtaining efficiency gains that a small firm could not manage on its own' (Wu, 2005: 3). It is further suggested that the spatial clustering of related industries and skilled workers allows the development of an innovative environment likely to lead to a competitive and specialized local economy. Co-location offers benefits in terms of coherence with a shared learning process, path dependence, complementary resources and technological opportunities (Bathelt *et al.*, 2004). Co-operation and competition take place simultaneously as there is a common pool of labour, knowledge, information and ideas (Wu, 2005).

Banks *et al.* (2000) argue that the market for creative products is volatile and creative firms are not solely profit-orientated, but are also keen to remain innovative. As formal support structures such as banks and business support organizations are generally ill-equipped to help with the needs of creative industries, networks are seen as necessary to temper risk and inspire trust. Informal and untraded relations are often more important in creative industries than are formalized interactions (Bayliss, 2007). For instance, in her study of creative industry firms operating in the lace market in Nottingham, Crewe (1996) identified the use of informal networks and gentlemen's agreements to derive more secure tenancy arrangements. With the advent of the knowledge economy there has been a shift from permanent to freelance and contract employment. Short-term and temporary collaboration is a corollary of a more reflexive and flexible economy, and the creative industries exemplify this trend. Firms are active in a volatile environment and so an adaptive nature and networking capabilities are needed to help overcome these weaknesses. This leads 'to the rejection of large hierarchical organizations in favour of networks of small firms able to respond and adapt quickly to changes' (Antcliff *et al.*, 2005: 6). For example, within the advertising industry campaigns are increasingly responding to current events and face increasing competition for media time and space. Workers need to come together on projects with little notice and on an ad hoc basis (Grabher, 2004). There are several characteristics of this shift. Project work takes place over a limited timescale and consists of interrelated tasks (Sydow and Staber, 2002). Meeting deadlines is the main criterion of evaluating performance (Grabher, 2002a). Importantly, project members tend to be assembled by a project manager and are often made up of past collaborators from the same network of contacts. In this way it is inter-personal rather than simply inter-firm relations which form the basis of the networks coming together to work on projects (Ekinsmyth, 2002).

The structure of project-based work can be described as 'flexible networks, or latent organizations consisting of groups of workers from different occupational groups, who come together repeatedly to work on successive projects' (Antcliff *et al.*, 2005: 15). These networks are characterized by mutuality, trust, shared expectations and norms governing behaviour (Antcliff *et al.*, 2005). The findings of Antcliff *et al.*'s (2005) study of workers in the audio-visual industry in the United Kingdom suggested that individuals in this sector sought out reconstructable employment relations through their involvement in and use of networks. The trust and reciprocity engendered by stable networks, built up over time, were used to offset the risk associated with the erosion of stable employment. These findings are consistent with a study of TV content production in two media regions in Germany by Sydow and Staber (2002) who found that, although firms come together to work on particular projects, typically their business relations extend for a much longer period than this. Commonly, firms and individuals who have worked together in the past will reassemble for further project work aided by their past experiences and expectations, even when they can only meet for short periods of time. Grabher (2002a) contends that it is know-who rather than know-how which dominates these networks and therefore it is essentially a reputation business. Projects can provide access to training and acquiring skills, but a reputation can be built once the core of long-term relationships is accessed (Grabher, 2002b). Projects are likely to favour proximity amongst participants for the regular face-to-face contact, which is thought to encourage the transfer of tacit knowledge. The creative industries are argued to be knowledge-intensive, with a far greater reliance on the transfer of tacit information or know-how. Unlike codified knowledge which can be transmitted globally, over long distances and at low cost, tacit knowledge tends to be 'sticky', non-articulated and embedded and is considered best transferred by those co-located in clusters (Bathelt *et al.*, 2004). Face-to-face exchange gives rise to what Bathelt refers to as an information and communication ecology, which can be described in a number of ways such as 'industrial atmosphere', 'noise' or 'buzz' (Bathelt, 2005). Co-location helps firms translate and understand local buzz transmitted through tacit knowledge. He argues that tacit knowledge is automatically accessed by those firms located within a cluster (Bathelt, 2005).

Some networks are highly place-specific due to the difficulty and high cost of transmitting tacit knowledge and also due to locally based cultures and traditions (Sydow and Staber, 2002). Those actors who are located in the pool are exposed to noise, including rumours, impressions, recommendations and trade folklore, which allows them to become enculturated (Grabher, 2002a). The more short-term the project, the more important co-location of project partners becomes (Grabher, 2002a). Proximity encourages the development of untraded interdependencies, which are of benefit to creative workers who work part-time or via contracts. Watson (2008) suggests in his study of London's music industry that organizational connections can offer, at best, only a very partial substitute for geographical proximity, particularly those already embedded in communities of practice. Proximity is also useful for meeting material resource requirements, such as access to studio space. This clearly has a spatial rationale that again points to the primacy of co-location for the creative industries.

Creative industries are regarded 'high-touch' as well as high-tech, meaning that the ability to meet lifestyle preferences and network in informal surroundings is seen as crucial to the success of firms (Montgomery, 2007). The creation of an institutional structure is often stimulated by local buzz, leading to the development of communities of practice. Co-location allows the development of shared structures: language, technical attitudes, interpretative schemes and 'communities of practice' (Bathelt *et al.*, 2004). Grabher (2002a) describes this process as 'hanging out'. The development of communities of practice, based around agglomerations of skilled workers, can provide an informal training ground, which allows participants access to the knowledge needed to become an insider. Individuals within this community will share norms of values, tastes, lifestyles and ways of doing things (Ekinsmyth, 2002: 233). These cannot be transmitted mechanically and so personal and collective stories are important (Santagata, 2002: 12). As O'Connor comments, the 'creative industries are seen to be highly sensitive to embedded cultural knowledge whose mobilization depends on being "inside" a place' (2004: 132). The symbolic nature of the products also depends on the knowledge of different sub-cultures, which can be accessed via socializing through networks within the range of alternative cultural and social scenes provided in urban locations (Reimer *et al.*, 2008).

These factors would suggest that the co-location of firms in this sector leads to the development of a sophisticated environment for creative production, which is reliant on the ability to build networks to successfully transmit knowledge. The evidence from existing studies would suggest that creative production is likely to be focused on global centres and raises the question as to whether other locations can support this economic sector.

The UK computer games industry: how does the games industry fit into the wider creative industries sector?

In many ways the computer games sector seems to reflect the characteristics of the creative economy and is often held up as a paradigmatic success story representing the wider creative economy. In 2008, the United Kingdom constituted the third largest computer games development territory by revenue and employed almost 10,000 people contributing £1 billion to GDP (Bakhshi and Mateos-Garcia, 2010). The United Kingdom is home to the studios that have developed games such as *Grand Theft Auto IV* (the fastest selling entertainment product of all time), *RuneScape*, the *Fable* series, *Broken Sword* and *LittleBigPlane* (TIGA, 2012). According to the DCMS, almost 60 per cent of the UK population plays video games. The sector has also been the focus of increased policy attention, for instance with the announcement in the 2012 budget that the sector would receive specialist relief from taxation from April 2013 (alongside animation and TV production). It has been estimated that over five years a games tax relief could create and protect 1,650 studio jobs and increase the games development sector's contribution to UK GDP by £280 million (DCMS, 2012a). In the same budget, investment plans for spatially targeted ultra-fast broadband connections were outlined for Birmingham, Bristol, Leeds and Bradford, Newcastle, and Manchester along with the four UK capital cities (DCMS, 2012b). There has been strategic funding targeted at higher education institutions including the Universities of Abertay, Dundee and Salford. Scotland has seen significant and explicit state support through the establishment of the Scottish Games Alliance.

Significant emphasis in the literature is placed upon the common characteristics of the creative industries sector, which in turn are likely to produce a shared spatial logic. It is therefore important to explore the commonalities between the different activities included under the banner of the creative economy and determine how far these are shared by the computer games sector. Whilst not being exclusive to the sector or shared by all the component parts, these characteristics tend to be seen in the activities involved. This section suggests there are several ways in which the UK computer games industry reflects the key attributes associated with the broader creative industries sector. These relate to the nature of the product, organizational structure and employment trends.

The nature of the product

Firstly, a commonly identified quality of the creative economy rests on the nature of the creative product which tends to be of a high value-added quality derived from the knowledge-intensive aspects involved in its creation, namely production, marketing and distribution. Creative products tend to possess symbolic or sign value, which can be ideas, experiences and images, rather than solely utilitarian functions (Scott, 2004). The markets tend to be niche and the products are highly customized. This is very much reflected within the computer games sector in the United Kingdom where technological innovation intimately supports content delivery and business model development (Bakhshi and Mateos-Garcia, 2010). In fact, within the games industry the lifecycle for a single product averages several years, in many ways suggesting that the sector offers a paradigmatic example of a knowledge-intensive production process (Tschang and Vang, 2008).

The nature of organizational structure

Creative industry firms are asserted to be small and agile, operating within a networked chain of interrelated activities (Rantisi *et al.*, 2006). Small firms and individuals are regarded as suitable for providing the model of flexible specialization and so, structurally, the majority of creative industry firms are small and are complemented by only a few large establishments (Scott, 2004). Reflective of these trends, in the United

Kingdom, the computer games sector comprises 220 businesses with only 5 per cent possessing a workforce of over 200 and only a quarter with a workforce of more than 50 (Skillset, 2010).

The nature of employment

In terms of workers in the creative industries, there are seen to be specialized demands which must be met by highly skilled, talented and committed individuals. The workforce is disproportionately young and well educated, with about 43 per cent passing through some form of higher education (Leadbeater and Oakley, 1999). The computer games workforce has an even younger age profile than the wider creative industries with 59 per cent aged under 35 in 2010, although there is evidence that the workforce is aging as this proportion was 76 per cent in 2005 (Skillset, 2010). The computer games workforce is also highly qualified with 80 per cent of employees possessing a degree qualification.

The sharing of these attributes suggests that the computer games sector is likely to reflect many of the spatial habits of the wider creative economy as already discussed such as an appetite for proximity, a tendency to co-locate and a preferencing of global cities. The next section considers the available evidence regarding the spatial habits of the games industry.

The spatial logic of the UK computer games sector

Within the UK, there is also a strong trend towards the concentration of creative activities in London. According to the Work Foundation's (2007) research, by far the greatest concentration of employment in the creative industries is located in London and the south east of England. These two regions together account for 46 per cent of the creative industries workforce, a significant over-representation given that the two regions account for 27 per cent of the total UK workforce. In some of the sectors there is a particularly strong regional skew: for example 40 per cent of UK advertising is based in London alone. The distribution of turnover in these industries is likely to be even more imbalanced than employment, because of the larger proportion of the more specialized and higher value-added activities being located in London and the south east. Export activity is also dominated by London and the south east. The London bias would be even more significant without public funding (Work Foundation, 2007). The evidence suggests that the computer games sector diverges from this general pattern. There is a more even distribution of the sector's workforce across the United Kingdom than within other components of the creative economy with just 19 per cent based in London compared with 46 per cent within the wider creative industries sector (Skillset, 2010;

see Figure 1.1). One explanatory factor regarding the less privileged position of London could be related to employee wages. Wages in the sector are higher in general than in the rest of the creative economy and thus paying staff London wages could be seen to be a significant burden over and above this (Cornford and Naylor, 2001; Skillset, 2010).

In terms of firm distribution, existing studies have found greater levels of dispersion across the United Kingdom than the creative industries sector as a whole. A study by de Propis *et al.*, published in 2009, looked at firm distribution across travel to work areas (TTWA) and found that there were hubs of software, computer games and electronic publishing activity in the cities of Bristol, Edinburgh, Manchester, Brighton, Oxford, Wycombe and Slough, Cambridge, Guildford and Milton Keynes.

There are several industry-specific explanations for the divergence of the spatial patterns of the computer games sector from the wider creative economy. One important factor is that the product lifecycle

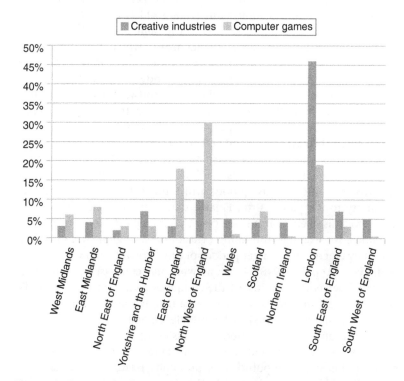

Figure 1.1 Proportion of computer games workforce and wider creative industries workforce by nation/English region (taken from Skillset, 2009, 2010)

is frequently lengthy due to its complexity, often taking between one-and-a-half to four years to bring a game to market, depending on the size of the team (Tschang and Vang, 2008). This can be seen to reduce the requirement to share information between firms as well as increasing the level of secrecy around product development. As the production time is longer, there is a further tendency towards relying on in-house capacity and so the proportion of freelancers and temporary staff is lower than in other creative industries (Tschang and Vang, 2008).

Despite some divergence from the patterns of the wider creative economy, there is some evidence of a tendency towards co-location within the computer games industry. Within the de Propis *et al.* (2009) study, greater levels of concentration of activity were found in another part of the study where location quotients were calculated. This is a measure which aims to show the relative degree of concentration of activity within a geographical area. This measure is a well-established index for comparing an area's share of a particular activity with a national or other benchmark. Location quotients are widely used partly because they are easy to understand. 1.0 means the same degree of presence in a local area as the average for the wider area in which it is situated, 2.0 means twice the proportion for the wider area, 3.0 means three times and 0.5 means only half as much as the wider area. Of all the creative industry sectors reviewed in the study, software, computer games and electronic publishing were the most concentrated across a small number of regions, namely London (1.31), the south east (1.4) and to a lesser extent the east of England (1.13) (see Table 1.1).

A feature which may influence spatial location is that there is a high propensity for spin-offs from larger firms. This may account for some patterns of co-location as spinoffs will tend to be located in relative proximity to the parent firm. Finally, due to the nascent character of the sector it is likely that it is affected by some, more arbitrary location decisions, for example the home of a founder. Agglomeration economies may emerge over longer periods of time which favour certain hubs of activity (Appold, 1998). Previous work has emphasized differences in spatial behaviour not just of the computer games sector as a whole, but also the different functions contained within it. For example, Cornford *et al.* (2000) noted that games development companies lacked an inclination to cluster. Patterns of clustering they identified within the study were more attributed to spinoffs or rationalizations and acquisitions rather than compulsions for proximity related to ideas sharing, 'buzz', 'thick' labour markets and other factors of agglomeration commonly attributed to the creative economy.

Table 1.1 Location quotients for software, computer games and electronic publishing and the firm location of the total creative industries by region/nation 2007 (de Propis *et al.*, 2009)

Region/nation	Software, computer games and electronic publishing	Total creative industries
London	1.31	1.37
South east of England	1.4	1.09
South west of England	0.93	0.95
East Midlands	0.79	0.82
West Midlands	0.84	0.84
East of England	1.13	0.97
Yorkshire and the Humber	0.7	0.79
North west of England	0.81	0.94
North east of England	0.56	0.91
Wales	0.59	0.75
Scotland	0.7	0.94

The Dundee example reflects this in many ways. The emergence of the sector in the late 1980s was around the time that Timex, the watchmaker, had turned over its Dundee factory to producing Sinclair ZX Spectrum computers, which, unlike other computers of the time, could be programmed spawning an interest in computer-games design. The first notable success in Dundee was realized by David Jones, a former Timex employee, who set up the company DMA Design in 1988, which was responsible for the huge hit *Lemmings* in 1991 and *Grand Theft Auto* in 1997. Many of the developers involved in DMA went on to set up further computer games companies including Visual Sciences and Realtime Worlds, which in turn have spawned Ruffian Games, Tag Games, Proper Games and others. The regular pattern of spin-outs has had strong institutional support with the University of Abertay capitalizing on the green shoots of the industry by launching the world's first master's programme in software engineering for computer games technology in 1996 and a BSc in 1998. Further funding and support have been derived from the Scottish Games Alliance, Interactive Tayside and European Regional Development Fund, which has facilitated a greater embedding of the sector in the city.

A heterogeneous sector?

There is a dearth of illuminating empirical evidence for a spatial logic for the computer games sector, which can lead to the emergence of a rather contradictory picture as we have discussed above. The indications available tend to suggest that the games industry behaves distinctly from some of the accepted patterns of the wider creative economy. There are, however, huge deficiencies within the current state of knowledge about the spatial behaviour of the games industry and the creative industries more broadly, which pose challenges for research. De Propis *et al.* (2009) utilized a rather broad definition, namely software, computer games and electronic publishing. The challenge of a lack of clarity regarding definitions and a tendency to aggregate activities into larger groupings which lack utility in analysis will be discussed in this section. In conceptual terms, there is contention regarding their definition and treatment as a homogeneous group, particularly in terms of what activities should be included within it (Flew, 2002; Galloway and Dunlop, 2007; UNCTAD, 2008). A corollary of this is that measurement of the sector is quite difficult. There are gaps in data provision and significant problems arise from the outmoded nature of existing statistical classifications.

The diversity of definitions of the creative industries and the activities included within it has led to 'terminological clutter' (Galloway and Dunlop, 2007: 19). Definitional questions can be divided along breadth and depth lines. In terms of breadth, the divisions can be drawn differently, depending on whether activities such as the gaming industry, tourism and sport are included or not (Pratt, 2005). With regard to questions of depth, decisions over what is included can be drawn along several lines, including content origination, exchange, reproduction, manufacturing inputs, education and critique and archiving (Pratt, 2005). How different activities are categorized is particularly relevant for funding. For example, there are differences in specialized tax breaks for the different sectors. As it is considered more cultural, the film industry is more likely to be funded than the computer games industry. The shift to using the term creative industries has tended to broaden the definition of which sectors and activities are included. As mentioned in the last section, computer games have often been subsumed into a wider category which includes software development, electronic publishing and even computer consultancy activities. Some see this as an attempt to overstate the economic weight of the sector and overemphasize its homogeneity for purposes of political expediency and instrumental gain (Oakley, 2004; Selwood, 2006). Tepper (2002) asserts that definitions tend to aggregate a wide breadth of activities and concentrate measurement on outputs. Even a slight alteration in a category of activity or output can result in a huge change in the statistical figures. This can do more to obscure than reveal generalizable trends. Garnham (2005) asserts that, in the DCMS mapping document, the whole of computer software was included and further argues that it was possible, only on that basis, to make claims about size and growth stand up. Divergence from the high-level trends of the creative industries has been illustrated using the example of spatial organization in this chapter. There are, however, a number of other ways in which the overstatement of commonalities across these activities could be highlighted. For example, the creative economy is often associated with fostering diversity. In particular, the creative industries can be felt to promote the gender balance as a significant number of women work in the production of arts and crafts, fashion-related areas and the organization of cultural activities (UNCTAD, 2008). Within the games sector representation of women is very low (around 6 per cent of the workforce) along with individuals from a black, Asian and minority ethnic background who account for around 3 per cent of the workforce (Skillset, 2010). Critics have highlighted socially constructed aspects of the computer games sector and, in particular, have identified an overly 'boosterish' tone to reports (Cornford *et al.*, 2000). Creating a semblance of the bigger picture may 'satisfy the requirements of accountability; might be persuasive in terms of justifying subsidy; or might serve the purposes of advocacy by proving that the cultural activities make a substantial contribution to GDP' (Selwood, no date: 1).

A further challenge in researching the creative industries, linked to definition, is that of measurement. Measuring the sector is an extremely difficult thing to do. There are different histories of data collecting, gaps in reporting, no relevant national industrial classification and a lack of shared mechanisms for collecting data. The Annual Business Inquiry (ABI) is commonly used to identify the spatial organization of the creative industries sector and tends to form the basis for the majority of quantitative analyses of firms in the creative industries. This database, however, suffers from a number of drawbacks. Much of the data in the ABI is based on estimates from a sample survey, leading to relatively large standard errors at disaggregated levels. Whilst not unique to the ABI, the Standard Industrial Classifications (SIC) are somewhat outdated, being rooted in past industrial structures and revised only when new sectors of the economy have become well established. Problematically, many of the classifications mix together, to differing extents, creative and non-creative activities within single codes.

Positively, in January 2008 the SIC codes were updated from SIC 2003 to SIC 2007. Some old codes were removed from the list as they were no longer relevant, new ones were added as new industries emerged, and others were moved around, split up or aggregated with others. This included the removal of certain SIC codes from the software/electronic publishing sector, including computer consultancy activities and business and domestic software development. The structure of the classifications means that, for some SICs, identification of creative industries within whole industrial codes is required. In the past computer games were part of an aggregate category 'software, computer games and electronic publishing', but due to demand there have been attempts to develop a more focused coding. The result of that is the creation of the category 'digital and entertainment media'. Whilst this signifies an improvement and greater level of detail, it is still not possible to distinguish computer games from other aspects of digital media. Further to this, due to the modifications, the estimates in the most recent release are not comparable with estimates from previous reports posing difficulties for creating any time series data.

Conclusion

The issues with definition and measurement, as outlined in the previous section, have further implications for policy developed to grow and nurture the sector. As Pratt (2005: 35) recognizes, 'a "one size fits all" creative industries strategy may be ineffective'. The limitations of accurately defining and measuring the sector raise important questions regarding the suitability of schemes aimed at boosting growth in these industries. These issues relate primarily to the diversity of activities and types of firms included under the umbrella term of the creative industries, which make uniform policy unlikely to be successful. As Tepper (2002: 163) suggests, 'the sector is heterogeneous, and effective policy must be informed by thorough analysis of the component parts of the system and their interrelationships'. So, the lesson is that aggregating might be good for politics, but disaggregating is essential for policy and understanding.

There are also many factors which are likely to influence spatial patterns over the coming years with digitization and convergence prospects disrupting as well as shaping business models in these industries. There is a clear mandate for detailed research, but there remain issues with the availability and utility of data which can be used for studying the sector. It is important to strive for greater disaggregation of data and steer away from the social construction of the sector as homogeneous. By recognizing, measuring and accepting diversity appropriate and targeted interventions can be used to help secure a stronger and more sustainable creative economy.

References

Antcliff, V., Saudry, R. and Stuart, M. (2005) Freelance worker networks in audio-visual industries, *Lancashire Business School Working Papers*, Preston: University of Central Lancashire.

Appold, S.J. (1998) Labor-market imperfections and the agglomeration of firms: evidence from the emergent period of the US semiconductor industry, *Environment & Planning A*, 30(3): 439–62.

Bakhshi, H. and Mateos-Garcia, J. (2010) *The Innovation Game: Adjusting the R&D Tax Credit: Boosting Innovation in the UK Video Games Industry*, London: NESTA.

Banks, M., Lovatt, A., O'Connor, J. and Raffo, C. (2000) Risk and trust in the cultural industries, *Geoforum*, 31: 453–64.

Bathelt, H., Malmberg, A. and Maskell, P. (2004) Clusters and knowledge: local buzz, global pipelines and the process of knowledge creation, *Progress in Human Geography*, 28(1): 31–55.

Bathelt, H. (2005) Cluster relations in the media industry: exploring the 'distanced neighbour' paradox in Leipzig, *Regional Studies*, 39: 105–27.

Bayliss, D. (2007) The rise of the creative city: culture and creativity in Copenhagen, *European Planning Studies*, 15(7): 889–903.

Champion, K. (2008) The business of creative cities, *Journal of Urban Regeneration and Renewal*, 2(2): 111–23.

Champion, K. (2010) Hobson's choice? Constraints on accessing spaces of creative production in a transforming industrial conurbation, *Creative Industries Journal*, 3(1): 11–28.

Cook, G.A.S. and Pandit, N.R. (2007) Service industry clustering: a comparison of broadcasting in three city-regions, *Service Industries Journal*, 27(4): 453–69.

Cornford, J., Naylor, R. and Drive, S. (2000) New media and regional development: the case of the UK computer and video games industry, in A. Giunta, A. Lagendijk, and A. Pike (eds), *Restructuring Industry and Territory: The Experience of Europe's Regions*, Norwich: Routledge, pp. 83–108.

Cornford, J. and Naylor, R. (2001) *Cutting edges in strange places: new media debates and the computer and video games industry in the UK*, CURDS Discussion Paper 01/1, Centre for Urban and Regional Development Studies, University of Newcastle upon Tyne.

Crewe, L. (1996) Material culture: embedded firms, organizational networks and the local economic development of a fashion quarter, *Regional Studies*, 30(3): 257–72.

DCMS (2001) *Creative Industries Mapping Document*, London: DCMS.

DCMS (2011) *Creative Industries Economic Estimates Full Statistical Release*, London: DCMS.

DCMS (2012a) Budget boost for creative industries, http://www.culture.gov.uk/news/news_stories/8932.aspx.

DCMS (2012b) Ten super-connected cities announced, http://www.culture.gov.uk/news/news_stories/8931.aspx.

de Propis, L., Chapain, C., Cooke, P., MacNeill, S. and Mateos-Garcia, J. (2009) *The Geography of Creativity*, London: NESTA.

Drake, G. (2003) 'This place gives me space': place and creativity in the creative industries, *Geoforum*, 34: 511–24.

Ekinsmyth, C. (2002) Project organization, embeddedness and risk in magazine publishing, *Regional Studies*, 36(3): 229–43.

Flew, T. (2002) Beyond *ad hocery*: defining creative industries, Paper presented at the Second International Conference on Cultural Policy Research, Te Papa, Wellington, New Zealand, 23–26 January.

Florida, R. (2002) *The Rise of the Creative Class*, New York: Basic Books.

Galloway, S. and Dunlop, S. (2007) A critique of definitions of the cultural and creative industries in public policy, *International Journal of Cultural Policy*, 13(1): 17–31.

Garnham, N. (2005) From cultural to creative industries: analysis of the implications of the 'creative industries' approach to arts and media policy making in the United Kingdom, *International Journal of Cultural Policy*, 11: 15–29.

Grabher, G. (2002a) The project ecology of advertising: tasks, talents and teams, *Regional Studies*, 36: 245–63.

Grabher, G. (2002b) Cool projects, boring institutions: temporary collaboration in social context, *Regional Studies*, 36: 205–14.

Grabher, G. (2004) Learning in projects, remembering in networks? Communality, sociality, and connectivity in project ecologies, *European Urban and Regional Studies*, 2: 103–23.

Helbrecht, I. (1998) The creative metropolis: services, symbols, and spaces, *International Journal of Architectural Theory*, 3(1): 1–10.

Higgs, P., Cunningham, S. and Bakhshi, H. (2008) *Beyond the Creative Industries: Mapping the Creative Economy in the United Kingdom*, London: NESTA.

Horkheimer, M. and Adorno, T.W. (1944) *Dialectic of Enlightenment*, London: Verso.

Hutton, T. (2004) The new economy of the inner city, *Cities*, 21(2): 89–108.

Hutton, T. (2009) Trajectories of the new economy: regeneration and dislocation in the inner city, *Urban Studies*, 46: 978–1001.

Landry, C. (2000) *The Creative City: A Toolkit for Urban Innovators*, London: Comedia.

Leadbeater, C. and Oakley, K. (1999) *The Independents: Britain's New Cultural Entrepreneurs*, London: Demos.

Leadbeater, C. and Oakley, K. (2001) *Surfing the Long Wave: Knowledge Entrepreneurship in Britain*, London: Demos.

Markusen, A. (2006) Urban development and the politics of a creative class: evidence from a study of artists, *Environment and Planning A*, 38: 1921–40.

Matarasso, F. and Landry, C. (1999) *Balancing Act: 21 Strategic Dilemmas in Cultural Policy*, Strasbourg: Council of Europe Publishing.

Mommaas, H. (2004) Cultural clusters and the post-industrial city: towards the remapping of urban cultural policy, *Urban Studies*, 41(3): 507–32.

Montgomery, J. (2007) *The New Wealth of Cities: City Dynamics and the Fifth Wave*, Aldershot: Ashgate.

Oakley, K. (2004) Not so cool Britannia: the role of the creative industries in economic development, *International Journal of Cultural Studies*, 7(1): 67–77.

O'Connor, J. (2000) The definition of the 'cultural industries', *The European Journal of Arts Education*, 2(3): 15–27.

O'Connor, J. (2004) 'A special kind of city knowledge': innovative clusters, tacit knowledge and the 'creative city', *Media International Australia, Incorporating Culture and Policy*, 112: 131–49.

Pratt, A. (2005) Cultural industries and public policy: an oxymoron? *International Journal of Cultural Policy*, 11(1): 31–44.

Rantisi, N., Leslie, D. and Christopherson, S. (2006) Placing the creative economy: scale, politics and the material, *Environment and Planning A*, 38: 1789–97.
Reimer, S., Pinch, S. and Sunley, P. (2008) Design spaces: agglomeration and creativity in British design agencies, *Geografiska Annaler, Series B, Human Geography*, 90(2): 151–72.
Santagata, W. (2002) Cultural districts, property rights and sustainable economic growth, *International Journal of Urban and Regional Research*, 26(1): 9–23.
Scott, A, J. (2001) *Global City-Regions: Trends, Theory, Policy*, Oxford: Oxford University Press.
Scott, A. J. (2004) The cultural products industries and urban economic development: prospects for growth and market contestation in global context, *Urban Affairs Review*, 39: 461–90.
Selwood, S. (2006) A part to play? The academic contribution to the development of cultural policy in England, *International Journal of Cultural Policy*, 12(1): 35–53.
Selwood, S. (no date) ESRC Seminar at LSE, http://www.lse.ac.uk/collections/geographyAndEnvironment/pdf/Sara_Selwood.pdf#search=%22esrc%20seminar%20lse%20sara%20selwood%22.
Skillset (2009) *2009 Employment Census*, London: Skillset.
Skillset (2010) *Computer Games Sector – Labour Market Intelligence Digest*, London: Skillset.
Stolarick, K. and Florida, R. (2006) Creativity, connections and innovation: a study of linkages in the Montreal region, *Environment and Planning A*, 38(10): 1799–817.
Sydow, J. and Staber, U. (2002) The institutional embeddedness of project networks: the case of content production in German television, *Regional Studies*, 36(3): 215–27.
Taylor, C. F. (2006) Beyond advocacy: developing an evidence base for regional creative industry strategies, *Cultural Trends*, 15(1): 3–18.
Tepper, S. (2002) Creative assets and the changing economy, *The Journal of Arts Management, Law and Society*, 32(1): 159–68.
TIGA (2012) *UK Video Games Industry*, http://www.tiga.org/about-us-and-uk-games/uk-video-games-industry.
Tschang, F.T. and Vang, J. (2008), *Explaining the spatial organization of creative industries: the case of the U.S. videogames industry*, Paper presented at The 25th DRUID Celebration Conference 2008 on Entrepreneurship and Innovation, Copenhagen, Denmark.
UNCTAD (2008) *Creative Economy Report 2008*, Geneva: UN.
Watson, A. (2008) Global music city: knowledge and geographical proximity in London's recorded music industry, *Area*, 40(1): 12–23.
Work Foundation (2007) *Staying Ahead: The Economic Performance of the UK Creative Industries*, London: DCMS.
Wu, W. (2005) Dynamic cities and creative clusters, *World Bank Policy Research Working Paper* 3509, New York: World Bank.

2
Commercial Business Models for a Fast Changing Industry

Gregor White and Nicola Searle

Introduction

Standing in line at the supermarket checkout, clutching the latest in Activision's *Call of Duty* series, is not particularly unusual as millions of people do the same during launch week. Collectively, we contribute to the £490 million of sales in the week following *Call of Duty*'s release. Standing in line feels anachronistic in a world where 'on demand' has come to mean games at your fingertips, any genre, any format, any platform.

Consumers of digital content have high expectations. No longer content with having to go to the high street to buy a physical product off the shelf, consumers expect to have the choice to extend their experience. They want to do so with additional content or be able to acquire experience or items that will allow for progression through the game more quickly. Consumers want to play alone or with friends or with strangers, cooperatively or competitively, and are prepared to pay.

If it can be done online, then why can it not be done on the console? Increasingly, this is the case as games studios developing for the retail market are waking up to the potential of business models being pioneered by online games developers. However, it is strange that a sector that considers itself innovative and technologically ground-breaking continues to wrestle with old-world service delivery problems. Relations between retailers, publishers and developers have been strained by the growing conflict over the sale of pre-owned games. This conflict has resulted in large sections of the computer games development sector seeking ways to short-circuit the route to the consumer and circumvent intermediaries while retaining a larger proportion of the profit. Complicit in these developments are consumers who benefit from improved access and cheaper prices than online publishing and purchasing have delivered.

Games developers and consumers have driven a series of innovations in both products and services in a synergistic relationship that has regularly thrown up counter-intuitive and unexpected solutions to business models and market challenges. In many cases, it is the desire amongst consumers to have a more flexible or diverse marketplace that has driven the development of new business models and the casual gaming boom. Dissatisfaction with the traditional retail model has driven the try-it-and-see, freemium and online subscription models. As gamers get older their tastes mature and disposable time to spend playing games shrinks. Changes in consumer behaviour and demographics, as much as technological innovation, have moved game-play into social situations where party games and motion controllers are dominant, and onto mobile phones and tablets where consumption time is typically shorter.

This chapter examines the evolving relationship between games developers, business models and consumers, not as a commercial or exploitative one, but as the engine for the evolution of the games marketplace and the products and services that have emerged and continue to emerge from that space. This relationship will be the lens through which we will consider how business models have been adopted by games developers over the last decade, in order to expose the nature of consumer-led change in computer games products, services and business models, and the role of the player as catalytic in the evolution of the market.

The chapter has three main themes: it will discuss the changing profile of the consumer, highlight some of the disruptive technologies that have influenced the market and look at ways in which the market has responded. Initially we will highlight how an understanding of the role of the consumer is increasingly important across the stages of the games value chain, from influencing games design and features to driving business model strategies and levels of service. The next section will look at recent demographic change in the consumer population and explore how the consumer's interaction with new technologies, markets and services has driven the demographic range of the game-playing community in every direction. We will consider the changing retail environment and emerging pricing mechanisms that have been developed in response to changes in consumer demand and expectation.

Consumer-led change

Change in digital media is often framed in the context of service- or consumer-led innovation. Computer games have traditionally been considered goods, or more specifically, experience goods. However, online innovation shifted the focus to games as a service. As sales of boxed products decline, the popularity of social network gaming, downloadable content and online gaming have risen. Recent innovation in computer games has concentrated on service elements of the business model: delivery channels, revenue streams and value proposition (Osterwalder and Pigneur, 2010). These business model innovations allow for producers in the computer games industry to expand their audience base, increase revenue opportunities and shift market power.

The market shift from product to service necessitates changes in the business models of computer games. The rise of social gaming via platforms such as Facebook has expanded the reach of gaming to populations not typically associated with gaming. As we will discuss later, this has caused a revolution in the demographics of consumers of games, technology and pricing mechanisms.

Change has long been cast as industry-led innovation. However, while firms may produce an initial innovation, it is often consumers who develop the innovation that leads to new service models. Consumers in the computer games industry have long understood this phenomenon. The fast pace of change in the computer games industry means that consumers themselves are in a state of perpetual upgrade (Ashton, 2011) as new technologies and new versions of software require new skills. This perpetual upgrading of skills helps create the constant innovation and change we see in games.

Consumers of games, also known as gamers, take this perpetual change even further through user-generated content and modding (the practice of creating modified versions of games). Advances in software and platforms have lowered the barrier for game making. While a console-based blockbuster game may require an experienced team many years to produce, software such as YoYo Game's *GameMaker* allows inexperienced programmers singlehandedly to develop games of their own. This has allowed the relationship with the consumer to spawn entirely new, co-creation-based business models.

The role of the consumer also changes as the line between producer and consumer blurs. The creation of digital content, often used in games, has also opened up to users and producer-consumers (prosumers). Software such as *Poser*, a rendering and animation software, incorporates an online marketplace where users of the software can sell their content. As Darkin (2012) notes, a user with successful content selling online may be able to earn back the price of the software itself. In addition to individual contributions, community-based collaborations, such as

Wikipedia (Bruns, 2008), also provide opportunities for consumer-led change in online spheres. This harnessing of the creative power of consumers has spurred further innovation in business models such as Wikipedia's consumer-based production.

A classic example of consumer-led innovation in computer games is that of *Counter-Strike*. As Ashton (2011) describes, *Counter-Strike* began as a modification of the game *Half Life*. While this represents the extreme in modification, an entire game generated by users from the game engine of another, it hints at the power of user-led innovation in games. Observations on how games are used by players, for example in *machinima* (Lowood, 2006), can influence game play and generate new forms or genres. Indeed, *machinima* is going mainstream with Hollywood director John Woo launching a *machinima* series (Bhushan, 2011).

The computer games industry has a flexible approach to business models and the role of the consumer. While consumers, as noted above, continually innovate, game developers excel at experimentation with business models (Humphreys *et al.*, 2005). As innovation drives the games industry forward, it also poses challenges for the business models and the role of players. In the next sections, we will examine demographic change in consumers, changes in the retail environment and the industry's innovative pricing response.

Changing consumer

Interest in audience data for the computer games sector has increased in recent years. As the proportion of transactions being conducted online and directly through consoles and proprietary services like Xbox Live and PlayStation Network increases, so does available data. This has resulted in a highly detailed picture of consumer behaviour and demographic distribution. Combined with the ability to respond to user demand through downloadable content (DLC) and iterative version release, the games industry has become highly sensitive to player preference. This helps create ideal conditions for consumer-led innovation to establish itself in production models.

Although individual companies might jealously guard detailed user information and analytic data about individual products, it is possible to discern macro-level trends in product and service developments from published data. Market research organizations, such as The Nielsen Company and the Pew Research Center for the People and the Press, aggregate large quantities of consumer data and user behaviour information.

These organizations conduct this research on behalf of the Entertainment Software Association (ESA) and Interactive Software Federation Europe (ISFE), who report annually to their industry members. In 2008, the UK Office of Communications (Ofcom) included games data in the annual Communications Market Report for the first time (Ofcom, 2008). The data was included under the general heading of 'Convergence', due to the capability of next generation consoles to deliver online services including video and audio content, and, in 2010, as 'Internet and Web Based Content' (Ofcom, 2010). For the purposes of this chapter, the demographic data used will include the most recent data available in the ESA Sales, Demographic and Usage Data Reports from 2007 to 2011, the ISFE Video Gamers Europe Report from 2010, and the Ofcom Communications Market Reports from 2008 to 2011.

Consumer demographic change is one of the most significant factors in both driving and responding to innovation in products, services and business models in the games sector. The profile of the games audience is complex and highly dynamic. Where consumer-led innovation and disruptive technologies and services are characteristic of the sector, the resulting mutations make longitudinal trends difficult to discriminate. The manner in which the market adapts to assimilate change and exploit the new conditions suggests that the market ecosystem continues to evolve.

Our understanding of consumer demographics at the national level has improved over the last decade. In 2005, the BBC (British Broadcasting Corporation) undertook the first demographic study of game-playing consumers in the UK. *Gamers in the UK: Digital Play, Digital Lifestyles* (Pratchett, 2005) established a range of measurements, behaviours and definitions that have persisted as significant elements of demographic reports ever since. The report defined a gamer as 'someone who had played a game on a mobile, handheld, console, PC, Internet or interactive TV at least once in the last six months' (Pratchett, 2005: 2). Although this definition persists, many data analysts have found it useful to subdivide this group in terms of regularity of game-playing episodes, and game purchases over defined periods. The ISFE Gamer Commitment Index (ISFE, 2010) divides gamers into six sub-groups from 'committed' gamers who play for more than one hour every day and have purchased more than three games in the preceding three months, to 'intermittent' gamers who play irregularly and have purchased one game or fewer in the preceding three months.

The size of the market is better documented as these reports regularly report market size. In 2011, ISFE reported that 25.4 per cent of

Europeans are gamers, while ESA (2011) reports that 72 per cent of American households belong to the category defined by one play/ one purchase in the last six months. Over the period from 2008 when the ESA first uses the measure, the US market has grown by seven percentage points, from 65 to 72 per cent of households. This growth corresponds to an increase in the value of the US games sector from $9.5 billion in 2007 to $25.1 billion in 2010. Even after a perfunctory review of the data, it is obvious that there is no clear relationship between market size and market value. This suggests that growth in the sector is not dependent on selling more products to more consumers, but on changes in consumption habits, audience demographics and extending product value.

Since the ESA first conducted its research in 2007, the characteristics of the game-player audience have changed in many significant ways. Interestingly, there appears to be little variation in the headline figures of gaming households, gender balance and age distribution over the period. Table 2.1 most notably shows the significant change in the number of gamers playing on mobile devices and the number of individuals paying to play online. The lack of direct correlation between market value and user trends would seem to suggest that the overall market is significantly segmented, and that audience and product have diversified over time.

Analysis of the demographic data will offer support for the proposition that significant developments in the production and business of computer games are directly related to changes in consumer behaviour and

Table 2.1 US profile of gamers

	2007	2008	2009	2010	2011
% of gaming households	67	65	68	67	72
Average age	33	35	35	34	37
Gender balance					
Female	38%	40%	40%	40%	42%
Male	62%	60%	60%	60%	58%
Under 18	28%	25%	25%	25%	18%
18–49	48%	49%	49%	49%	53%
50+	24%	26%	26%	26%	29%
Playing on mobile	34%	36%	37%	42%	55%
Pay to play online	–*	22%	23%	17%	19%
Value $billion	9.5	11.7	10.5	15.9	–

Source: ESA (2007–2011).
* 2004 value is 8 per cent.

profile. The nature of innovation in this environment is synergistic and dynamic and is located between the creativity of the producer and the creativity of the consumer.

Despite the increasing availability of data, it is difficult to paint a clear picture of where the industry stands. Publicly available reports frequently present conflicting data; details and more extensive data are often privately held and therefore unavailable, and key variables are ill-defined. To illustrate, the UK Interactive Entertainment Association (UKIEA, 2012) and ESA (2011) report sales of £2.8 million and £1.9 million, respectively, for computer games industry sales in 2010. Both reports use GfK Chart-Track, but the ESA report uses IHS Screen Digest media intelligence for its estimates of digital sales. However, this alone should not account for the UKIEA estimate being 50 per cent more than the ESA estimate. Thus, it is difficult to draw firm conclusions about the size, impact and nature of the industry's sales.

Analysis of the demographic and consumption habits of gamers is also challenged by a lack of consensus. As noted earlier, the definition of a gamer as 'someone who has played a game in the last 6 months' (ISFE, 2010) is a broad one, which potentially includes those playing analogue games as well. Drawing meaningful conclusions from such a wide range of potential consumers is problematic. Based on similar definitions, we have estimates of the portion of the population considered to be gamers as 25 per cent of the adult European population (ISFE, 2010), 72 per cent of American households (ESA, 2011) and 59 per cent of 6- to 69-year-old UK residents (Pratchett, 2005). Potentially, these numbers are not contradictory; however, it is difficult to draw conclusions from such heterogeneous values.

Notwithstanding the lack of consistency in publicly available games industry data, the availability of data and the insights gleaned from the research continue to improve. Longitudinal data using the same definition, such as the ESA game-playing audiences, clearly shows that the consumer demographic for games is changing. In the next section, we will examine some of the changes that have brought this about.

Interaction of technology, business models and demographic changes

Demographic changes have been caused in part by changes in games technology and business models. In the last decade there have been four significant technological disruptions in the games sector. These disruptive technologies and products have had a profound impact on the extension of the games audience and the diversity of the consumer demographic.

They occurred within the space of four years:

2005: *Club Penguin* becomes the first of a number of successful online virtual worlds for children;
2006: Nintendo launches the Wii console which deploys the first mass-produced motion controller;
2007: Apple launches the iPhone (and the App store in June 2008);
2009: Facebook emerges as a gaming platform.

Online virtual worlds for children

The growth and success of online virtual worlds and massively multi-player online role-playing games (MMORPG) have driven the overall age profile of pay-to-play consumers down. Products such as *Club Penguin* (Disney) and *Moshi Monsters* (Mind Candy), aimed at children as young as six years old, have been key to this change. Typically, online worlds offer social network features and chat services, as well as customizable avatars and habitats, mini-games and other media content. Almost all virtual worlds and MMORPGs deploy the freemium business model that offers two levels of access and service to the player. These two levels are free and premium. These worlds incorporate social features and competitive play that has seen this demographic segment move to virtual worlds from browser-based games. The single most influential factor in determining which games and services this age group will access and play is their parents. ISFE reports that parents of young children who play games online closely monitor which games their children are playing. As ISFE (2011) notes, 'approximately 80 per cent of parents monitor games played by 4–7 year olds, this drops as the age of the child gets older; 50 per cent (Gamer Parents) and 37 per cent (Non-Gaming Parents) monitor games played by their children aged 16–17'.

The most successful products in this space not only offer the features and services children expect, but are associated with parent or affiliate organizations with good reputations for child safety: *Poptropica* is distributed by Pearson Education, *Club Penguin* is a Disney product and Moshi Monsters added credibility to their service by advertising on children's television channels. Other, more established brands have moved into this space and enjoyed some success, including *Build-a-bear*, *Lego*, *Barbie*, and a number of Disney brands. All of these brands enjoy a reputation for child safety and age-appropriate content. An interesting spin-out effect of this part of the sector is the growth of cross-licensing models. Cross-licensing has seen virtual world brands diversify into other product lines and markets including physical goods like toys, action figures and magazines, and other media including broadcast and online linear media. These ventures provide additional revenue streams to brand owners. Virtual worlds for children have successfully monetized what had been a free-to-play segment of the online games audience.

Consoles and motion controllers

The seventh generation of games consoles was launched in 2005 (Microsoft Xbox 360), and 2006 (Sony Playstation 3 and Nintendo Wii). Sony and Microsoft were both building on the success of the previous generation models (Playstation 2 and Xbox), whereas Nintendo's previous Game Cube console had been a critical and commercial flop. The build-up to the release of the Nintendo Wii was characterized by scepticism about the console and its revolutionary Wiimote motion controller.

This scepticism was unfounded. In 2010, eight of the top 20 selling titles were family multi-player or party game formats (ESA, 2011). Games like *Wii Sports Resort, Just Dance* and *Mario Kart* are designed to appeal across family age ranges and encourage competitive and co-operative game play and real-world social interaction around the console. Nintendo's Wii console was the unexpected leader in hardware sales of the seventh generation consoles with 89.36 million units sold worldwide as of Q4 2011 (Nintendo, 2011), which compares favourably to Xbox 360 with 57.6 million units sold (Microsoft, 2011), and PlayStation 3 with 56 million units sold (Sony Computer Entertainment, 2012). In 2010 both competing consoles moved aggressively into the party game space with a new range of sports and fitness titles and new control systems. Microsoft launched Kinect, a camera-based motion sensor; and Sony launched Move, an accurate motion control system.

The Nintendo Wii remains the console of choice for the non-traditional gamer demographic. For example, Reggie Fils-Aime, President of Nintendo America, reported that 80 per cent of female console users play on Nintendo Wii. During a presentation delivered at a BMO Capital Markets event he told attendees that this 'didn't happen by accident [...]. It's the result of a deliberate attempt to expand the market' (Kotaku, 2009).

Unlike its competitors, the Wii also attracts a much younger age group. It is the most popular console for 6- to 11-year-old boys and 25- to 34-year-old women (Nielsen Wire, 2009). Since the launch of the Wii console in 2006, a measurement of family game play habits in 2007 found that the percentage of parents reporting that they play computer games with their children rose from 36 to 45 per cent (ESA, 2011).

Anecdotally, the reason for the appeal of Wii amongst younger and older players is the accessibility of the control system (O'Brien, 2007). The intuitive functionality of the remote control lowers the barrier to the experience by eliminating the complex manual controls common to traditional joy pads.

The iPhone and App Store

Having already established its innovation credentials, and more recently turned the digital distribution model for music on its head, Apple opened its App Store on 10 July 2008 via an update to iTunes. On 11 July of the same year, the iPhone 3G was launched.

Bringing mobile phone functionality to the iPod was not the innovation. Apple brought many of the successful service features from the iTunes store to the App Store. Additionally, Apple reproduced iTunes's closed system that incorporates a reassuringly secure system for purchase and account management, while ensuring customer loyalty through proprietary technology. The success of Apple products builds on their ease of use and accessibility. By addressing these issues with the App Store/iPhone service, Apple removed two of the biggest barriers to mobile games purchases. In doing so, the iPhone liberated smartphone technology from its niche and created a market environment where both hardware and software markets could become competitive. The percentage of gamers playing on handheld or mobile devices has leapt from 36 per cent in 2008 to 55 per cent in 2011 as noted in Table 2.1.

Increasing sophistication of product and service has led to increasing sophistication of use. The augmented scale of the market place has driven down costs and barriers to entry for the high consumption 16–24 demographic. As noted by Ofcom (2011), the top three activities and functions used regularly on mobile phones are social networking (62 per cent), listening to music (62 per cent) and playing games (50 per cent).

At the time of writing, the iPhone is not the bestselling smartphone. In November 2011, the iPhone, with 11.2 per cent of the market, was the fourth bestselling smartphone after the Samsung (25.6 per cent), LG (20.5 per cent) and Motorola (13.7 per cent) handsets (ComScore, 2011). But the App Store has proved an attractive outlet for app developers and has by far the largest and most diverse app market with over 590,000 apps available and more than one billion downloads every month. This compares with the Android Market's 320,000 apps and

Windows Marketplace with 40,000 apps (E2, 2011). The App Store has established the financial models and viability of the market, and driven much of the product and business model innovation in mobile gaming.

Online social networks

The final disruptive service to have a significant impact on changing the game player demographic is the emergence of Facebook as a gaming platform. As a rule, most statistics about Facebook and its use are mind-bogglingly large, so it comes as no surprise that the Facebook games data conforms to this expectation. Facebook has more than 800 million active users covering almost all demographic groups. Ofcom estimates 'that around 40 per cent of time spent on Facebook globally is spent playing games, provided by third-party developers such as Zynga or Playfish' (Ofcom, 2011: 224).

Particular to social network games (SNGs) is the facility to play cooperatively with personal friends. Popcap's research into social gaming shows that '62 per cent of social gamers play social games with personal (real world) friends, followed by 56 per cent who play with online friends, and 37 per cent who play with online strangers' (PopCap, 2010: 42). To play with personal friends seems to be a feature that appeals to a more mature demographic. This may be due to game play on SNGs being more accessible through the incorporation of turn-based mechanics and features familiar in popular board games. Social network games have shifted the age demographic of players upward. The average social game player is 43 years old with almost 60 per cent of social game players above the average gamer's age of 37 (PopCap, 2010: 6).

Many SNGs also feature collectables, wealth accumulation and high levels of customization and personalization. These are features that promote player retention in games but also appeal to female gamers more than to the traditional demographics. This has resulted in more female gamers playing social network games, 55 per cent female as opposed to 45 per cent male gamers (PopCap, 2010: 5). Again, we find that the changes in technology and business models have led to changes in the consumer demographics.

Collectively, the rise of online children's virtual worlds, developments in console technologies, Apple's market innovation and the success of online social networks have resulted in significant changes in the consumer demographic for games. The diversity of the demographic has increased as both younger and older consumers play more games. This change in the demographic of gamers can be attributed to the impact of new delivery channels and customer relationships on the business models of games. In the next section, we focus on pricing mechanisms as a means to examine the business model response.

The changing context of games retail

In 2011, the retail computer games sector in the United Kingdom reported sales worth £1,420 million (Parfitt, 2012). The figure, according to the Entertainment Retailers Association (ERA), represents a 7 per cent reduction on 2010 and a continuing long-term decline in physical sales from the 2008 high of £2,136 million (ERA, 2011). As a sector, computer games retail is under assault from various directions, notwithstanding the financial crisis affecting the major global games markets in the United States, Japan and Europe. The sector has been under further pressure from new distribution technologies and a publishing sector which regards traditional retail models as unfairly exploiting their products beyond the initial sale value. The accusation most often levelled at the boxed-product games retail sector is of promoting 'pre-owned' over 'new' because of the greater margin for the pre-owned product. In this section, we will examine the context of the changing retail environment for games.

The technological advances and expansion of the Internet have dramatically impacted retail business models. The channels through which consumers discover, evaluate, purchase and receive goods and services have radically changed (Osterwalder and Pigneur, 2010). The Internet means that marketing of new games is heavily diversified with amateur and professional review sites now having a key role in consumer awareness of games. Price comparison sites have reduced the ability for retailers to charge different prices online; this impact is also felt in bricks-and-mortar outlets where the ability to charge a recommended retail price (RRP) is limited by the prevalence of discounted goods. The purchasing environment is changing as repeat customers can purchase with a single click. One advantage bricks-and-mortar retail maintains over online is the immediacy of delivery; online provision entails shipment and delivery.

What 'is wrong' with retail? The answer depends on who is being asked. When looking for evidence of consumer-led developments in business models, the catalytic factors in the retail space are most apparent in the debate over the pre-owned games market. As noted in Brown (2010), the issue 'resurfaced early in 2011 when the Electronics Arts UK Managing Director Keith Ramsdale attacked pre-owned retailers for "deliberately extending the reach of their pre-owned offers"'. Pre-owned games are a physical product that has been bought new from a retail outlet (high street or online) that has a trade-in value most commonly redeemed against another new title. Traded games are then re-sold, sometimes multiple times, by the retailer at a reduced price. A similar model can be found in used book and music stores. Almost all games retailers and, increasingly, general entertainment retailers and supermarkets, have moved into offering pre-owned trade-in services. Pre-owned game purchases are estimated to constitute 23 per cent of the US retail market and 20 per cent of the EU retail markets. This compares to 65 per cent of the retail market that is new boxed product and 12 per cent downloaded through online retail services (NewZoo, 2011).

As a result, computer games developers creating physical product for the retail market have access to a continuously shrinking share of consumer spend in the market. In response to these conditions, the games sector has developed new business models. Further, the necessity of finding new customers and developing the game-playing audience has led to the emergence of new products and platforms designed to meet new customer expectations. These new models, discussed below, have brought significant pressure on computer games developers who had grown in size over time in response to the demands of developing products for new generation consoles and advances in 3D gaming. Many larger studios now find it difficult to maintain the level of investment needed to meet the increasing cost of development for the triple-A (high-quality, high-cost, blockbuster-type games) games market. Fahey, in his discussion of the closure of Black Rock Studios, concludes that 'developing top-tier console games has never been more expensive, and it's never been more risky [... and ...] never been less attractive to publishers' (Fahey, 2011). In response to these pressures there are a number of strategies typically being adopted by development studios.

The blockbuster model has emerged in the form of large-scale release into the Q4 market of very high production value franchises including *Call of Duty/Modern Warfare, Assassin's Creed* and *Saints Row*. Variations of this model, used by Crytek GmbH and Bioware (EA), have technology business strands that support longer games development times. Rockstar employs a stable of studios and staggers development periods and release dates across the group. Trading on the success of the franchise and the reputation of the studio, the companies can insulate themselves against risk. The rewards in this space are still considerable as these titles consistently feature in the top ten selling video games every year. Fahey (2011) further notes that 'you can simply accept that the market isn't growing and costs are rising, and respond by trying to extract more money from each of your consumers. The last option is one being embraced by every publisher in the industry. It's the reason for the proliferation of DLC and in-game purchases'.

Unbundling

A trend seen across console, social network and smartphone models is the unbundling of content. The emergence of downloadable content (DLC) as part of major release titles is of considerable interest as it is an example of the cross-fertilization of business models in the games sector. DLC usually takes the form of additional missions, characters or items that can be accessed online and downloaded to the console. Initially available through early networked consoles, Sega's Dreamcast and Sony's PlayStation 2, DLC only became a regular feature of game releases with the emergence of console-affiliated marketplaces. The three major consoles each have a dedicated online market. Microsoft's Xbox 360 connects directly with the Xbox Live Marketplace through the console's user interface. Likewise, Sony's PlayStation Store and Nintendo's Wii Shop Channel allow players to download DLC and other services through an Internet connection.

DLC capability through networked consoles has allowed development studios to begin to exploit a range of business models that have emerged in other markets. Until this point, retail pricing models had fixed the RRP of computer games, the income potential for the studios and publishers and the amount of money that individual consumers could spend. Now, DLC accounts for 12 per cent of the console consumer market value in the United States and 9 per cent in the European Union with 54 per cent of console users regularly downloading content (NewZoo, 2011). Early iterations of the DLC model were based on the Buy-the-Box model that is familiar to MMO players. Buy-the-Box games are normally played online through a PC-based client (a stand-alone interface on a user's computer which communicates with servers).

The market leaders in this space are *World of Warcraft* (Blizzard), with over 10 million subscribers, and *Guild Wars* (NCSoft) with over 5 million units sold. These games exploit variations of the DLC market to generate income to support the continued development of the game. *World of Warcraft* is based on a subscription model where players subscribe to game time (£8.99 per month in the United Kingdom as of 2012) and can purchase expansion packs. *Guild Wars* is subscription free and uses micro-transactions in the in-game market to fund on-going development and operational costs.

More recent iterations of the Buy-the-Box model have been introduced by companies in the retail space. As these companies look for ways to extend product value through the sale of additional content, they introduce unique identification systems that will enable them to recoup some of the pre-owned deficit of the product. Late in 2009, John Riccitiello, CEO of Electronic Arts (EA), gave the green light to 'Project $10' in response to poor retail sales, an over-dependence on the shrinking retail market and the loss of revenue to the pre-owned market. 'Project $10' uses games DLC as a reward to customers who buy new games. Included with the physical product, the customer receives a unique product code that unlocks DLC free of charge. However, anyone buying a pre-owned copy of the game will have to purchase a new code in order to unlock the DLC. EA's Chief Finance Officer Eric Brown claims the scheme is vital to the company's future and is broadly accepted by customers. As reported in Meer (2010), Brown notes: 'The price is $10, which seems to be gaining user acceptance – the acquisitions, the take rates are quite high, well north of 60 per cent on the titles we've seen so far.' However, the revenue generated by the pass is a fraction of the revenue generated by standard DLC on EA games. The company has reported DLC revenue at 70–80 per cent of retail on individual titles, and recognizes the significance of networked consoles in bringing flexibility to the company's business models. Brown also argues that 'the online functionality of triple-A titles [is] leading to enormous revenues' (Meer, 2010).

Pricing strategies

As EA's '$10 Project' experiment suggests, the changes to retail market and demographics have affected the pricing strategy elements of business models. These strategies allow sellers to sell games at different prices to different consumers. The second-hand games market, for example, allows retailers to capture unmet demand by consumers unwilling to pay the full retail price at launch, but willing to wait for a discount. This represents third-degree price discrimination as the market is segmented by time. As the industry shifts from a product-based to a service model, we will see more changes in the pricing structure.

More subtle pricing in computer games comes via additional content. Many models, including the boxed product and freemium games approaches, incorporate a standard game at the entry level. Further content, in the form of maps, DLC, multi-player online environments and in-game assets, can then be purchased by the user. This represents two new pricing strategies in the industry. First, by breaking the game up into different goods and services, rather than using product-bundle pricing, sellers are able to cater to, and capture value from, consumers at different points along the demand curve. Second, the industry is moving to a two-tiered pricing structure where there is an initial fixed fee (which, in the case of freemium, is zero) and a supplementary charge for additional content. For example, the *Smurfs Village* iPhone application represents both unbundled content and tiered pricing as it is free to download, but additional content can be purchased in $4.99 to $99.99 increments (Kang, 2011).

Activision, publisher of the popular *Call of Duty* (COD) franchise, reports a sometimes one-to-one ratio of boxed games sales and DLC. The total sales of the *World at War*, *Modern Warfare 2* and *Black Ops* (the 2008, 2009 and 2010 instalments of the COD franchise) amounted to 51 million copies. Sales of additional content in the form of maps (downloadable multi-player levels) for these instalments totalled 38 million (Orland, 2011). This suggests that, in terms of sales volume, the DLC accounts for 43 per cent of the total. NewZoo (2011) estimates that 54 per cent of American games consumers also purchase DLC and notes that the figure is roughly the same in Europe. Generalizing this to the reported COD sales, this would mean that the average map-purchasing player purchases 1.4 maps.

Games pricing strategies further incorporate micro-transactions, also known as micropayments. The advent of digital technology has meant that very small transactions (such as £0.25) are now feasible as transaction costs have decreased. This has opened up the market for small, one-off payments for digital content and goods within games. It enables the two-tiered pricing model discussed earlier to capture more fully the scope of willing consumers.

Further pricing strategies can be found in the pricing of additional content. Some items can be paid for by experience points earned through gameplay, which is referred to as soft currency. Other items can be paid for via in-game currencies often linked to real-world currencies, known as hard currency. Items may be priced as solely available via soft, hard or both currencies, known as 'dual currency items' (Erez, 2011). The differences between the two currencies are not always distinct, as, for example, Zynga, the makers of *Farmville*, offer both their hard and soft currencies, cash and coins, for sale in exchange for real-world currencies (Farmville Freak, 2010) and as earned currencies. This duality of in-game currencies allows for games to appeal to both the cash poor-time rich and time poor-cash rich consumer demographics.

The development of pricing strategies and in-game currencies has led to the rise of virtual economies. These are particularly prevalent amongst MMORPGs where in-game currencies exhibit the signs of real economies by having inflation, exchange rates and fraud. Gold-farming, in which farmers play games with the purpose of earning in-game currency which is then sold for real-world currency, is the black market equivalent of virtual economies. Trade in virtual currencies is another revenue stream for the games industry as the games businesses sell the currencies and, less commonly, take a percentage of transactions as a fee.

The unbundling of content and use of two-tiered models enables differentiated pricing. It allows games sellers to capture more of the consumer demand for computer games. Much of this differentiated pricing is only possible in the digital era where delivery of additional content can be performed quickly and at low cost.

Conclusion

The games industry has undergone significant changes in business models and technology in the last decade. These changes have both been led by, and resulted in, changes to the demographics of games consumers. The industry itself has adapted to a changing retail environment quickly as it experiments with different pricing structures. Our discussion has highlighted the fact that the games industry continues to evolve and has not yet reached a steady state. This adaptability should be considered a badge of pride for the industry as it seems better positioned than similar digital media sectors.

Under investigation, initial assumptions about the growth of the games market proved to be overly simple. Long-term trends that show a steady increase in the average age of gamers and minor fluctuations in gender balance mask the complexity of demographic diversification. Where the steady growth of the hard-core gamer segment of 18- to 34-year-old males should be apparent in the figures, they fail to register because of the growth of other demographic segments. Technological and service innovation have seen a strong growth in female gamer numbers, and in hours spent in active gaming in social network gaming and party game titles developed for the Nintendo Wii. At the extremes of the age range, Nintendo has captured non-participant audiences through the release of titles aimed at the family and the development of accessible controls in the motion sensitive Wiimote.

Similarly, the boom in online gaming has seen the traditional gamer profile shift significantly due to the increase in product diversity and the willingness of parents to pay to ensure the safety of their children in online social environments. The success of child-friendly virtual worlds has seen an increase in regular active game-play in children as young as four years old. At the other end of the spectrum social network games record the age profile of players as significantly older than the traditional demographic. Where the boom in mobile gaming does not skew to a particular demographic, it has contributed to the significant growth in consumption of games and has resulted in an increasingly large number of small to medium-sized games development studios. The mobile app market has also pioneered a number of new business models and monetization strategies.

Given the combination of technological and demographic change experienced by the games industry, the response, in terms of the development of new business models such as the blockbuster model and approaches based on DLC, is to be expected. New delivery mechanisms, via new platforms such as social media networks and smartphones, have widened the scope of gaming consumers. As we have detailed, the changes in the retail market have led to conflict within the industry and to innovation in pricing strategies. The evolving strategy of the games industry includes new pricing mechanisms such as freemium, micro-payments and the unbundling of content. These new forms of cash flow will continue to shape the future of the games industry as it adapts to new demographics and new platforms.

The disadvantage of the fast-changing nature of the games industry is that it limits our predictive ability. It is unlikely that, ten years ago, we would have foreseen the massive changes imposed on the games sector by the advent of smartphones and social networking websites. Indeed, the trends noted in this chapter will likely change as the games industry continues to refine itself.

References

Ashton, D. (2011) Upgrading the self: technology and the self in digital games perpetual innovation economy, *Convergence*, 17(3): 307–21.

Bhushan, N. (2011) John Woo launches animated web series *Seven Brothers* with Liquid Comics, *The Hollywood Reporter*, http://www.hollywoodreporter.com/news/john-woo-launches-animated-web-275697.

Brown, J. (2010) The pre-owned market, *7outof10*, http://www.7outof10.co.uk/preowned-market/19/04/2010/.

Bruns, A. (2008) *Blogs, Wikipedia, Second Life and Beyond: From Production to Produsage*, New York: Peter Lang.

ComScore (2011) US mobile subscriber market share, *ComScore Reports*, http://www.comscore.com/Press_Events/Press_Releases/2011/12/comScore_Reports_November_2011_U.S._Mobile_Subscriber_Market_Share.

Darkin, C. (2012) Create poster content for sale in online marketplaces, *3D Artist*, 37: 78–9.

E2 (2011) 'How many apps?' *2011 Market Review*, http://www.e2save.com/community/news/how-many-apps-2011/.

Entertainment Retailers Association (ERA) (2011) Yearbook introduction, http://www.eraltd.org/info-stats/overview.aspx.

Erez, Y. (2011) Micro transactions: does it really work? http://digi-boom.blogspot.com/2011/02/micro-transactions-does-it-really-work.html.

Entertainment Software Association (ESA) (2011) *Sales Demographic and Usage Data: Essential Facts 2010*, Washington, DC: Entertainment Software Association.

Fahey, R. (2011) Rock and a hard place, *Games Industry Business*, http://www.gamesindustry.biz/articles/2011-05-06-rock-and-a-hard-place-editorial?page=2.

Farmville Freak (2010) Zynga adds more currency options for *FarmVille* and others, http://farmvillefreak.com/farmville-upgrades/znyga-add-more-currency-options-for-farmville-others.

Humphreys, S., Fitzgerald, B., Banks, J. and Suzor, N. (2005) Fan based production for computer games: user led innovation, the 'drift of value' and the negotiation of intellectual property rights, *Media International Australia incorporating Culture and Policy*, 114: 16–29.

Interactive Software Association Europe (ISFE) (2010) *Video Gamers in Europe 2010*, http://www.isfe.eu/sites/isfe.eu/files/video_gamers_in_europe_2010.pdf.

Kang, C. (2011) In-app purchases in iPad, iPhone, iPod kids' games touch off parental firestorm, *Washington Post*, 8 February 2011, http://www.washingtonpost.com/wp-dyn/content/article/2011/02/07/AR2011020706073.html?sid=ST2011020706437.

Kotaku (2009) Nintendo boasts 9 million player advantage among female console gamers, http://kotaku.com/5411707/nintendo-boasts-9-million-player-advantage-among-female-console-gamers.

Lowood, H. (2006) High performance play: the making of machinima, *Journal of Media Practice*, 7(1): 25–42.

Meer, A. (2010) EA: DLC revenue 'above and beyond' physical sales: FIFA DLC earned $30m, *GamesIndustry.biz*, http://www.gamesindustry.biz/articles/2010-09-15-ea-dlc-revnue-is-above-and-beyond-physical-sales-fifa-dlc-earned-USD30m.

Microsoft Corporation Earnings Release (2011), http://www.microsoft.com/investor/EarningsAndFinancials/Earnings/Kpi/fy12/Q1/detail.aspx.

NewZoo (2011) *Topic Report: DLC, Pre-Owned & Digital Distribution*, http://www.slideshare.net/New7zoo/newzoo-topic-teport-dlc-preowned-digital-distribution-9976665.

Nielsen Wire (2009) Every gaming system has its fans, but women like wii, http://blog.nielsen.com/nielsenwire/consumer/every-gaming-system-has-its-fans-but-women-like-wii/.

Nintendo Co. Ltd. (2011) Consolidated sales transition by region 2011, http://www.nintendo.co.jp/ir/library/historical_data/pdf/consolidated_sales_e1112.pdf.

O'Brien, J. (2007) Wii will rock you, *CNN Fortune and Money*, http://money.cnn.com/magazines/fortune/fortune_archive/2007/06/11/100083454.

Ofcom (2008) *Communications Market Report 2008*, London: Office of Communications.

Ofcom (2010) *Communications Market Report 2010*, London: Office of Communications.

Ofcom (2011) *Communications Market Report 2011*, London: Office of Communications.

Orland, K. (2011) Activision Blizzard reports digital sales growth, 18m *Black Ops* map pack sales, *Gamasutra*, http://www.gamasutra.com/view/news/36985/ Activision_Blizzard_Reports_Digital_Sale.

Osterwalder, A. and Pigneur, Y. (2010) *Business Model Generation: A Handbook for Visionaries, Game Changers, and Challengers*, New York: John Wiley and Sons.

Parfitt, B. (2012) UK games retail sinks 13 per cent in 2011, *Develop News*, http:// www.develop-online.net/news/39427/UK-games-retail-sinks-by-13-in-2011.

PopCap Games Information Solutions Group (2010) Social gaming research 2010, http://www.infosolutionsgroup.com/2010_PopCap_Social_Gaming_ Research_Results.pdf.

Pratchett, R. (2005) *Gamers in the UK: Digital Play, Digital Lifestyles*, London: BBC New Media and Technology.

Sony Computer Entertainment Inc. (2012) Corporate information PlayStation3 worldwide hardware unit sales since April 2006, http://www.scei.co.jp/ corporate/data/bizdataps3_sale_e.html.

UK Interactive Entertainment Association (UKIEA) (2012) Strong quarter four sees 2011 video games sales up on forecasts, http://ukie.info/content/strong-quarter-four-sees-2011-video-games-sales-forecasts.

3
The Role of the Consumer: From Sales to Co-production

Peter Zackariasson and Timothy L. Wilson

Introduction

In 2012 Tim Schafer raised more than \$1 million in less than 24 hours towards his next video game development – not from a big-name publisher, but from fans alerted to the project on Twitter and Facebook (Snider, 2012). Reflecting on this rapid response, industry analyst Wanda Meloni commented: 'I think there is a growing pent-up demand for really good, creatively designed games that aren't coming out of the big publishers' (Snider, 2012: 5B). This development signals a full circle return of the importance of the consumer in video game development. In the initial stages of the industry developers and consumers were peers – individuals programming computers for their own entertainment. As commercial interests grew, users became the targets for sales and thus the indirect sponsors of development. Now, as Tim Schafer's experience shows, they are becoming more directly involved in the financing of games. Always, however, it was the consumer who both provided and was a user of value in these games.

In this chapter we discuss how the consumer is made part of the development of video games, from sales to co-production. The role of the consumer, however, is neither straightforward nor easily defined because video games, similar to other cultural products, do not follow a simple development pattern of definition and production. A discussion of the role of the consumer in the context of cultural products, and of video games specifically, is consequently of particular importance. In this chapter we will therefore focus on the person for whom games are ultimately created for, the gamer. Like any other industry, the video games industry comprises a large number of different actors, and the value chain in the development of video games (Zackariasson and

Wilson, 2012) could be described as follows: developer – publisher – distributor – retailer – customer – consumer. But the consumer, as end user, is not merely the final participant in the value chain. The consumer is an important actor for sending feedback back along the value chain, in order for value to be created throughout the process of delivering a video game.

Developing a consumer perspective

Characterizing the nature of video games in a basic, satisfactory sense remains a challenge. In our initial paper on this topic, we suggested that massively multi-player online games (MMOGs) could possibly be described as part of the services industry, specifically as a tourism service[1] which involves people going somewhere and participating in different activities (Zackariasson and Wilson, 2004). But instead of a physical setting we were exploring the mental and cognitive tourism involved in many different forms of media interaction. The virtual world in general, and MMOGs specifically, give participants a place to go to and they go there apparently for the same reasons that tourists visit places, for activities, for events and because of the surroundings. The difference between conventional and virtual tourism is that the consumer must be encouraged to come back again and again, for instance as an actor in an action adventure like *Battlestar Galactica* or as a participant in a social setting like *Friends* to enjoy the set and company. Further, within the general regime of games it is clear that labelling them as services does not capture the nuances developed across the spectrum of available games. There is thus a need to develop a consumer perspective on video games and to explore what they, as service users, get from these games. In one of the classic papers on software development, Boehm (1988: 63) reflects that 'I can't tell you what I want, but I'll know when I see it'. This quote to a large extent describes the nature of video game consumers. Potential purchasers may not be able to describe what they want, but they surely know what it is when they see it, as evidenced in worldwide industry sales which were valued at approximately $52 billion per year in 2009, expected to grow to $80 billion in 2015 (DePrato *et al.*, 2012: 223).

The background to understanding this consumer perspective comes from Hesmondhalgh (2007), who has provided a valuable overview of the cultural industries and their commercialization, and Colbert (2007) who relates the cultural industries with marketing to consumers. These studies suggest that the cultural industries are characterized by two, sometimes conflicting, development logics: production logic and marketing logic. Video games fall into this category of industries. When applying production logic the point of departure is the competence of the organization to deliver the product or service, followed, after production, by aggressive promotion techniques that are applied to create sales. This logic can also be described as an engineering way of doing business and it is used in a large number of organizations today. The benefit of this approach is that production is based on existing knowledge within the organization, resulting in a product or service that is more likely to be of high quality. The downside of the engineering perspective is that there is not necessarily a correlation between what an organization has in the way of knowledge to develop a product or service and what the customer would actually like to have.

The alternative to production logic is to apply a marketing logic to the production of the offering. The difference between production logic and market logic is that the latter is based on a consumer focus sustained throughout the entire production process. Instead of taking internal capabilities as a starting point in the organization, the needs and wants of consumers are what drive production. Need is defined by Kotler *et al.* (2008: 8–9) as states of felt deprivation; want is defined as the form that human needs take as they are shaped by culture and individual personality. More specifically needs and wants relate to the American Marketing Association (2012) definition of consumer motivation as 'the positive or negative needs, goals, desires, and forces that impel an individual toward or away from certain actions, activities, objects, or conditions. It is the needs and wants of the individual, the driving force, guided by cognitions, behind the behavior to motivational approach to attitudes [sic] purchase, approach, or avoid products and ideas and things.'[2]

With the consumer as a starting point, an organization has the potential to find the appropriate way to satisfy his or her needs or of determining these needs. Nevertheless, once a product or service has been developed, promotional activities are required in order to communicate with consumers. Compared to the hard sell that takes place at the end of a production logic, developing a product based on the needs and wants of consumers will involve a much smoother communication process.

These dichotomies are valuable as models for thought, but it is rarely the case that any producer strictly follows either one or the other logic. Any firm would rather have a foothold in both the production assets of the organization as well as understanding the needs and wants of the consumer. Nevertheless, if we go back to the value chain referred to earlier (developer – publisher – distributor – retailer – customer – consumer), firms will display a dominant logic, operating as if reading the value chain from left to right (production approach to development) or from right to left (suggesting a marketing logic to development). The following section discusses how video games can be understood in terms of these logics.

Watershed moments in the video games industry

The video games industry has seen a shift in logic. Reflecting on the evolution of the industry towards a marketing approach to consumers, two events come to mind (Zackariasson and Wilson, 2010).[3] There have been watershed moments in the industry as it has shifted to a consumer-based approach. These events may be called paradigm shifts, as first described by Kuhn (1996 [1969]). An early, yet significant, shift during the evolution of the industry was the formation of Activision in 1979 as a third party video game developer-publisher (Kent, 2001). The old paradigm of having a vertically integrated company dominating an industry, while at the same time contracting specialists who could do portions of the work better, was simply no longer adequate. Further, an arrangement where games software for games consoles was exclusively published by the producers of these consoles was unlikely to develop a marketing logic aiming towards consumer satisfaction. The introduction of the Internet to commercial activities in the mid-1990s created the second watershed moment for the games industry. It opened up possibilities for video games that supported many people playing the same game, from a handful to many thousands. While modems had made this possible since the late 1970s, the Internet eventually became technically more advanced and significantly cheaper for the user. With these new possibilities two new genres of video games evolved, the Massively Multiplayer Online Role-Playing Game (MMORPG) and the Massively Multiplayer Online Social Game (MMOSG). What characterizes these is that the game has a persistent world that can be accessed at any time over the Internet and that the game centres on the development of a digital representation (an avatar) in this virtual world. In effect, consumers not only entered these games holding virtual identities, but they had also become involved in co-producing them.

The nature of the video games market

There are some known facts about the consumer market for video games. The demographics, for instance, are well known. Statistics from the Entertainment Software Association (ESA, 2012), a US games industry organization, summarize the key characteristics as follows:

- The average gamer is 30 years old and has been playing for 12 years. Again, 68 per cent of gamers are 18 years of age or older.
- Of all players, 47 per cent are women, and women older than 18 years of age are one of the industry's fastest growing demographics.
- Today, women represent a greater portion of the game-playing population (30 per cent) than boys age 17 or younger (18 per cent).
- Of the gamers, 62 per cent play games with others, either in person or online and 78 per cent of these gamers play with others at least one hour per week.
- Social games are played by 33 per cent of gamers.
- Gamers play on-the-go: 33 per cent play games on their smartphones, and 25 per cent play on their handheld device.

We also know about the motivation of gamers. Yee (2007) suggested, building on the work of Bartle (1996), that these motivations could be characterized into three main components, which were in turn composed of ten sub-components. The main components were achievement, social aspects and immersion. Yee summarizes these as follows:

1. Achievement
   - *advancement*: progress, power, accumulation, status;
   - *mechanics*: numbers, optimization, templating, analysis;
   - *competition*: challenging others, provocation, domination.
2. Social
   - *socializing*: casual chat, helping others, making friends;
   - *relationship*: personal, self-disclosure, finding and giving support;
   - *teamwork*: collaboration, groups, group achievements.
3. Immersion
   - *discovery*: exploration, lore, finding hidden things;
   - *role-playing*: story line, character history, roles, fantasy;
   - *customization*: appearances, accessories, style, colour schemes;
   - *escapism*: relax, escape from reality, avoid real problems.

What has yet to be determined is a market segmentation approach that is useful for game developers to approach their task. In a previous study (Zackariasson *et al.*, 2006) the main objective of the game development studio we studied was to develop games that were fun and immersed their gamers. Thus, the developers operated with the same kind of uncertainty that characterizes most other cultural undertakings (Caves, 2000). In this context fun and immersion have to be defined as the games are built, and normally it is the project team that ascertains the potential for fun and immersion. In our study the in-house approach that was set up ascertained whether fun was being built into the game as it was developed (Zackariasson *et al.*, 2006). Every two weeks the portions of the game that had been developed were placed into a build, a playable version of the game. Our conversations with other actors in the industry suggest that today it is standard to apply agile project structures, for example SCRUM,[4] to handle these uncertainties in the development process.

Based on these considerations, the market could be segmented along the axes of fun and immersion, defining a desire for fun and immersion as a conceptual space for games development (see Figure 3.1). Clusters in this space are as yet to be determined, as are ways of quantifying 'fun' and 'immersion'. Market segmentation thus remains an area for future research.

The closest we have come is to identify possible clusters that are associated with existing games. There is a larger cluster comprising individuals who get a lot of fun from and are immersed in MMORPG and MMOSG games. It remains to be seen whether this is a single cluster

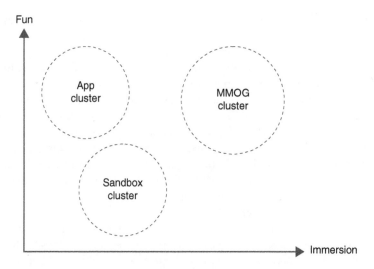

Figure 3.1 Conceptual space for segmenting the gamer market

or two, and it is not clear how closely present games are serving the segment or segments. Another cluster comprises gamers who are fun oriented, but who do not get highly immersed in app games that may be downloaded on their portable devices. And there are other clusters in the spaces in between – and beyond – these main clusters which are represented as a single sandbox cluster in Figure 3.1. Their locations and characteristics would provide a clear and practical target for developing a game, or games, as the location of the cluster on the fun and immersion axes would provide insight into gamers' wants and needs. It is useful to return to the marketing definition of need cited earlier which emphasizes the needs and wants of the individual as the driving force, guided by cognitions, behind the individual's attitude to purchase, approach or avoid products, ideas and things (American Marketing Association, 2012). Developers who best understand those needs and wants and develop offerings that most closely meet them are assured a significant element of success.

Finally, and importantly, it is worth noting that the largest single cluster in this space comprises the many and as yet unspecified non-player clusters. The reality is that more and more non-players are being drawn into playing. Consequently, all clusters in this space are growing and new clusters will be developed as well.

Getting the consumer's influence into the game

While our understanding of the market place in which games operate is not yet fully developed, we are still faced with the need to understand present marketing approaches and requirements. We therefore turn to some practical matters. First, it is suggested that a video game is partly an artistic production and partly a commercial production, similar to other products in the cultural industries (for instance music, television, and film). This combination of art and commerce means that production will place more emphasis on the abilities and visions of the group creating the game than on those consuming the product. Nevertheless, the outlook of the consumer must be inserted into the development process. This insertion has been accomplished by having gamers develop games, as illustrated in early studies conducted in a Swedish games developing studio (Zackariasson, 2003). Here, nearly everyone working in the company was also a gamer, that is to say, if you wanted to work there you had to play video games. This pattern has been confirmed by other studies (Dovey and Kennedy, 2006). That all developers in our case company were gamers was highly visible.

Playing games seemed to be part of the work, and that meant playing games developed within the firm as well as those developed by other studios. The sound of gunfire or of games crashing somewhere in the office was constant, and interviews confirmed that being a gamer was a prerequisite for work in the studio. The CEO of a Swedish game studio explained that those producing games also had to have a great deal of experience in playing games. This experience, he suggested, equipped the individual developer with insight and capability that no formal education can provide. If he had to choose between a technically highly skilled person and a devoted gamer, he would in most cases choose the latter because it was easier to train a gamer to produce graphics for games than it is to train a skilled graphical artist to produce good game graphics (Zackariasson, 2003). Collins (2001) refers to this as a matter of getting the right people on the bus. In this case, the right people were on the bus indeed, as they not only had functional skills, but were evidently gamers as well. They had the ability to evaluate results, the knowledge required to take the next step in the development process, and the commitment to take that step. Having studied the development of technology, Akrich (1992, 1995) suggests that the developer often takes on the dual role in the product development process of developer and expert user, resulting in a method of development described by Akrich (1995) as I-methodology. In that approach designers of new products anticipate and represent the envisioned user. It is tempting to accept this suggestion because elements present in the development process often meet anticipated wants or needs of developers. However, this approach, we argue, does not capture the dynamics of producer-user involvement adequately. A more appropriate analogy for describing the process is provided by Simon (1996) who suggests that making 'complex designs that are implemented over a long period of time and continually modified in the course of implementation has much in common with painting in oil. In oil painting every new spot of pigment laid on the canvas creates some kind of pattern that provides a continuing source of new ideas to the painter' (Simon, 1996: 162–3). Video game development, as observed in this firm (Zackariasson, 2003), appeared to follow this type of approach, and for two reasons. First, there was the fuzzy front end. As an initial step, the game was sketched out only roughly. Developments were centred upon features that the games would provide and not upon some final design. Second, both technology and expectations of consumers were likely to change over the two-year period it would take to develop the game. Consequently, progress was driven by the ten-day evaluations described in a number of previous studies, including Zackariasson *et al.* (2006), where the interim build became Simon's pigment on the canvas to which the development team reacted. Game development does not proceed on a random or ad hoc basis. The process of developing video games traditionally follows a number of distinguishable and separate stages (Sellers, 2003): concept, pre-production, production and post-production. This process has evolved from a traditional waterfall model of organizing product development, using a standard project management method. This project model, used in widely different situations (Meredith and Mantel, 2003) presupposes a definition of the product, followed by the planning, execution and evaluation stages. However, game studios have abandoned this project model and are using, almost exclusively, agile project models such as SCRUM. This shift occurred because of the problem of defining the end result of a game, just as in any other cultural product (Caves, 2000). In an agile project model it is possible to improve the game incrementally throughout the entire project cycle (Shore and Warden, 2008; Walfisz *et al.*, 2006; Zackariasson *et al.*, 2006). In brief, the different stages involve the following:

- at the concept stage the content of the game is identified;
- in pre-production a production team is staffed and the game idea is specified with regard to how this idea will be developed;
- in the production stage the game is built;
- in the post-production stage the game is evaluated and polished for release.

It is worth noting in this process that in textbooks on game development it is argued that the consumer should be made part of the development, from pre-production until post-production phases. Sellers (2003: 256) summarizes as follows:

> During pre-production, early mock-ups and prototypes should have been given exposure to players to look for interest and comprehension – is the game going to be fun and will players understand it? During production, gameplay testing of individual levels, modules, or systems also helps hone the design and keep implementation on track. Now [post-production], with the entire game in place, full gameplay testing begins in earnest.

The argument made by Sellers (2003) is that if consumers are involved early in the development process there will be a higher likelihood that the game will attract the defined target segment. This approach does not necessarily involve a marketing logic in development, but rather anchors game concepts that are sketched internally with consumers which have the ability to attract interest early and maintain it throughout production. Succeeding with this agenda could mean building a game that meets the expectations of intended consumers as their on-going involvement equally creates their high expectations and ensures that they can be met (as discussed further below).

The most concrete and hands-on impact that consumers have on the development of video games is in post-production. Post-production of games requires a number of deliverables. In two of these deliverables, the alpha and beta versions of the game, consumers are invited to participate as game-testers before the final version, gold master, is released; the gold master is thus the version that consumers would buy. These play-testers have a dual role in evaluating games, much in line with the film industry's usage of panel audiences in film screening. Frequently this is the first time anyone other than the game studio or publisher have the opportunity to experience the actual game. Consequently, it is a crucial moment to establish to what extent the design intentions of the game meet the needs and wants of the intended consumer. Will the intention of the developers be understood by consumers? Will the consumers enjoy the game features? Will they understand these features? Will they use them correctly? The degree of fun experienced by gamers is next to impossible to define or quantify. Since fun involves a subjective opinion the process of developing games has largely, until this point, been based on the opinions of those involved in the game development project. One of the objectives of play-testing is thus to determine whether the game is indeed fun. The second aspect of play-testing is to test technical issues of the game, how it performs and how failsafe it is. Any software project contains thousands upon thousands of lines of code. Making all lines failsafe and making them all work smoothly is next to impossible. There may be processes for making code that is easy to revise, code that is structured and where bugs should be fairly easy to locate. Despite the knowledge of developers and the sophistication of the tools they use to create games, it is not until the moment when they place consumers in front of the game that the code is truly pushed to its limit. Successful alpha and beta releases will push the game forward in developing content that is appreciated by the target consumer, an interaction between the consumer and the game interface that satisfies initial goals and ensures that the code does not contain errors. The result is a game that is both market adapted and technically failsafe.

Finally, firms have moved to a form of product management in the development process (Zackariasson and Wilson, 2006). Concepts of this form of organization go back to the US consumer products industry of the 1920s (Kotler, 1972, 2000). Essentially an individual is given responsibility for harmonizing the various activities surrounding a product, particularly with regard to professionalizing the development process. Although one might suspect that this type of organization would be product logic-oriented, in practice it can have a consumer-oriented bias. This is the case with game development.

Conventionally, the product manager is responsible for ensuring that the product is appropriate for the intended market and for implementing a programme that is suitable for its marketing. Also, conventionally, he or she is an influence in that process. That is to say, the individual has the responsibility of project management without the authority to get things done. He or she works through people as opposed to having people work for him or her. In the development process referred to in Zackariasson and Wilson (2006), it was the project manager who had authority, but the product manager had influence in bringing intermediate feedback back from the marketplace:

> What we are saying to developers is that we're not inventing this observation; it is a 'fact'. That is why developers today accept what should be changed, what should be added. (Zackariasson and Wilson, 2006: 234)

On the other hand, he acknowledged that sometimes discussions were required:

> Sometimes they (the developers) do not want to hear what marketing has to say, then we have to be convincing. Maybe we are wrong also, so we need to say the consumers were saying this. Is it really a good idea? Then there is a discussion between marketing and the developers. (Zackariasson and Wilson, 2006: 234–5)

And of course there are times when a project manager has difficulty in exercising any influence:

> Additionally, marketing does not have as much influence over the developer that has had a few good games as they might have over a developer that is making his first game for us. (Zackariasson and Wilson, 2006: 235)

Conventional marketing concerns

Much of this chapter has been devoted to reflecting on the incorporation of a marketing logic into game development. We see this as the present, prime marketing challenge and anticipate a regime of benefits when it is achieved. At the same time, conventional concerns such as promotion, pricing and distribution of games cannot be overlooked. In order to be successful, an appropriate package must be put together for the particular game and segment of interest. Most frequently this package is put together by the publisher (Readman and Grantham, 2006).

Sometimes marketing and promotion are thought of as being synonymous. They are, of course, not and over half this chapter has been devoted to discussing how marketing enters the development process. Promotion is, however, important. It not only makes potential consumers aware of the product, but raises expectations of the product – buzz, as it were. Among the large publishers (for instance Activision, Electronic Arts and Ubisoft) typically 50 per cent of revenues are ploughed back into promoting business in one aspect or another (Zackariasson and Wilson, 2012). The package is similar in some respects to that used for film and books. Since promotion affects unit sales, the amount spent on any one game is a function of expected sales, a circular practice that produces self-fulfilling prophecies. TV gets some emphasis, but a two-step process through independent reviewers and publication is important. Naturally alpha and beta results play an important role in these reviews.

With respect to the message in promotion, there is some advantage in going back to considering games as services (Zackariasson and Wilson, 2004). That is, service theory is based on the premise that consumers' concepts of both quality and satisfaction are based on an actual versus expectations comparison (Zeithaml and Bitner, 2000; Grönroos, 2007). That is to say, individuals have some inherent expectation of what is to be experienced. If actual experience and expectations are the same, they tend to be satisfied; if actual is better than expected they tend to be very satisfied. Expectations can be managed through promotion, hence considerations in this area are vitally important. It is suggested that increasing expectations before the game is released will generally result in consumer satisfaction being higher. The reason for this, argues Oliver (1997), is that if the outcome does not match expectations the previous increase will still generate a positive satisfaction. This should be compared with a game where consumers have no previous experience and any negative satisfaction has the potential to lower overall satisfaction.

With regard to pricing, only when the game is distributed directly via the Internet to the consumer does the publisher, or developer, have direct control. Otherwise it is a retail function and tends to go by game classification and thus expected popularity. The function is clearly important. In a study of Swedish game development Sandqvist (2010) showed that, despite the high revenues among developers, profit is low or non-existent for game developers. Revenues are instead generated in other parts of the value chain. Subscriptions to MMORPGs and MMOSGs remain popular and depend upon adding features to sustain loyalty. The key change in this area has been to give the game away and rely upon purchases of items within the game for revenue. The industry must wait to see if Schafer has hit on something by having consumers prepay for a game that is yet to be developed – individuals who pledged $15 will get a free download and access to the ongoing video and discussion group (Snider, 2012).

Finally, distribution of games has been featured as either traditional specialty and discount brick and mortar stores, online retailers, or downloads. Breakthroughs in service distribution, however, tend to enlarge and markedly change industries, for instance ATMs in retail banking, Federal Express and package distribution. The breakthrough in games has been the use of social networks in distribution, as is the case with Zynga[5] through Facebook. Latest results, however, suggest that Zynga has underperformed expectations, which in turn has produced underperformance in Facebook's financial results (Thurm, Raice and Demos, 2012). Further, Zynga no longer has the field to itself, receiving competition from Gree and DeNA in mobile games (Wakabayashi and Ante, 2012). A second-hand (used) games market has not become a large, commercial sector, perhaps because of technology advancement in games, but GameStop has indicated it will explore its development (Molina, 2012).

Concluding comments

It is difficult writing chapters on video games that retain currency – the industry itself moves so rapidly. Nevertheless, we have taken our shot here in dealing with the relevance of marketing, particularly a marketing logic, in video game development and final sales. Following the line of argument made in this chapter, two things seem especially important. Firstly, the video game industry needs consumer involvement in order to grow to a position where the actors in the industry can carve out stable and sound business ventures. Secondly, as video games are cultural products there is a need to expand upon who will participate in the interpretation and creation of symbols of society. Each of these considerations is important on its own. Taken together they bring out both the economic and cultural importance of customer involvement in video game development.

In a commercial sense, the development of video games has to acquire and sustain a profit motive. It is true that the industry consists of people with a passion for games: eating, drinking and sleeping and always thinking of games. But even these people have to fund their livelihood somehow. Most games are developed in order to generate money, at least to break even. Unfortunately we have heard game studios passionately urging eager game development students to follow their passion and – take any job available just in order to build the games they want. This approach might work as an entrance to the industry, but game development has to grow into something more than an activity that lingers on the border between business and hobby. Further, as suggested by Dymek (2012), this paradigm results in most games being developed for gamers. Our premise is that involving consumers will produce games that have a wider attraction in the marketplace, decreasing the misses and wasted development that is always involved in developing games.

Setting aside the economic importance of involving the consumer in game development, there is an academic cultural importance that is equally important. Video games are cultural products, in the same way as film, art and music also are cultural products. It has been suggested, however, that all cultural production is symbolic production (Hesmondhalgh, 2007). This correlation means that whoever is defining the content, in a painting, musical lyrics or a video game, some aspect of society is being interpreted and thus, that individual is offering his or her understanding, or critique, in the final product. In the development of a video game there is a rather homogenous set of persons defining digital worlds for a heterogeneous set of consumers (see Zackariasson, Chapter 6 in this volume). The result is that consumers are forced into an understanding of society as viewed from a very narrow viewpoint. Much of the nuances that exist in our physical world are lost, leaving only a distilled version for millions of consumers to interact within.

Finally, although we have focused our thoughts on how the consumer is, or might be, involved in development, we made some observations on marketing as it exists today in the industry. The one thing that is certain is that changes will be made – perhaps by the time this chapter comes to market. That is one of the attractions, however, in the field.

There are individuals in the industry out there pushing change and it is our pleasure to be on-lookers to their efforts.

Notes

1. As the authors commented in Zackariasson and Wilson (2012a), leisure is also used to categorize video games. It is, of course, a matter of definition. But we believe that the leisure terminology has an unfortunate similarity to what Huizinga (1950 [1938]) describes as the magic circle. This bounds an activity and shields it from the outside world, thus disconnecting the content of the activity from the outside. We believe that this does not fully serve in the understanding of video games.
2. http://www.marketingpower.com/_layouts/Dictionary.aspx?dLetter= M#motivation.
3. We are ignoring here the transition of graphics from dots on oscilloscopes to icons on a screen and the commercial transition of the product.
4. Scrum is based on the concept that software development is not a defined process, but an empirical process with complex input/output transformations that may or may not be repeated under differing circumstances. The name is derived from a rugby play where the teams attempt to move against each other in large, brute force groups (Boehm and Turner, 2004: 168).
5. Zynga, the company formed by Mark Pincus in 2007, has been a game changer in the industry. Basically, it has permitted play for free, but its audience of 150 million players (September 2011) have the opportunity to buy chickens for $5 in Farmville or pay $3 for skyscrapers in Cityville. Facebook provides the social base that gives Zynga appeal: players use friend connections on it to find other players (Wingfield, 2010: A1 and A4).

References

Akrich, M. (1992) The de-scription of technical objects, in W.E. Bijker and J. Law (eds), *Shaping Technology/Building Society: Studies in Sociotechnical Change*, Cambridge, MA: MIT Press, pp. 205–24.

Akrich, M. (1995) User representations: practices, methods and sociology, in A. Rip, T.J. Misa and J. Schot (eds), *Managing Technology in Society: The Approach of Constructive Technology Assessment*, London: Pinter Publishers, pp. 167–84.

American Marketing Association (2012) *Online dictionary*, www.marketingpower. com.

Bartle, R. (1996) Hearts, clubs, diamonds, spades: players who suit MUDs, www. mud.co.uk/richard/hcds.htm.

Boehm, B.W. (1988) A spiral model of software development and enhancement, *IEEE Computer* (May 1988): 61–72.

Boehm, B.W. and Turner, R. (2004) *Balancing Agility and Discipline*, Boston, MA: Addison-Westley.

Caves, R.E. (2000) *Creative Industries: Contracts between Art and Commerce*, Cambridge, MA: Harvard University Press.

Colbert, F. (2007) *Marketing Culture and the Arts*, Montreal: HEC.

Collins, J. (2001) *Good to Great*, New York: Harper Business.

DePrato, G., Lindmark, S., and Simon, J.-P. (2012) The evolving video game software ecosystem, in P. Zackariasson and T.L. Wilson (eds), *The Video Game Industry: Formation, Present State and Future*. New York: Routledge, pp. 221–43.

Dovey, J. and Kennedy, H. W. (2006) *Game Cultures: Computer Games and New Media*, Berkshire: Open University Press.

Dymek, M. (2012) Video games – a subcultural industry, in P. Zackariasson and T.L. Wilson. (eds), *The Video Game Industry: Formation, Present State and Future*, New York: Routledge, pp. 34–56.

ESA (2012) *2012 Essential Facts About the Computer and Video Game Industry*, http://www.theesa.com/facts/gameplayer.asp.

Grönroos, C. (2007) *Service Management and* Marketing, 3rd edition, New York: John Wiley.

Hesmondhalgh, D. (2007) *The Cultural Industries*, London: Sage.

Huizinga, Johan (1950 [1938]) *Homo Ludens: A Study of the Play Element in Culture*, Boston, MA: The Beacon Press.

Kent, S.L. (2001) *Ultimate History of Video Games*, Rocklin, CA: Prima Publishing.

Kotler, P. (1972) *Marketing Management*, 2nd edition, Englewood Cliffs, NJ: Prentice Hall.

Kotler, P. (2000) *Marketing Management*, Millennium edition, Upper Saddle River, NJ: Prentice Hall.

Kotler, P., Armstrong, G., Wong, V. and Saunders, J. (2008) *Principles of Marketing*, 5th European edition, Harlow: Prentice Hall.

Kuhn, T.S. (1996 [1969]) *The Structure of Scientific Revolutions*, Chicago, IL: University of Chicago Press.

Meredith, J. and Mantel, S. (2003) *Project Management: A Managerial Approach*, 5th edition, Hoboken, NJ: Wiley.

Molina, B. (2012) GameStop exploring digital game resales. Online USA Today, http://content.usatoday.com/communities/gamehunters/post/2012/07/gamestop-exploring-digital-game-resale-space/1.

Oliver, R.L. (1997) *Satisfaction: A Behavioural Perspective on the Consumer*, New York: McGraw-Hill.

Readman, J. and Grantham, A. (2006) Shopping for buyers of product development expertise: how video games developers stay ahead, *European Management Journal*, 24(4): 256–69.

Sandqvist, U. (2010) *Digital Dreams and Industrial Development: The Swedish Computer and Video Game Industry 1980–2010*, Doctoral thesis, Department of Economic History, Umeå University, Sweden.

Sellers, M. (2003) The stages of game development, in F.D. Laramée (ed.), *Secrets of the Game Business*, Hingham, MA: Charles River Media, Chapter 4.1.

Shore, J. and Warden, S. (2008) *The Art of Agile Development*, Sebastopol, CA: O'Reilly Media.

Simon, H. (1996). *The Sciences of the Artificial*, 3rd edition, Cambridge, MA: MIT Press.

Snider, M. (2012) Game designer gets financed by the players, *USA Today* (10 February): 5B.

Thurm, S., Raice, S. and Demos, T. (2012) Social-media frenzy fizzles, *Wall Street Journal* (July 28–29): B1 and B3.

Wakabayashi, D. and Ante, S.E. (2012) A land grab for mobile games, *Wall Street Journal* (14 June): B1 and B2.

Walfisz, M., Zackariasson, P. and Wilson, T.L. (2006) Real-time strategy: evolutionary game development, *Business Horizons*, 49(6): 487–98.

Wingfield, N. (2011) Virtual products, real profits, *Wall Street Journal* (9 September): A1 and A4.

Yee, N. (2007) Motivations of play in online games, *Journal of Cyber Psychology and Behavior*, 9: 772–5.

Zackariasson, P. (2003) *Cyborg Leadership: Including Nonhuman Actors in Leadership*, Licentiate Thesis, Umeå School of Business and Economics, Department of Business Administration, Umeå University, Umeå, Sweden.

Zackariasson, P. and Wilson, T.L. (2004) Massively multiplayer online games: a 21st century service? Other Players Conference, Copenhagen, Denmark, 6–8 December 2004.

Zackariasson, P., Walfisz, M. and Wilson, T.L. (2006) Management of creativity in video game development: a case study, *Services Marketing Quarterly*, 27(4): 73–97.

Zackariasson, P. and Wilson, T.L. (2006) Marketing of video games 'A': a product managers view, in J. Chapman (ed.), *Association of Marketing Theory and Practice (AMTP) Proceedings*: pp. 231–6.

Zackariasson, P. and Wilson, T.L. (2010) Paradigm shifts in the video game industry, *Competitiveness Review*, 20(2): 139–51.

Zackariasson, P. and Wilson, T.L. (2012a) Introduction, in P. Zackariasson and T.L. Wilson (eds), *The Video Game Industry: Formation, Present State and Future*, New York: Routledge, pp. 1–14.

Zackariasson, P. and Wilson, T.L. (2012b) Marketing of video games, in P. Zackariasson and T. L. Wilson (eds), *The Video Game Industry: Formation, Present State and Future*, New York: Routledge, pp. 57–75.

Zeithaml, A. and Bitner, M.J. (2000) *Services Marketing*, 2nd edition, New York and London: McGraw-Hill.

4
Business Growth, the Internet and Risk Management in the Computer Games Industry

Neil McGregor

Introduction

According to Wasserman (2011) the growth of the Internet has transformed the software industry in a wide variety of ways. These include the creation of new business opportunities as well as significant impacts across software business processes such as software development, distribution and product support. This chapter examines one significant sub-sector of the software industry, the computer (or video) games industry, and focuses on the impact on games development companies of the opportunities created by developments in Internet and mobile technologies.

The computer games industry has grown rapidly since the first games were developed in the 1960s. In this chapter we define the computer games industry to include games played on a computer (PC games) as well as those played on a games console (such as Playstation or Xbox), or on a handheld device. The industry has grown into a multi-billion dollar global business comparable in scale to the global film industry (Johns, 2005). We will illustrate how the Internet has altered computer games production networks and how the associated new business models, adopted by games development businesses, introduce the potential for significantly increased rewards. However, these opportunities do not come without associated risks. Utilizing evidence from the games development cluster in Dundee, Scotland, the chapter illustrates that these new business models, if they are to succeed, require businesses to understand, evaluate and manage the associated risk exposure. Ultimately, this involves the acquisition of key management competencies in order to manage exposure to market and price-related risks, which were previously borne by other stakeholders in the games production network.

Games production networks and changing business models

The computer games industry in the United Kingdom has experienced remarkable growth over the past decade. However, the games industry is undergoing an important transition as many games development studios begin to move away from the old work-for-hire (WFH) based business models to strategies geared towards creating and exploiting their own intellectual property (IP). These new and emerging business models are largely a result of the opportunities (and threats) associated with the Internet and other mobile technologies. A report by IFF Research (2008) undertaken for the Skills for Business Network in the United Kingdom highlighted the key changes in the games industry in the mid-2000s. These are the emergence of digital downloads (either to a PC or console) as a means of distributing the product to the customer, and the development of user-generated content platforms and online communities.

The first of these has had a significant impact on the way businesses in the games development sector operate and are structured. The digital download route to market represents an opportunity for businesses of all sizes. Investment in new skills, and for smaller businesses the acquisition of critical hardware, are seen as necessary pre-requisites to the exploitation of these opportunities. The second trend is a newer development and most businesses in the sector are beginning to explore and, in many cases, exploit its potential. Due to the uncertainties associated with the scale and dynamics of these opportunities, games developers are not yet able to quantify fully the growth associated with these two developments. Even the largest employers that are at the forefront of the sector's online offerings consider the extent of the impact of recent developments to be unpredictable (IFF Research, 2008). While the new business models have the potential to offer significantly greater rewards, there are associated risks for the businesses. The current study utilizes data derived from a series of interviews with key stakeholders, as well as a range of secondary data sources, to identify how the business models are changing and to assess what the games developers need to do to make these new, higher risk business models work.

The traditional computer games developer business model: work-for-hire

Prior to the proliferation of Internet-afforded opportunities for the games industry, the standard business model for games developers was similar to that illustrated in Figure 4.1. According to Stolz (2008), a video game typically becomes attractive to consumers due to the variety and the originality of the game software, even if it is true that hardware innovations are also relevant to innovative game development. Due to the mutual dependence of hardware (for instance Sony, Nintendo and Microsoft) and software producers, their relationship has been described as symbiotic (Johns, 2005). Game software is typically produced by game software publishers (some of which can also be hardware manufacturers) or specialized, independent software firms. The independents develop and produce game software on their own and sell their products to the hardware producers, usually on a WFH basis. Besides these, there are also smaller software houses which, due to resource and capacity constraints, tend only to develop the software and then to transfer production and marketing to the publishers. The traditional industry model is presented in Figure 4.1.

Figure 4.1 illustrates a critical aspect of the traditional games production network – that the games developers do not have direct access to distribution networks or consumer markets. In the traditional model either the publishers or the console manufacturers themselves will contract the developer to produce a game. The main implication of the WFH model for the developer is that revenues are often fixed irrespective of the success or otherwise of the product in the marketplace. From a risk management perspective the removal of the uncertainties over cash flows associated with the sales of the product effectively removes market risk for the developer,

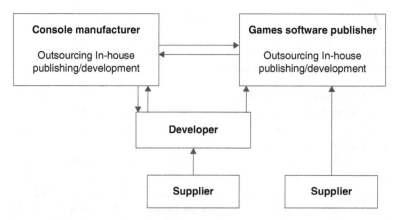

Figure 4.1 Business-to-business relationships within the traditional games industry model (based on Stolz, 2008)

while other sources of risk, faced by any business, remain (for instance credit risk and operational risk). The WFH model therefore helps to reduce the portfolio (combined) risks for the games developer. The down-side for the developer is the associated reduction in potential returns.

The impact of Internet and mobile technologies

The Internet and other technological developments (such as mobile technologies) have created significant opportunities in the computer games industry. The observation by Barnes (2002) suggesting that the Internet and related technologies are developing into the communication system of choice across a wide range of business sectors, has proved to be correct. Similarly, the convergence of Internet and wireless technologies has extended the proliferation of these business opportunities, particularly in business-to-consumer markets. These opportunities are increasingly being realized in the computer games industry.

New on-line gaming portals and communities are emerging and represent key opportunities for games developers. Perhaps the best known of these is currently the Apple App Store, although a number of other portals such as STEAM (an on-line version of X-Box from Microsoft), Greenhouse and, potentially, an on-line gaming portal available via Google also represent new and developing opportunities for computer games developers. However, these Internet and mobile technology based opportunities present challenges for games development businesses in that, as they move towards the IP-based model, they will have to think more and more about selling the product. A number of businesses have recognized this and have identified weaknesses in capabilities such as on-line marketing.

The new Internet-based games developer business model: intellectual property model

The development and proliferation of Internet and mobile-based technologies has led to the emergence of a wealth of opportunities for games developers. These opportunities stem largely from the new marketing and distribution channels that these technologies open up for them. The games sector is facing fundamental issues associated with the ambitions of many of the games companies to move away from their current WFH-based business models towards an IP-focused model. For many games companies in the United Kingdom, their business model has tended to concentrate on generating revenues by undertaking work contracted by large publishers (such as EA Games for example) and/or

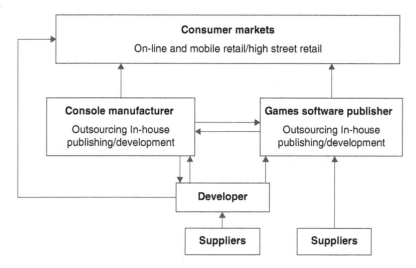

Figure 4.2 Changing relationships and business models within the games industry

for large platform developers (such as Sony and Microsoft). This business model is relatively low risk, but is also associated with lower returns (see Figure 4.1). Some in the industry have begun to move away from this approach towards a strategic business model whereby they not only develop games (and other digital) content but now also maintain ownership of the IP. This approach, while opening up the potential for significantly greater rewards, brings with it inherent risks and uncertainty which have the potential to wipe out cash flows accumulated over many years of operation – termed war-chests in the sector – and may put the survival of the business in jeopardy. In addition, in order to fully exploit the opportunities associated with the new business model, businesses will need to acquire different sets of skills, at all levels of the organization. In particular, on-going changes in the consumer market for games are, as outlined above, offering new opportunities for content developers to sell direct (or via a gate-keeper) to consumers on-line (see Figure 4.2).

The new business models, made possible by the increasing proliferation of the Internet and mobile technologies, are based on a range of emerging opportunities such as:

- SMEs being able to deliver a product directly to the consumer without the need for a publisher;

- extending the life span of 'on shelf' games through digital add-ons;
- utilization of community forums and social networking sites to manage the marketing process;
- increased potential for tracking consumer behaviour and improving the conversion rate of users visiting a web site;
- increased potential for monitoring the user response to elements of a product (for instance beta testing);
- unlocking new market demographics, such as female gamers as a result of short session, casual gaming; and, under-18s through the development of store-bought points or subscriptions;
- new revenue streams opening up through being able to release re-branded packs digitally;
- the rise of advergames (and their potential for obtaining marketing information).

Enterprise risk management in IP-based business models

As discussed above, the Internet and associated mobile technology booms have presented games developers with an array of opportunities. These opportunities, however, are associated with a change in the risk exposure of the businesses themselves. As a result of this, for the new business models to succeed the games developers must be in a position to understand, evaluate and manage these new sources of risk. The Casualty Actuarial Society (2003) identifies four main types of risks in the context of enterprise risk management, namely: hazard, financial, operational and strategic risks, as summarized in Table 4.1.

The list of risk types in Table 4.1 identifies the main categories of risk and examples of the typical sources of risk in each. The approach to enterprise risk management (ERM) principles adopted by CAS (2003), however, does not attempt to provide an exhaustive list of risks nor does it engage in debates about which category of risk each specific source of risk might best be associated with. Instead, the ERM approach emphasizes the need to consider enterprise risks from a portfolio perspective. Specifically, CAS (2003) states that the portfolio view of enterprise risk involves an understanding that portfolio risk is not just the sum of the individual risk elements as it involves an understanding of each individual risk as well as the interaction between risks. Furthermore, the risk associated with the entire organization (portfolio risk) is relevant to the critical decisions of the enterprise.

In light of the ERM approach, it would appear at least sensible, and potentially critical, for games developers to understand the impact on

Table 4.1 Types of risk

Hazard risks

- Fire and property damage
- Weather and other natural perils
- Theft, crime, personal injury
- Business interruption
- Disease and accident
- Liability claims

Financial risks

- Asset prices, foreign exchange, input/commodity prices, interest rates
- Liquidity and cash flow
- Credit
- Hedging/basis risk

Operational risks

- Business operations
- Leadership and empowerment
- Information technology
- Regulatory information requirements

Strategic risks

- Reputation
- Competition
- Regulatory and political
- Social and demographic trends
- Access to capital
- Market demand and customer wants

Source: Adapted from CAS (2003).

portfolio risk associated with the shift from the WFH model to the IP-based model. While each games developer would have to undertake the analysis and management of their risk portfolio on an individual basis we can draw some generic conclusions on risk exposure associated with the shift in business model. Based on the list of risks presented above and the foregoing analysis it is reasonable to assume that the enterprise portfolio risk associated with a games developer moving to the new business model potentially alters risk exposures across a range of factors.

Risk as opportunity

The implication of the above is that a change in strategy to follow an IP-based business model will result in significantly increased portfolio risk exposure for the developer. Many games developers have been very successful and have grown significantly by following the WFH model. However, the CAS (2003) view of enterprise risk provides one generic rationale for opting to take on the higher risk IP-based strategy, namely, risk as opportunity.

CAS (2003) identifies a shift in attitudes towards risk across organizations generally. Historically organizations may have tended to emphasise the downside of risk and therefore to adopt a predominantly defensive attitude, viewing risks as situations to be minimized or, even better, avoided. More recently organizations have recognized the notion of up-side risks and the potential value-creating opportunities associated with certain types of risk. This attitude change has, over time, led to the development of increasing sophistication in organizational capacities to identify, assess and manage the risks they face as well as increased access to information about risk. This has led many organizations actively to seek out risks as they become more familiar with the nature of the risks they face and confident in their ability to manage them.

This shift in risk attitudes identified by CAS (2003) at least in part provides a rationale for games developers moving to the IP-based business model. One other factor that is likely to contribute towards a desire among games developers to adopt the new business model is that the IP-based model places far greater emphasis on creativity and freedom of expression in games development. This is likely to have been more constrained by the contractual terms of reference set out by the client under the traditional WFH model. This art rather than profit attitude towards games development appears to be common across games development enterprises. Many developers see the development of a game not as a product to be sold but more as an artistic creation and something that they would personally enjoy playing and that they want to share with like-minded games-players – rather than something which is a way to make profit.

Risk implications of the emerging business models

Game development is risky and the commercial success of a game under development is uncertain (Banks *et al.*, 2002). Even where revenue streams are generated by commercial games developed to the specifications of clients (for instance, publishers or console manufacturers) via the WFH business model the commercial and financial constraints for small studios are significant. The route to growth for many ambitious games developers involves the creation and eventual exploitation of their own products with sovereignty over this IP work (Hotho and Champion, 2010).

As illustrated in Table 4.2, the consequence of a shift away from the WFH model to the IP-based model involves a change in the specific risks involved and hence the portfolio risk exposure of the games developer. Firstly, the IP-based model involves the allocation of resources to higher value IP creation through explorative innovation. Secondly, the investment of funds into IP creation involves significant resources and games developers following this approach often need to seek external financing, often via the venture capital route. Finally, and perhaps most critically, the move to the IP-based model exposes the games developer to new risks associated with cash flow uncertainties. In the WFH model the games developer would not be exposed to risks associated with the product demand and their cash flows would be fixed via the contractual agreement with the publisher or the console manufacturer. The shift to the IP-based model assumes that the games developers will, facilitated by the proliferation of internet and mobile technologies, attempt to sell their products direct to the market. This fundamental shift in the business model exposes the games developer directly to product cash flow uncertainties and risks associated with pricing and sales.

Shifting to the IP-based model requires shifts in business strategy and operations that involve either experimentation with flexible organizational forms, changes in workforce skills and scale, a decision on whether to undertake a total shift from the old to the new business model, or structural arrangements designed to enable both explorative (IP-based) and routine (WFH) activities simultaneously. These structural and organizational demands reflect the tensions between exploration and exploitation. Computer games developers face the innovator's dilemma of having to strike a balance between exploration and exploitation (Edwards *et al.*, 2005; Nooteboom, 2000), but this challenge is exacerbated in an industry with a fast-paced, creativity and technology-driven, innovation imperative. This conflict is reflected in the differing portfolio risk associated with the alternative games developer business models. A games developer adopting the WFH business model will attempt to build a portfolio of regular and guaranteed work for a stable set of clients, but in so doing will sacrifice the ability to act dynamically and flexibly to exploit market opportunities as they emerge (Tushman and O'Reilly, 1996). The ability of the organisation to engage in both exploitation and exploration is viewed as being of particular importance for the games industry (Raisch, 2008; Raisch *et al.*, 2009). The ability to manage

Table 4.2 Examples of differential enterprise risk exposure variation between WFH and IP-based games developer business models

Potential new risk exposure	Examples of differential risk exposure with shift in business model	
Hazard risks		
Theft, crime	Risk of counterfeiting/IP theft	
Financial risks		
Foreign exchange	Exposure to foreign exchange risk if overseas sales	
Liquidity and cash flow	Exposure to cash flow risks as revenues generated via sales only	Exposure to liquidity problems as up-front investment funds required for product development
Credit	Remove exposure to counter-party risk as bypassing publisher/console manufacturer and going straight to market	Exposure to financial distress and credit default risk as a result of increased debt levels if investment financed via borrowing
Operational risks		
Business operations	Introduction of new ways of working and enterprise culture change to encourage innovation and creativity	New skills and competencies required in terms of product development
Leadership and empowerment	Managerial capabilities and experience	Management of change and corporate culture transformation
Information technology	Product demand dependent on popularity of technology platform	Impact on relationship with former client and subsequent access to information on technological developments (for instance, in console design and compatibility issues)
Strategic risks		
Reputation	Product quality directly attributed to developer by consumer rather than publisher/console manufacturer	Poor investment returns and/or financial distress
Competition	Loss of traditional WFH clients to rivals	Direct competition with publishers, console manufacturers and other IP-based games developers

(*continued*)

Table 4.2 Continued

Potential new risk exposure	Examples of differential risk exposure with shift in business model	
Social and demographic trends	Need to address changing customer base/profile/ fashions etc.	Importance of access to and effective interpretation of market information
Access to capital	Strategy may become dependent on external capital	Access to capital markets may mean dilution/loss of managerial control
Market demand and customer wants	Price/unit sales volatility and hence cash flow uncertainty	Importance of access to and effective interpretation of market information

Source: CAS (2003) and author's own analysis.

successfully the transition from an organization focused on the ability to develop products to order to an organization with the capability to both develop and market innovative products is at the heart of the enterprise risk management issue discussed in this chapter. How to develop such dynamic capability and how to manage it has not yet been addressed in this industry sector (Hotho and Champion, 2010).

The Dundee computer games industry

This section examines the relevance of the foregoing analysis for games developers in the context of a specific location. The case of Dundee's computer games industry is adopted here as it represents a microcosm of the issues raised in the foregoing analysis and illustrates the dilemmas faced by games developers across the global games development sector. The following case material has been developed from a range of sources including on-line blogs (for instance Gamesblog), newspaper articles (including articles available from *The Guardian* on-line) as well as previous research undertaken by McGregor *et al.* (2010).

The city of Dundee, and the games and technology companies based there have played a significant role in the history of computer games development. Personal computing became popular in Dundee in the early 1980s; the reason for this is, at least in part, due to the manufacture of the Sinclair ZX series of home computers at the Timex factory in Dundee. The shortage of readily available software for Spectrum resulted in a boom in simple games programmed in living rooms and bedrooms across the city. One of these young pioneers set up his first company DMA Design and released its first game, *Menace*, in 1988. By

1997 DMA had launched *Lemmings* and *Grand Theft Auto* selling more than 70 million units and making DMA one of the most successful developers in the world. The success of DMA placed Dundee on the world stage, studios sprang up around the city and the constant stream of talented programmers and artists graduating from local universities ensured that Dundee's games development companies have thrived (McGregor *et al.*, 2010, 2011).

The first generation of games development studios in Dundee were responsible for the production of some of the most successful titles and franchises in the history of the medium. While Vis Studios enjoyed success with the *State of Emergency* series, DMA created *Lemmings* and probably the best-known games franchise, *Grand Theft Auto*. Following generations of studios including Visual Sciences, Cohort, 4J, Realtime Worlds and Ruffian established new business and production models working for global publishers like Electronic Arts, Sony and Microsoft amongst others. The major departure from the WFH development model was led by Denki in 2000. The company was set up to be a design-driven development studio, focused on the creation of digital toys and games. Denki's intention was to develop games for a variety of smaller platforms, including the Game Boy Advance, which the company saw as opening the games market up to a new, more casual audience. In 2005 Dynamo Games published *Championship Manager* for mobile phone and spawned a new generation of developers in the city focused on games development for mobile phones and handheld consoles.

The case of Realtime Worlds

By 2010 Realtime Worlds (RTW), founded by *Grand Theft Auto* creator Dave Jones, had grown to become the largest games development company in Scotland, employing over 300 people based in their Dundee studios. The company's rapid growth was based on the development of IP. RTW, having already demonstrated significant potential (for instance in producing the hit title *Crackdown*) and having an experienced management team, secured over $100 million of venture capital funding. RTW was the giant of the Dundee games community, the lynchpin amid a thriving cluster of development studios, many of which were off-shoots of Jones' original company, DMA Design. However, by August 2010 the developer had become insolvent and had entered into administration (broadly equivalent to Chapter 11 status in the United States), following an initial restructuring announcement in June of that year. This restructuring announcement came a few weeks after the launch of its massively multiplayer online game (MMOG) *APB*. How did this happen to RTW? According to Stuart's posting on Gamesblog/*The Guardian* (2010) '*APB* was going to be the *Grand Theft Auto* of the 21st century – a freeform cops 'n' robbers shootfest, taking place in a massively multiplayer universe where player characters were infinitely customizable.' The strategy for RTW was high risk in that they were putting if not all, then certainly a lot of eggs in one basket – with the success of a single key product representing a critical factor in the future success of the business. So what went wrong?

An analysis of various games-based blogs, Twitter feeds as well as more traditional media coverage, indicates that the main contributing factor was that the product, *APB*, was not good enough. Stuart (2010) notes '[w]hen APB was released on 29th June 2010, it was clear the game was nowhere near ready. The shooting mechanism didn't work, the vehicle handling was sluggish, the match-making system was hopelessly inaccurate ... the game wasn't good enough.' An ex-RTW employee observes (Stuart, 2010):

> We were getting the data every week and we could see what the sales were like. It was very clear to us a number of weeks ago that the game was not selling in the quantities that the projections told us it would. Couple that with the feedback we were getting on the forums and add in the reviews ... it wasn't painting a great picture. And it became clear that APB was not sustainable given the revenues it was generating. But because of the reviews, the rumours, the disappointing beta tests, there weren't enough players. That was the killer. And you've just got to ask again, how did this happen?'

And Gamespot (Wordpress, 2012) notes:

> there were issues that APB just wasn't fun enough, but it was believed that (as had happened with Crackdown) things would fall into place right before launch. As such, capital reserves were spent to the point that RTW had little in the bank when APB launched on 29 June 2010 and attracted around 130,000 players. Things didn't fall into place and sales fell short of expectations.

There is no doubting the calibre of the *APB* team. Lead designer EJ Moreland came in from Sony Online Entertainment where he worked on *Everquest II*; before that, he was a designer on the formative *Ultima Online* franchise. Brian Ulrich, the company's director of development, came from EA Sports. As for the rest, within two days of the administration announcement, the likes of Sega, Blitz and Activision were flying up to Dundee to set up recruitment events. This was a talented, respected outfit. Another part of the problem, it seems, was the money. There was simply too much of it, and no one had come up with a plan on how to spend it effectively. 'Having too much money is as much a curse for start-ups as having too little,' says Nicholas Lovell of business blog Gamesbrief (2010). Lovell further notes:

> Instead of identifying clear market opportunities, focusing resources and worrying about delivery, too much money gives you the licence to meander, experiment and play, and the absence of direction can be masked by the money for a very long time. This clearly happened in the case of RTW. The company meandered ... with no clear sense of direction. That makes sense on a Facebook game with a budget of US$300,000, or the original budgets of *Lemmings* and *Grand Theft Auto*, but not anymore.

A former RTW employee explains (Stuart, 2010):

> There wasn't enough discipline [...] We got all this money, and it made us relax, when really it should have focused our attention on making sure we had a really good approach to managing the project, to ensuring the design was exactly what it needed to be, to focus on testing early on, and just proving that we were doing the right thing, rather than taking the old 'it'll be done when it's done' attitude.

There are many question marks over the demise of this in games developer terms massive company. Why was there not a strict development structure in place? Why were the problems within *APB* not spotted earlier and dealt with properly? How could the whole issue of latency, especially with an action game running predominantly on the server rather than client side, not have been adequately predicted? How could this happen? In the end, it would appear to be a story of hubris and mismanagement, of artistic vision clashing with the realities of the need to make *APB* a commercial success. As a lot of reviews pointed out, it is likely that *APB* would have been a hugely successful game back in 2006. However, by 2010, smaller companies with greater agility were doing more interesting, coherent things in the MMOG sector.

The case of RTW illustrates some aspects of the changing portfolio risk exposure associated with the shift towards the IP-based model. In this case RTW were heavily reliant on the success of a single product in the marketplace, and directly reliant on cash flows arising from sales of that product.

For a variety of reasons, the product simply did not perform as expected. Had RTW adopted a WFH model to the development of *APB* there would have been far more certainty associated with cash flows arising from the project. The contributing factors appear to stem from a conflict within RTW between the way things had been done in the past and how things needed to change. This change ultimately required a complete cultural transformation within RTW and it was this transition in strategic and operational approaches which proved too difficult to achieve. From a risk management perspective it appears that RTW recognized the need to address a new set of risk exposures and took action to deal with these, for example by bringing in expertise from outside the business. However, RTW failed to identify and manage effectively the significant changes in portfolio risk brought about by the new business model, or more specifically in this case, the rapid expansion associated with the IP-based model.

The case of Cohort Studios

In contrast to the IP-based approach adopted by RTW, Cohort Studios, formed in 2006 following the demise of Visual Science, has until recently been focused on undertaking WFH for a single client, Sony. The company employs over 50 people in their Dundee studio. On the back of the Sony WFH, which accounted for about 95 per cent of total turnover in 2010, Cohort have expanded rapidly in recent years (recruiting around 20 graduates in the past three or four years). Despite the success to date, Cohort's Managing Director, Lol Scragg, explains that their future strategy will involve a gradual shift from WFH projects towards self-publishing titles (i.e. the IP-based model): 'Ideally we would want to be 100 per cent IP-based but the main barrier is finance. We need WFH for cashflow so our aim is to move gradually towards self-publishing. In 2011, for example, we will be looking for 80 per cent WFH and 20 per cent IP.'

The Cohort Studios approach involves a more measured and gradual transition from the WFH model to the IP-based model. The implication is that, not only would the more gradual shift lead to greater cash flow certainty than an immediate shift to a 100 per cent IP-based model but it would also allow the enterprise to evolve culturally in a more organic way. This minimizes the potential culture shock for both managers and employees associated with the new business model and promotes the opportunity for a period of organizational learning which means that risks, if they materialize, are less likely to lead to the failure of the enterprise. The gradual shift in business model allows the business to take the consequences, learn from the experience as an organization, and adjust its strategic and/or operational approach appropriately, without exposing itself to unacceptable portfolio risk levels that have potential solvency implications.

Conclusions: lessons from enterprise risk management

The implications of the foregoing analysis suggest that the development and proliferation of internet and mobile technologies has represented a significant opportunity for computer games developers, and is likely to continue to do so. In order to exploit these opportunities games developers are moving from a WFH based business model towards an IP-based model. This shift, while representing the potential for significantly enhanced returns, exposes the enterprise to new and different sources of risk and overall is likely to significantly increase portfolio risk exposure for the business.

These risks emerge in a variety of ways and relate to issues associated with a change in the traditional value chain relationships within the games production network, including: cash flow uncertainty and marketing/ distribution channels; financing and access to capital; managerial competencies and skills; and corporate culture changes, amongst others. It is evident that the shift to the new IP-based business model acts to significantly alter the risk-return profile of the games developer. It is clear from the views and actions of games development firms themselves that there is a strong desire to move towards an IP-based model. It is also evident that, for this shift to succeed, businesses need to be aware of their changing risk exposure as well as how to manage these differential risks effectively. The pace of transition from the WFH model to the new model, following an Internet and/or mobile technology based distribution channel strategy, needs to be carefully considered by the games development business managers. The concept of enterprise risk management can help businesses recognize the risk exposure implications and provides the tools for undertaking the systematic evaluation of alternative business models. However, the experience of businesses like RTW in Dundee should not discourage games developers from attempting to exploit their own IP and the risks presented by the new business model should be embraced as an opportunity. But success will only flow from those enterprises that identify, assess and manage the inherent risks effectively.

References

Banks, M., Calvey, D., Owen, J. and Russell, D. (2002) Where the art is: defining and managing creativity in new media SMEs, *Creativity and Innovation Management*, 11: 251–60.

Barnes, S.J. (2002) The mobile commerce value chain: analysis and future developments, *International Journal of Information Management*, 22: 91–108.

Casualty Actuarial Society (2003) *Overview of Enterprise Risk Management*, Committee of the Casualty Actuarial Society: CAS.

Edwards, T., Delbridge, R. and Munday, M. (2005) Understanding innovation in small and medium-sized enterprises: a process manifest, *Technovation*, 25: 1119–27.

Hotho, S. and Champion, K. (2011) Small businesses in the new creative industries: innovation as a people management challenge, *Management Decision*, 49(1): 29–54.

IFF Research (2008) *The Impact of Online Trading*, Research Report July 2008 for the Skills for Business Network.

Johns, J. (2005) Video games production networks: value capture, power relations and embeddedness, *Journal of Economic Geography*, 6(2): 1–30.

Lovell, N. (2010) Hubris, ambition and mismanagement: the first post-mortem of Realtime Worlds, Gamesbrief, http://www.gamesbrief.com/2010/08/hubris-ambition-and-mismanagement-the-first-post-mortem-of-realtime-worlds/.

McGregor, N., White, G. and Farley, P. (2010) The University of Abertay Dundee and the games industry in Dundee: Case Study 5, in D. Docherty (ed.), *The Fuse: Igniting High Growth for the Creative, Digital & Information Technology Industries in the UK*, London: Council for Industry and Higher Education, p. 22.

McGregor, N., White, G. and Farley, P. (2011) Successful industry-higher education collaboration: the Dundee games cluster and Abertay University, Paper presented at the ICABE 2011 Conference Proceedings, University of Piraeus, Piraeus, http://www.icabe.gr/downloads/ICABE_2011_PROC.pdf.

Nooteboom, B. (2000) *Learning and Innovation in Organizations and Economies*, Oxford: Oxford University Press.

Raisch, S. (2008) Balanced structures: designing organizations for profitable growth, *Long Range Planning*, 41: 483–508.

Raisch, S. Birkinshaw, J., Probst, G. and Tushman, M.L. (2009) Organizational ambidexterity: balancing exploitation and exploration for sustained performance, *Organization Science*, 20(4): 685–95.

Stolz, C. (2008) Dynamics in innovation systems: evidence from Japan's game software industry, *Research Policy*, 37: 1480–91.

Stuart, K. (2010) Realtime Worlds: an inside story, Gamesblog/*The Guardian*, 27 August, http://www.guardian.co.uk/technology/gamesblog/2010/aug/27/realtime-worlds-collapse.

Tushman, M.L. and O'Reilly, C.A. (1996) The ambidextrous organization: managing evolutionary and revolutionary change, *California Management Review*, 38(4): 1–23.

Wasserman, A.I. (2011) How the Internet transformed the software industry, *Journal of Internet Services Applications*, 2: 11–22.

Wordpress (2012) *Great MMO company collapses of cur time – RealTime Worlds*, http://unsubject.wordpress.com/2012/06/16/great-mmo-company-collapses-of-our-time-realtime-worlds/.

5

'Some Companies Are Fine One Day and Gone the Next': Sustaining Business in the Digital Games Industry

Sabine Hotho

Introduction

While the overall global economic outlook since 2007 has remained pessimistic, the computer games industry continues to display remarkable resilience. In November 2012, for instance, NPD Group, reporting a 22 per cent year-on-year sales growth in digital games in the US market, described this industry as the only bright spot in an otherwise depressed economy. With its offering of affordable, easy-to-access entertainment and a still relatively youthful customer base, few industries seem to be as capable of recession proofing as the games industry. Constant technology updates and innovations diversify opportunities for development and routes to market, and consequently offer ever more opportunities for new enterprises. The industry's growth trajectory remains exceptional as technological advances relating to platforms, their capacities and functionalities, and their potential for compatibility remain unpredictable (*ParisTechReview*, 2012).

But such global optimism masks variation in company fate: in the United Kingdom, the growth rate of games developers is still disappointing and the industry is overpopulated with micro enterprises. The business mortality rate is high. Between 2008 and 2011, 208 studios were created in the United Kingdom but there were also 197 failures (TIGA, 2012), and this is confirmed in industry *fora* reports regularly published online such as GamesIndustry International. The same applies to other locations including Canada, France and Germany.

Increased competition is a factor in this highly polarized industry (Kerr, 2006). Large studios use existing brand-building intellectual property (IP) to maximize efficiencies and reduce production costs, while small developers are exposed to growing competition from micro firms exploiting the lowered entry barriers afforded by new platforms and direct routes to market. While the market space is getting ever more crowded, uncertainties relating to tax relief allocations in the United Kingdom and internationally highlight the industry's need for government support and the vulnerability of regional studio clusters to 'subsidized competition' from abroad (Boxer, 2008). In the current economic climate, the games industry is thus, simultaneously and paradoxically, a promising and a difficult entrepreneurial space to be in. To survive and grow, a combination of financial, technical, market, business and management capability is required, the precise nature of which is not yet understood.

This chapter contributes to the emerging literature that examines the evolving nature of the industry, its ever changing actors and their management practices and its sustainability. Specifically, the aim is to examine how managers of small independents, the creative driving force of the industry, make sense of business challenges and directional choices for their organizations. Therefore a social constructivist perspective is adopted which is based on the notion that social reality is constructed in an ongoing interpretation process as actors make sense of, and attribute meaning to, experiences individually or collectively in interaction (Berger and Luckman, 1966). It is argued that insight into such sense-making will extend our understanding of the industry as a collective of actors who are, simultaneously, constituting and enacting their industry, its discourses and structures. It is proposed that this can establish a base from which a discussion of effective (strategic) management practice may develop which can sustain business success.

A case study approach is chosen to explore emergent themes in the day-to-day and strategic management practice of games studios, and to capture layers of organizational reality in the reflections of key decision makers within game development studios (mostly owner managers) as they face a rapidly changing environment.

The chapter is organized as follows: the next section will provide a review of the relevant literature that can be drawn upon to understand the business challenges faced by small businesses in fast-changing environments, with the view of establishing how existing research can shape the interpretative approach taken for the case study. Data from the case study will then be discussed, using the extant literature as reference points. The concluding section argues that greater emphasis should be placed on understanding internal dynamics and tensions created by assumptions on how to do business that are taken for granted in the industry.

Sustaining the business of a small business

Industry-specific studies concerned with factors facilitating and hindering the success of small businesses are as yet limited (Alvisi, 2006; Holt and Macpherson, 2006), in part because of the relative youth of the digital games industry and also in part because many of these factors seem to be generic, with differences in degree rather than in kind between the games and other industries, including high-tech industries.

In any sector young businesses, and in particular micro-businesses, are especially vulnerable, and the relative youth of the industry and its high proportion of micro businesses may account for the particular level of business exit in the digital games industry (Kerr, 2006). As noted by Persson (2004), the likelihood of business survival increases with age and company size, and three to five years is the critical period. Whether businesses survive or cease to exist depends on the extent to which their managers recognize that strategic inflection points are reached, and this is confirmed in the context of high tech businesses in particular (Berry, 1996). While many games studios survive that period, many also fail, confirming the significance of these critical junctures in this industry context. As Berry (1996) argues, managers' ability to recognize these inflection points is central to the survival of high-tech businesses, and it is important to explore this argument further in the context of the digital games industry.

Factors affecting small business success can be classified into three groups, factors relating to the external environment, to organizational characteristics, and, in the case of younger businesses in particular, to the individual characteristics of the founder, owner-manager or key decision makers (Brüderl *et al.*,1992). External factors including government policies, access to funding, access to human capital and networks (Ahlström-Söderling, 2003; Beaver and Prince, 2004; Pullen *et al.*, 2008), but also access to professional advisors and industry advisors (Mole and Keogh, 2009) are relevant for the survival and growth of small businesses in all sectors. In addition, the contextual factors relating to the competitive environment and the specifics of industry structure and region (Fritsch *et al.*, 2006) have been shown to be as important as access to resources, notably for the games industry (NESTA, 2008). In the high-tech sector new and emerging technologies, combined with growing customer expectations, pose an additional challenge, be it as an opportunity, a cost or resource factor, or as a dynamic capability issue (Berry, 1996). The digital games industry illustrates this paradigmatically: pace of technology, cost of production and access to the right skills at the right time are among the reasons most widely cited by industry insiders and academics (Kerr, 2006) to explain why small independent studios fold.

Significant internal factors related to the entrepreneur's (or dominant group's) human capital include education and training, prior industry experience, self-employment experience and leadership experience (Brüderl *et al.*, 1992), in addition to business orientations ranging from the motivation for setting up the business to the orientation towards business growth and risk, and strategic orientation (Salavou *et al.*, 2004). These complement the ability to recognize opportunities and niches in the market, an ability to draw on past experience (and avoid the repeat of errors) and the experience of having motivated people. Such factors – and the list could be extended further – are seen as prerequisites for small business growth and success. More recently the interest in internal capabilities that determine small business performance and growth has expanded, moving the focus of analysis from the level of individual entrepreneur characteristics to that of the firm. Lee *et al.* (2001) for instance identify pro-activeness, innovativeness and entrepreneurial orientation, but also tacit capabilities, such as quality control, as key determinants of success among high tech small businesses, combined with financial endowments and network access.

A quasi-bridge between these two levels of internal analysis is created by the literature concerned with management practice. This literature aims to explore the management skills and practices that affect small business performance. Notably, small businesses have been recognized as lacking in marketing skills, and hence as having a limited understanding of opportunities, risks or customer changes and behaviours. Similarly, small businesses in all sectors tend to have patchy human resource strategies and policies, or commitment to training and development, in part a reflection of resource constraints (Keogh and Evans, 1998). This results in reduced exploitation of human capital for growth and learning (Keogh and Evans, 1998). Finally, there is evidence of small businesses' reluctance to engage in business planning and strategy formulation, once more a consequence of size, age and entrepreneurial orientation. This is the case in small businesses in general, and in high-tech businesses in particular (Berry, 1996). In young games businesses the resource and experience base on which planning and forecasting can be based is limited (Ries, 2011) and the pace of technology innovation makes resource flexibility imperative. The meaning – and our understanding of – strategic management in the context of this industry is therefore at best emergent. Yet the importance of strategic thinking as providing the integrating dynamic capability that combines the ability to recognize opportunity, sense future trends and leverage and reconfigure resources accordingly has been identified as one of the most important capabilities to provide sustained business (Brinckmann *et al.*, 2010) and the presence or absence of this capability is a significant factor in all industry contexts.

The digital games industry, while experiencing specific challenges, shares many of the issues typically faced by small businesses, but here these issues may be more sharply profiled. This applies in particular to one of the most fundamental challenges faced by *all* businesses, namely the tension between managing efficiency-generating routines (the exploitation of existing capability, processes, markets) required for profitability and opportunity-seeking exploration of new markets, products or ways of doing things, which is required for innovation and future success. This tension is at the heart of all management. It can be traced back to Schumpeter (1934) and beyond, was extensively discussed in the context of organizational survival by March in 1991, and is central to the concept of the ambidextrous organization (Birkinshaw and Gibson, 2004; Tushman *et al.*, 2004). Exploitation is commonly associated with activities such as refinement, improvement, incremental implementation, whereas exploration refers to risky activities such as search, variation, experimentation, risk taking and significant innovation. As March summarizes, 'an appropriate balance between exploitation and exploration is a primary factor in system survival and prosperity' (March, 1991: 71). Findings from the ambidexterity literature confirm the importance of this balance for business sustainability (Raisch, 2008; Raisch *et al.*, 2009) without underestimating the difficulty of achieving that 'appropriate balance'. If exploitation is required for profitability, exploration is required for sustainability; competing for scarce resources, both modes follow different logics (March, 1991) which map out the inherent management challenge contained in this binary. The ambidexterity literature expands on the different logics (Birkinshaw and Gibson, 2004; Güttel and Konlechner, 2009; Raisch *et al.*, 2009) and refers to ambidexterity as the organizational capability required to sustain a balance by transforming the exploration-exploitation dualism into a synergistic and profitable duality (Raisch *et al.*, 2009). The literature confirms that organizations have a tendency to move towards one of these poles, and its logic, as the management of exploration and exploitation as a duality is significantly more effortful (Güttel and Konlechner, 2009). The computer games industry provides a specific variation of this challenge: exploitation of current products and markets, and exploration of new ideas is framed around the issues of work for hire (WFH), normally client-commissioned repeat work on fast and short production cycles and IP work undertaken by the developer to generate their own intellectual property and thus their own value base (Hotho and Champion, 2010, 2011), with the additional layer of a routine versus creative work polarity as IP work is indeed largely non-routine, experimental work requiring novel solutions rather than repeat effects.

The ambidexterity literature to date is more concerned with quantitative analyses of structural and organizational variants than with management practice, but where organizational cultures for ambidexterity are discussed (Birkinshaw and Gibson, 2004; Güttel and Konlechner, 2009; Raisch *et al.*, 2009), similarities between this literature and the management of innovation and creativity emerge. Effective people management remains central to business success, in particular in innovation-driven high-tech industries. The innovator capability resides in the creativity, the tacit and explicit knowledge of the expert workforce (Drucker, 1993; Florida and Goodnight, 2005), and the computer games industry is once more paradigmatic. The deployment of appropriate management practices and appropriate structures and systems designed to nurture, develop and commercialize such expertise is recognized as a management imperative for innovative companies (Mumford *et al.*, 2002). There is consensus that this requires a management mindset and practices which are radically different from conventional approaches (Storey, 2005; Storey and Salaman, 2005; Isaksen and Tidd, 2006). Flexibility, networked structures, a celebratory culture, self-organized teams and projects, devolved decision making, autonomy and task ownership and tolerance of failure are among the defining features characterizing creative, innovative and ambidextrous organizations (Amabile, 1998; Birkinshaw and Gibson, 2004).

Business challenges are management challenges, and require appropriate responses if a business is to be sustained. These may be proactive or reactive, but responses are only possible *if* a challenge is recognized as such. The history of many failing businesses is evidence that this is not a taken-for-granted capability. Further, the effectiveness of a response depends not only on whether a challenge has been recognized but also on *how* it has been recognized, on how causes are attributed (Rogoff *et al.*, 2004), and contexts made sense of (Weick, 1995; Weick *et al.*, 2005; Brown *et al.*, 2008). It is, for instance, widely recognized that marketing skills are vital for sustained business. But to understand better how and why businesses succeed (or fail) requires more insight into *how, when* and *why* a business owner or manager realizes this need.

The preceding sections have provided an overview of business challenges, and related these to management challenges; links to the games industry as a specific industry faced with both generic and contingent challenges have been suggested. Our understanding of business sustainability in the games industry requires further examination of such aspects, based on an interpretive approach that draws on qualitative data produced in the reflections and interpretations of the key decision makers in games businesses.

Making sense of reality

Sensemaking refers to the ongoing process, undertaken by individuals and groups, of meaning construction, and the construction of plausible accounts, interpretations and explanations, the production of *post hoc* rationalizations of events, and consequently of social realities (Weick, 1995; Weick *et al.*, 2005). Through processes of sensemaking, meaning, coherence and continuity are given to otherwise disconnected phenomena: 'to engage in sensemaking is to construct, filter, frame, create facticity [...] and render the subjective into something more tangible' (Weick, 1995: 14). To that extent sensemaking creates spaces of shared understanding as much as of divergence (Brown *et al.*, 2008). As a cognitive process, it draws upon and alters cognitive frames of reference, and is characterized by subjective and institutionalized, deliberate and unintentional, processes of inclusion, exclusion, fore-fronting or marginalization of phenomena. These interpretative selections may be attributed to individually located ego defences (Brown *et al.*, 2008) or, equally, to the interpretative frameworks residing as shared consensus in social groups such as organizations or professions.

Sensemaking as a collective activity is present in the discourses and narratives of communities of practice as social groups that cut across organizational boundaries and are arranged around shared sets of values, ways of doing, language and generating knowledge (Lave and Wenger, 1990). Communities of practice standardize processes of sensemaking, resulting in greater efficiencies but also, importantly, in mindset rigidities which preclude alternative modes of thinking and doing, and might eventually reduce the innovative or regenerative potential of the respective collective, social group or organization (Mateos-Garcia *et al.*, 2010). Interpreting organizational data through the lens of sensemaking thus allows us to develop an understanding of how interpretations of phenomena such as business challenges are shared or divergent, and of the consequences such standardized sensemaking might have.

The case study

Over a period of three years, the author conducted qualitative interviews with senior members of games production studios in a local games cluster. Two complementary interviews with the local enterprise agency were conducted. The studios were comparable in size, age and evolution, with none older than 8 years or larger than just over 20 staff, and they recognized each other as members of the same local network. Interviewees used each others' companies as reference points for comparison and differentiation. All interviewees were entrepreneurs by default, having set up the company because their previous employer had ceased to exist. In this chapter data collected from five studios and 10 senior level interviews are used. The interviews were explorative to encourage free reflection on the business, its challenges and future trajectory. Thus rich data were generated which were subjected to open and aggregate coding (Strauss, 1987) to produce structuring interpretative brackets that could be linked to the literature.

'Some companies are fine one day and gone the next ...'

This section presents the emergent themes which enable us to take stock of how participants in the industry frame experiences, challenges and opportunities and how these are reflected in management practice. The themes are related to the strands identified in the literature review to the extent that they relate to specific orientations of key decision makers, the assessment of external factors, management capabilities and issues, and the notion of duality or dualism between exploitation and exploration and the value base of the business.

The environment – endless opportunities in a bounded field

The external environment figured strongly throughout the interviews as interviewees consistently selected four aspects of that environment: finance; publishers as both the required source of that finance, and as a barrier to business fulfillment; the customer as a seemingly homogeneous, passive target in that environment, access to which seems often impeded by the publisher, and finally technological change relating to platform and routes to market. The external environment was presented as a sequence of events to which the business had to align itself, or in terms of coincidence; often the environment was presented as determining business moves: when 'timings in the market place were good' and 'digital distribution took over' one company felt 'things aligned at once and that was about seizing the moment'; similarly, periods of crisis were described as events simply happening 'when the bottom fell out of the market'. As opportunities arise, so does success, again described without reference to agency, and as a surprise which created uncertainty and in itself posed a challenge to rethink strategic orientation: 'we sold concepts much faster than expected [...] so the decision had to be made do we stick to the original plan [...] I don't know if I think that was the wisest thing to do'. The most significant event for all interviewees was technological change – the 'key change in the market place' – with consoles coming out that 'allowed developers such as ourselves to sell games straight to the consumer through the console instead of having to go through a publisher'; interviewees reported how they responded to such opportunities almost accidentally, opportunistically and consequently uncertain of associated risk: 'the timing was coincidence [...] it was pretty much by chance'.

Competition in the market was recognized, and responses were consistent: interviewees saw competition as a consequence of cost-reducing technological change, resulting in greater opportunities for micro firms and garage developers. None of the interviewees expressed specific concern about such competition, indeed one interviewee described the fact that 'you can actually start up again with two or three people like you could 20 years ago' as if this was a return to the early days of the industry, occasionally sentimentalized as a 'golden age'. That doing business required differentiation was appreciated, but this differentiation was described in rather similar ways as amounting to 'doing things differently' either through bundling technology ('most developers I know develop for one or two of those screens whereas the way [we] are currently changing [our] strategy is we're going to position ourselves as a 3 screen developer and develop for all screens'), through a different business model ('going after these licenses is pretty unusual for small games developers'), or a different way of running and managing the company differently ('we seem to do things in a slightly different way to most games companies'). Ultimately, these attempts at differentiation were not seen as the basis for doing business, but as two tactical purposes: first, the purpose of circumvention, i.e. the purpose of escaping what all saw as the persistent threat (the publisher), and second the purpose of generating financial means or 'the war chest' required to produce IP because 'having control of your own IP is the only way to have any kind of value', a 'strategy from the start' for all.

The environment, from this evidence, is thus constructed as a perpetual, if unpredictable, source of opportunities. That reduced entry

barriers and reduced cost of producing IP might reduce such opportunity remains unrecognized as the ideal of the small garage start-up still
holds; the possibility to circumvent the publisher was seen as the most
central business opportunity, making it easier to produce IP which all,
with one exception, saw as the route to sustainable value (a theme
to which we will return later). What emerges is a sense of a firmly
bounded industry environment with an already given view of how to
leverage the opportunities it provides. The games industry is rendered
as closed, despite the perpetual changes that characterize it. Only the
enterprise agency interviewee made a sceptical comment about this,
noting almost as an aside that companies overestimated their 'luck',
and 'feel safe in the environment they know', a safety seemingly justified, of course, because 'now there are so many more opportunities
in the games sector'. But what games developers were not able to see
was their potential to transgress the boundaries of their industry, and
with that find further sources of success: 'what they did not appreciate
was that they had lots of skills and expertises that they could transfer
into other industries'. In an industry constructed as offering perpetual
opportunities the idea to transfer skills and business into another
domain simply does not arise.

The start, the plan, the strategy

The SME literature confirms the importance of the founding rationale
as direction-setting for a business, its growth orientation and direction,
and its culture. The business owners who were interviewed had set up
their business for the same reason: their previous owner had ceased to
exist, and the new company was set up 'following the collapse of X', by
bringing together a small core group of ex-employees determined now
to go it alone, sometimes within a matter of weeks. Early success was
described as luck, a consequence of 'a chance conversation' – founders
'were lucky and found the stars well aligned' to continue work for a previous client, WFH on quick turnaround schedules, often remembered
as 'fun'. Interviewees thus presented the motivation for setting up the
business as accidental and early success was often attributed to good fortune and coincidence rather than to commercial or production knowledge or skill or a business plan. Interestingly, almost all interviewees'
previous experience was that of having worked with a larger firm and all
but one shared the view that they did not wish to repeat that experience
('it was a conscious decision not to go back into having a large studio')
but preferred to remain 'quite a small studio'. One interviewee described
the prospect of a larger firm as 'this machine that you would need to

keep feeding and that is the one thing we want to stay away from a little bit'. This preference to stay small is in part technology-afforded, as games or apps no longer require large teams or 'a £20 million budget' – but a certain fear of size seemed deeply embedded in the psyche of industry actors. Because work in the industry is project-based, business size was seen as determined by specific project needs, and the size of the business was thus entirely flexible, expandable or shrinkable as the opportunity required, using 'interns', 'outsourcing' or 'contractors'. To that extent the interviewees merely confirm what we know. But the qualitative data convey a sense of perpetual provisionality and the constant expand-and-shrink cycle was accepted as standard behaviour and inevitable norm. This sense of provisionality is further expressed in the way interviewees talked about uncertainty beyond a current project, uncertainty about future funding, or about accidental discoveries such as 'only just having realized' that 'having a goal, a strategy, business goals is actually worthwhile'. Living on the edge is expected as the norm in the industry and there is a noticeable absence of industry actors trying to challenge, question or alter that norm.

This standardized sense of provisionality also serves a plan. For all interviewees the production of 'our own games', 'our own IP' is the sole purpose of the businesses, as discussed already: 'having your own IP is the only way as a developer to have any kind of value otherwise you are just a bunch of guys sitting in a room typing on computer keypads'. WFH, the client work that is actually commercialized, is the project work either done or outsourced to generate the 'war chest' for projects under the developer's own control, or IP. WFH is subordinate to the value residing in IP and is often seen as the goal that gets the business through tough times: 'everybody can see it [WFH] goes towards the greater good and if it does spin out then they know that the WFH will stop and the original IP will grow', or 'we are trying to get to a position where we are creating original small games. That is our priority. Therefore everything we do should be geared towards that [...] and doing that [conversion work] gives us the cash to do original work'. IP is strategy for most, 'our strategy is to get back on our feet with originality', but a strategy that can only be sustained until the war chest is empty, or for as long as it 'can be balanced' with WFH work, 'one project that pays the wages' even if 'we just have to suck it and get on with it, unfortunately'.

Thus there is a value proposition around which the businesses are built, 'our own IP' and much of the routine work seems accepted as a necessary, if unwelcome, chore to generate that value. This requires, and makes acceptable, the shrink-expand cycle, where the expansion phase can generate the 'war chest' for IP work. All interviewees talked, in more or less detail, about just *how* difficult it is to generate and extract commercial value from IP, but that value proposition is so deeply rooted as the sole business purpose that a remarkable resilience prevails in the face of disappointment if not failure. This was expressed in the acceptance of perpetual provisionality, and explicitly in reference to 'disaster plans', 'exit strategies' or, less dramatically, in describing the business as a sequence of trials and errors. The appetite for trying again was undiminished: '[IP] was the plan from the start, but it really took us about two years to have money to do a little thing, which did not work out, and then it took us another 18 months to get more money together to have another crack at it which was moderately successful, but still did not really make us any money, and now we are back in the phase of needing to build up more cash so it's really a hard cycle to be in' but 'we are quite happy to risk failure to be successful'.

The centrality of IP for a games developer is confirmed in all industry reports, economic analyses and the academic literature, and the focus on IP in our interviews is no surprise. But qualitative data can expose additional aspects of this widely accepted view: firstly, the powerful impact that the focus on IP has on developers' personal resilience (which is not the same as business resilience), and their willingness to risk it all or to keep trying in ever new reconfigurations; and secondly the unidirectional and homogeneous definition of IP as value. All interviewees defined IP as a value proposition to be taken 'to our consumers' from the developers' perspective. None of the interviewees described IP or 'the original game' from the customer or customer value perspective, and thus, from the perspective that decides whether or not a game is monetizable, and the business profitable.

The innovation imperative is thus written into the strategic discourse of interviewees as the IP imperative, and as such highlights a tendency in the industry to focus on the value of originality as an idealistic rather than a commercial proposition while, at the same time, using highly commercial language to frame the publisher rather than internal market knowledge or any other internal features as key barrier to success. The opportunity to go to market directly rather than capability, resources or an opportunity *in* the market seem the trigger behind strategic moves.

'We are now managers'

The notion that developers make games they want to play rather than sell is widely held and was, at times self-deprecatingly, confirmed by interviewees for instance when they talked about their 'love' for the game, or the 'fun' of working on original projects, but all emphasized the commercial dimension of their organization. All saw themselves as managers, albeit, in some cases, reluctantly: 'we suddenly had to turn into being managers and directors so that was actually quite difficult'. This applied even to the director of the smallest and youngest studio who used a more informal language than any of the other interviewees to describe his business as a 'bunch of guys' who more or less seemed to stumble upon opportunities and who enjoyed the 'freedom to make mistakes'. Yet management and control featured in all interviews, ranging from reflections on SWOT analysis to schemes such as Investors in People, and all seemed to be engaged in building a specific organizational culture that was aligned to the strategic purpose of the company. Counter to some preconceptions, none of the interviewees talked about the business as if it was a lifestyle business, or a business set up without commercial aspiration.

When asked to describe the company and talk about their management role, interviewees almost accidentally referred to functional skills and requirements, but talked more about actual tasks in hand, building the culture being one. That new functional skills were required as the business developed was recognized, reflecting the linear process and orientation typical of many small businesses. Professional HR or marketing skills were neither present nor appreciated in the earlier stages of the business, 'when we messed about with mobile games', and the need for such skills seemed at times to come as a surprise, if not in recognition that 'the games industry is notoriously bad at picking managers'. For some there was a sudden realization of a marketing challenge, and the recognition that 'we actually have to do market research now, which we have never really done before so there are all these different things that we have not done before.' Others recognized the need for a management team from the start, but with a focus on the product, and HR. Marketing and outward-facing or brand-building communication seemed a later addition in all companies ('we may have to look at bringing more specialist marketing people on board, sales people') and one mostly tentatively added 'to see what benefit we can get from each other there'. Thus, while interviewees saw themselves as being in charge of the business, the need for specific – functional – skills was emergent rather than integral from the start. Instead, much emphasis was placed initially on culture and culture building. Flexibility and a culture defined by 'doing things differently' were recurrent themes, often associated with sustaining 'the guys'' motivation – in other words, aspects that related to people management. Interviewees talked about their teams, 'the guys' and 'the girls' (!), 'creative people', the 'relaxed office' where 'fun games' or 'larger, darker, and more technical stuff' is produced and where 'we are always asking people for ideas and input into things', where 'flexi-time', 'normal working hours' and 'decent wages' are offered and where 'all can play at their computers at lunchtime'. Interviewees stressed the need to create a good working environment, and agreed that established working practices in the industry such as long hours, stressful project deadlines and casual work needed to be addressed if businesses were to flourish. To that extent, the interviewees took issue with taken-for-granted work practices in the industry, and the habituated practices closely linked to the early days of the industry and its garage culture. Indeed, several interviewees explained that a main driver behind their effort to build a company culture and introducing company values was to set their company apart from 'typical' companies in the industry, to make themselves more professional, and to set themselves apart from other companies nearby. Thus, there was a strong sense of managerial responsibility to create a good work environment, and there was clear evidence of deliberate attempts to create a supportive culture appropriate to the nature of work and the nature of the highly expert and creative workforce. Several interviewees described company values, enshrined in company handbooks and value catalogues. Culture building was embraced as a managerial task and executed as such, namely as a top-down effort of constructing the work environment.

But while there was emphasis on supporting the creative workforce through an appropriate culture, there was also a sense that people – 'the resource', as one of the interviewees put it – were 'the greatest challenge'. Again, some of the challenges mentioned are familiar from other studies of the new creative industries. Lacking commercial awareness among the designers ('the geeks'), the wish to make a game 'the guys' want to play, rather than a game the market wants to buy, the aspiration to work on IP as defining a professional career and professional success and the need for a flexible environment if creativity is to flourish are all themes discussed in the literature (Kerr, 2006; Bilton, 2007). Interviewees deplored that some of their teams 'are not really buying into what we are wanting people to be doing here'. It seemed at times that interviewees were dealing with recalcitrance, having to invest considerable effort in making employees see the purpose of projects or management decisions, with some slow recognition among the workforce: 'basically telling them why and why not we can or could not do certain projects [...] we are starting to be quite honest with them [...] so I think they are starting to understand'. However, 'staff' remained the challenge in different ways: 'this has been a big challenge to try to get the mentality that they feel like the company is their own and they are not stopping for lunch every time at 12'; we 'want them to share in our success or feel that they can share in our success and we are trying to work that out' as people 'are taking their jobs for granted'. Various responses to such challenges were mentioned, which at times sounded like tactics straight from an HR toolkit: Christmas lunches, brainstorming sessions, pitches, bonuses, 'inviting everybody's ideas', events, company celebrations, or flexi-time. Yet the 'studio full of geeks', the 'guys' remained recalcitrant. In dealing with people issues, interviewees were looking for and trying to adopt and adapt best management practice as promoted in the industry, in SME guidance or even online management guides. What is striking is the managerial language of control and direction underneath the discourse of flexibility and informality and the interviews suggest that the true management challenge lies in managing the tension between a need to control and direct and a need to gain and maintain people's buy in. Culture design efforts seem not to deliver: 'you've got to move away from this habit as a games designer that you are making a game for yourself. You're not. You need to know the market you are making the game for and make it for them. [...] I think that is a great challenge to people and I think the only way around that is to basically force the team into doing what you want them to do'. The soft language of management through values and an empowering organizational culture thus strikingly jars with the language of managerial control, reflecting an unresolved tension between gamers turned managers and gamer-designers. The former strove to create a homogeneous organization rallied around the unifying cause of producing original IP while trying to make their organization both more conventional in working practices and more conventionally corporate; the latter seemed to struggle with having to behave like corporate people and having to be creatives at the same time. To an extent, the IP imperative and the associated notions of value, identity, fun and creativity seem to create a particular perceptional hurdle for employees, and their managers, necessitating levels of managerial control that seem at odds with the informal, people-focused management discourse when interviewees talked about what they wanted the work environment in their organization to be. This became even more marked as interviewees focused on the innovation imperative, the need to produce IP.

'They have basically not learned their lesson yet...'

The games industry faces many competitive external challenges, but from these interviews 'people', 'the guys', 'the bunch of geeks' emerged as an internal challenge that has been rarely addressed. The issues, as previously mentioned, relate to gaining employee buy in, culture fit, value acceptance and motivation, but, significantly, in one case also to capability issues. Indeed, one interviewee expressed quite severe doubt over the capability of his staff to rise to the challenge of delivering an IP project on time, and to the desired levels of creativity, authenticity and quality. At that point in the conversation, 'people' had become 'a resource' and as such a depersonalized and disposable entity. The interviews revealed tensions which seem resistant to conventional management and people management practices. The purpose of this section is to explore further the nature and the dimensions of that tension. This requires, at times, that we read between the lines. The interviews suggest that some of the institutionalized assumptions about work and management practices in the industry, and strategic aspirations, might constitute drivers as well as barriers to sustained success (Mateos-Garcia *et al.*, 2010). This has been underestimated in the current literature.

The consistency with which interviewees, directly and indirectly, talked about 'culture', values, company handbooks, about 'chill out rooms', 'poker nights', 'company nights out and things', the determination 'to do stuff with the guys' and 'going to try and do some more stuff' speaks also of an urgency to stabilize the precariousness of the work context, and of an urgency to maintain managerial control. The precariousness of studios, their work and their organization, while contributing to their internal dynamics, seems to trigger, in gamers as managers, a desire for levels of managerial control not dissimilar to much more conservative organizations. Culture seems to provide the most appropriate discourse and techniques to exert this – albeit with ambiguous results. This is a paradox built into the industry: for as long as organizational precariousness is considered the norm (and all interviewees had personal experience of that precariousness), for as long as it is considered routine that businesses come and go, and that people can move in and out as companies shrink and expand, attempts at building a stable and unified organization are destined to fail – while, in order to sustain the business, these very attempts remain a necessity.

These tensions are most marked where the IP imperative is addressed, and made sense of. Interviewees emphasized the value of IP over

WFH, and agreed that IP would be more motivating and relevant for career building individuals. This built up strong expectations around IP as contributing to motivation, commitment and employee support because 'it is your own creativity', and 'it is just more fun and typically less pressure'. These assumptions seem widely shared – but the reality of IP work posed unexpected problems, resulting in tension or, repeatedly, in challenging 'balancing acts' between employee expectations and business necessities. In two cases, the developers had embarked on IP projects, seizing a market opportunity – but the nature of the IP project was met with almost an uproar: 'it's like some of the team are horrified that we are actually going to work on this. They don't understand what we are making ... so that is a challenge to me internally to persuade them that this is because you've got to move away from this habit as a games designer that you're making a game for yourself'. IP work, however desirable, clearly created an additional management challenge. If the IP project can easily combine with designers' preferences, the 'love for the game' will sustain it; where IP follows a commercial imperative that contradicts this expectation match, the managers of studios seem to face managerial challenges which frustrate ever more as they repeat themselves: 'we have been through this once and they have not learned'.

The IP imperative is thus an ambiguous value at most, and in some cases, exacerbates the tension between taken-for-granted and institutionalized notions of creative freedom, however bounded, and the need for control, a tension that cannot be removed for as long as IP retains its predominance in managers' and employees' mindsets. Indeed, this very predominance can challenge the sustainability of the business. This became most explicit in one case where the experience of IP work resulted in a relative sense of disenchantment among employees and managers: managers felt 'disappointed' by what their 'resource' could deliver, the IP projects seem to drag on unduly, levels of quality were only reached under tight project management control and employees articulated similar disenchantment. IP work resulted in remarkable levels of frustration and organizational strain. Indeed, the view was widely held that the previous WFH projects, with routines which allowed sufficient creative deviation, and timescales which resulted in satisfaction of getting a job done, were, after all, very worthwhile work. The uncertainties of IP, the risks involved had come too early for the company to cope with. Interestingly, staff capability was seen as the main cause of problems. And this, again, leads to the core of taken-for-granted work practices in the industry: building resource capability in an environment characterized by perpetual provisionality, and on projects which are deemed of lesser value than aspirational IP, poses a management task for which we do not yet have recipes, in part because the task is not sufficiently recognized.

Discussion

The interviews illuminate how industry actors make sense of their strategic environment, management and organizational issues, and the key determinants impacting on business success. Some of the typical features characteristic of small businesses in general were present: a linear move from product to business focus, a gradual move towards accepting the need for management and the realization that the business requires functions such as marketing and human resource management if it is to succeed, and a shared sense of financial resources as a constant struggle. As a result of the much celebrated growth opportunities in the market (see for instance, Gaudiosi, 2012), a lack of market and marketing awareness seemed almost justified, unlike in other industries, and the shared experience of business exit and rebirth might serve as further confirmation. However, underneath this mostly optimistic interpretation of the business environment, a distinct management discourse emerged that suggests that the games industry needs to address more specific challenges.

Across the interviews there were significant similarities relating to industry specifics and organizational responses, confirming that values, practices and organizational responses are highly homogenized and internalized in the games industry as a community of practice. The detrimental impact of such standardization of language, values, and management response has been pointed out by Mateos-Garcia and Steinmueller (2008) and Mateos-Garcia *et al.* (2010) in the context of innovation capability and innovation preferences. The interviews discussed here can take this argument a step further. Firstly, interviews highlighted limitations, in terms of strategic thinking and management practice, resulting in part from the bounded self-construction of industry actors; secondly they highlighted tensions as managers reiterated and reinforced some of these accepted values, practices and strategic aspirations, while simultaneously battling with the realization that these can only be sustained with great difficulty, or with increased managerial control, which goes against the shared self-understanding of the industry as creative, and its organizational cultures and structures as flexible and flat. Thirdly, from this emerges a sense of 'them and us', with managers setting the norms for 'the guys' and employees being reduced to, at times recalcitrant, workers who seem to be equally struggling with the mismatch of agreed values and practices, and the concrete demands of the business environment.

Strategic thinking and environmental sensing, central to business success as much as a market and marketing orientation that evolves as the business evolves (Berry, 1996), seemed much less of a priority as interviewees expanded on technology-facilitated opportunities. These were not articulated as markets, but appeared mostly as new routes to the same market – with limited recognition of customers as the constituents of that market. Successful high-tech businesses are advised to seek an integration of marketing and technological considerations (Berry, 1996). The interviews suggest that an equation of technology with opportunity prevails in the industry, and possibly to the detriment of a number of firms. Similarly, technology-push rather than market-pull drives strategic tactics rather than strategy, resulting in a hierarchical arrangement of WFH as subordinate to IP work. As long as these tactics determine how games studios manage their work, they sign up to perpetual provisionality – evidence from the interviews suggests that this has become deeply internalized. IP work is experimental, uncertain and needs to stop when the company runs out of money: learning, experience, and human capital as the basis of sustained and future success (March, 1991) of necessity remain marginalized. This is of consequence only for as long as it is *also* accepted as the norm that studios come and go, and that there will always be opportunity to start again. However, if technology creates the new opportunity, the likelihood is that the new business will also be technology-orientated rather than market-driven, with the risk of repeating the same fate as previous businesses which do not become sufficiently market-orientated (Berry, 1996).

The subordination of WFH to IP work meant that most adopted an either-or approach, depending on resource availability. Combined with the acceptance that companies would expand or shrink, depending on the projects, meant that the need for balance between the modes of exploitation and exploration, WFH and IP, was not recognized. Where IP and WFH took place simultaneously, this seemed accidental, opportunistic, and with resources randomly rather than purposefully allocated, a reflection of the liability of size, shared with all small businesses (Keogh and Evans, 1998) which probably precludes them from developing as ambidextrous organizations. The prospect of IP work as a motivator to get staff through the routine of WFH proved not sufficient to sustain staff motivation, nor did IP work deliver on the promise (of higher sense of esteem) when it actually took place. Indeed staff motivation seemed to require considerable effort, reflective of significant tensions between the need to control and the need to provide creative freedom, the promise of value and the realization that this is elusive as business realities become more pressing. Despite the tools and tactics characteristic of creative organizations (Amabile, 1998) there was a clear sense of managerial control being exerted – reflective of a struggle to sustain the organization as a business.

Conclusion

This chapter provides some insight into how gamers-turned-managers make sense of their industry and its challenges. Much further work is required to understand to what extent businesses in the digital games industry face similar or quite distinct challenges, and thus, to what extent current knowledge of business and management practice is adequate to drive growth and sustainability in digital games. While many of the challenges may be quite distinct, many, equally, seem self-generated by actors in the industry. The focus on IP work as the sole source of sustained business, for instance, and the resulting impact on employees and work organization has become so normalized that it is indeed time to question its very prominence (Mateos-Garcia *et al.*, 2010). Similarly, the acceptance of perpetual provisionality and the business birth-death-rebirth cycle deserves some critical consideration. As digitization offers ever more opportunities, even for conventional industries such as manufacturing, it becomes evident that the digital games industry is merely one of many potential new, or renewed, industries. Lessons we can learn from the digital games industry may prove useful for other twenty-first century industries yet to emerge.

References

Ahlström-Söderling, R. (2003) SME strategic business networks seen as learning organizations, *Journal of Small Business and Enterprise Development*, 10(4): 444–54.

Alvisi, A. (2006) The economics of digital games, in J. Rutter and J. Bryce (eds), *Understanding Digital Games*, London: Sage, pp. 58–74.

Amabile, T.M. (1998) How to kill creativity, *Harvard Business Review*, 76(5): 76–87.

Beaver, G. and Prince, C. (2004) Management, strategy and policy in the UK small business sector: a critical review, *Journal of Small Business and Enterprise Development*, 11(1): 34–49.

Berger, P.L. and Luckman, T. (1966) *The Social Construction of Reality: A Treatise in the Sociology of Knowledge*, Garden City, NY: Anchor.

Berry, M.M.J. (1996) Technical entrepreneurship, strategic awareness and corporate transformation in small high-tech firms, *Technovation*, 16(9): 487–98.

Bilton, C. (2007) *Management and Creativity: From Creative Industries to Creative Management*, Oxford: Blackwell.

Birkinshaw, C.B. and Gibson, J. (2004) Executive briefing: the ambidextrous organization, AIM Stage 3: http://www.aimresearch.org/publications/ambidexterous rpt.pdf.

Boxer, S. (2008) Games industry: arrested development, *The Guardian*, http://www.guardian.co.uk/technology/2008/oct/23/games-industry, 23 October 2008.

Brinckmann, J., Grichnik, D. and Kapsa, D. (2010) Should entrepreneurs plan or just storm the castle? A meta-analysis of contextual factors impacting the business planning-performance relationship in small firms, *Journal of Business Venturing*, 25: 24–40.

Brown, A., Stacey, P., Nandhakumar, J. (2008) Making sense of sensemaking narratives, *Human Relations*, 61(8): 1035–62.

Brüderl, J., Preisendörfer, P. and Ziegler, R. (1992) Survival changes of newly founded business organizations, *American Sociological Review*, 57: 1–15.

Drucker, P. (1993) *Post-Capitalist Society*, New York: HarperCollins.

The Economist (2008) Play on: video games have proved recession-proof – so far, http://www.economist.com/node/12815694, 20 December 2010.

Florida, R. and Goodnight, J. (2005) Managing for creativity, *Harvard Business Review*, 83(7/8): 124–31.

Fritsch, M., Brixy, U. and Falck, O. (2006) The effect of industry, region, and time on new business survival: a multi-dimensional analysis, *Review of Industrial Organization*, 28: 285–306.

Gaudiosi, J. (2012) New reports forecast global video game industry will reach $82 billion by 2017, *Forbes*, http://www.forbes.com/sites/johngaudiosi/2012/07/18/new-reports-forecasts-global-video-game-industry-will-reach-82-billion-by-2017/, 18 July 2012.

Güttel, W.H. and Konlechner, S.W. (2009) Continually hanging by a thread: managing contextually ambidextrous organizations, *Schmalenbach Business Review*, 61: 149–171.

Holt, R. and Macpherson, A. (2006) *Small Firms, Learning and Growth: A Systematic Review and Reconceptualiztion*, London: Advanced Institute of Management Research.

Hotho, S. and Champion, K. (2010) 'We are always after that balance': managing innovation in the new digital media industry, *Journal of Technology Management and Innovation*, 5(3): 36–50.

Hotho, S. and Champion, K. (2011) Small businesses in the new creative industries: innovation as a people management challenge, *Management Decision*, 49(1): 29–54.

Isaksen, S. and Tidd, J. (2006) *Meeting the Innovation Challenge: Leadership for Transformation and Growth*, Chichester: John Wiley & Sons.

Keogh, W. and Evans, G. (1998) Strategies for growth and the barriers faced by new technology-based SMEs, *Journal of Small Business and Enterprise Development*, 5(4): 337–50.

Kerr, A. (2006) *The Business and Culture of Digital Games: Gamework/Gameplay*, London: Sage.

Lave, J. and Wenger, E. (1990) *Situated Learning: Legitimate Peripheral Participation*, Cambridge: Cambridge University Press.

Lee, C., Lee, K. and Pennings, J.M. (2001) Internal capability, external networks and performance: a study of technology-based ventures, *Strategic Management Journal*, 22: 615–40.

March, J.G. (1991) Exploration and exploitation in organizational learning, *Organization Science*, 2(1): 71–87.

Mateos-Garcia, J., Grantham, A., Sapsed, J., Steinmueller, E.W. and Voss, G. (2010) Sticking to their guns: the impact of the culture and organizational practices of video games studios on the technological trajectory of the console games sector, Paper presented at DRUID Summer Conference 2010 on Opening Up Innovation: Strategy, Organization and Technology, 16–19 June 2010, London.

Mateos-Garcia, J. and Steinmueller, E.W. (2008) Open, but how much? Growth, conflict and institutional evolution in open source communities, in J. Roberts and A. Amin (eds), *Community, Economic Creativity, and Organization*, Oxford: Oxford University Press, pp. 254–82.

Mole, K.F. and Keogh, W. (2009) The implications of public sector small business advisers becoming strategic sounding boards: England and Scotland compared, *Entrepreneurship and Regional Development*, 21(1): 77–97.

Mumford, M.D., Scott, G.M., Gaddis, B. and Strange, J.M. (2002) Leading creative people: orchestrating expertise and relationships, *The Leadership Quarterly*, 13: 705–50.

NESTA (2008) *Raise the Game: The Competitiveness of the UK's Games Development Sector and the Impact of Governmental Support in Other Countries*, Games Investor Consulting, December 2008.

NPD Group (2012) Digital the only bright spot in an overall US games industry decline, http://www.gamasutra.com/view/news/181699/Digital_the_only_bright_spot_in_an_overall_9_US_games_industry_decline.php#.UQeyYr800mO.

ParisTechReview (2012) Video games and their very real economic wars, http://www.paristechreview.com/2012/03/12/video-games-real-economic-wars?med, 13 March 2012.

Persson, H. (2004) The survival and growth of new establishments in Sweden, *Small Business Economics*, 23: 423–40.

Pullen, A., de Weerd-Nederhof, P., Groen, A. and Fisscher, O. (2008) Configurations of external SME characteristics to explain differences in innovation performance, in *16th Annual High Technology Small Firms Conference Papers*, HTSF 2008, 21–23 May 2008, Enschede.

Raisch, S. (2008) Balanced structures: designing organizations for profitable growth, *Long Range Planning*, 41: 483–508.

Raisch, S., Birkinshaw, J., Probst, G. and Tushman, M.L. (2009) Organizational ambidexterity: balancing exploitation and exploration for sustained performance, *Organization Science*, 20(4): 685–95.

Ries, E. (2011) *Lean Start Up: How Constant Innovation Creates Radically Successful Businesses*, London: Portfolio Penguin.

Rogoff, E.G., Lee, M.-S. and Suh, D.-C. (2004) 'Who done it?' Attributions by entrepreneurs and experts of the factors that cause and impede small business success, *Journal of Small Business Management*, 42(4): 364–76.

Salavou, H., Baltas, G. and Lioukas, S. (2004) Organizational innovation in SMEs: the innovation of strategic orientation, *Journal of Marketing*, 38(9/10): 1091–1112.

Schumpeter, J. (1934) *The Theory of Economic Development*, Cambridge, MA: Harvard University Press.

Storey, S. (2005) Human resource policies for knowledge work, in S. Little and T. Ray (eds), *Managing Knowledge*, 2nd edition, London: Sage, pp. 199–220.

Storey, S. and Salaman, G. (2005) *Managers of Innovation: Insights into Making Innovation Happen*, Oxford: Blackwell.

Strauss, A. (1987) *Qualitative Analysis for Social Scientists*, Cambridge: Cambridge University Press.

TIGA (2012) TIGA promises successful future for UK games studios with targeted games tax relief, http://www.tiga.org/news/press-releases/tiga-promises-successful-future-for-uk-games-studios-with-targeted-games-tax-relief, 16 February 2012.

Tushman, M.L. and O'Reilly, C., III (2004) The ambidextrous organization: managing evolutionary and revolutionary change, in M.L. Tushman and P. Anderson (eds), *Managing Strategic Innovation and Change: A Collection of Readings*: New York and Oxford: Oxford University Press, pp. 276–91.

Weick, K.E. (1995) *Sensemaking in Organizations*, Thousand Oaks: Sage.

Weick, K.E., Sutcliffe, K.M. and Obstfeld, D. (2005) Organizing and the process of sensemaking, *Organization Science*, 16(4): 409–21.

6
The Role of Creativity

Peter Zackariasson

Introduction

The video games industry is rapidly becoming one of the fastest growing industries of the twenty-first century, at least if one is to believe the numerous reports from national and international trade organizations such as The Independent Game Developer Association (TIGA), Entertainment Software Association (ESA), European Games Developer Federation (EGDF) and International Game Developers Association (IGDA). However, policy makers, government organizations, economic data reports (UK SIC, 2007) and academics have reached the same conclusion (Beck and Wade, 2004; Mollick and Edery, 2009; Chatfield, 2010) and speak of undiminished growth in the industry. What makes the video games industry and its growth trajectory so fascinating is that it is a fairly young industry. It had its start in the early 1970s, with the spread of the arcade machine and gaming parlours which caught the attention of young and mostly male players (Herz, 1997; Poole, 2000; Kent, 2002; Demaria and Wilson, 2004; Donovan, 2010). Much of the production of games at that time was small scale, and the industry contained only a handful of developers. Today we are looking at an industry that was estimated to be worth around $56 billion in 2010, and is predicted to be worth $82 billion by 2015 (PricewaterhouseCoopers, 2011).

Despite clear similarities with other software industries, the video games industry has certain characteristics that separate it from these (O'Donnell, 2012), one of these being the very essence of the software programme itself: this is not a functional programme, but is all about fun and leisure. Because of this quality, it is assumed that the development of such software requires something in addition to merely engineering logics and technical skills of programming, namely creativity.

The digital games industry is consequently defined as a creative indus-try (UK SIC, 2007), thus joining industries such as 'book and magazine publishing, the visual arts (painting, and sculpture), the performing arts (theatre, opera, concerts, dance), sound recordings, cinema and TV films, even fashion and toys and games' (Caves, 2000: 1). Being a creative industry implies that the development of games is dependent on artistic skills, and the outcome of any production cannot easily be predicted. In other words, just as in the film industry, the sales of a game cannot be guaranteed at the outset, resulting in an industry where profits are notoriously difficult to predict and investment risks are high.

This chapter will discuss the role of creativity in the digital games industry. Defined as 'creative', it is often assumed that what happens in the production process in this industry is, in essence, dependent on a sequence of creative acts. Here, I will propose that there is a need to separate category from process: the category of creative industries from the process of being creative. Had the video games industry been catego-rized as a cultural instead of a creative industry, this issue would not have arisen, as category and process would have been separate. Being part of the cultural industries does not assume creativity, but cultural practice. As it is, the categorization of the games industry as a creative industry leads to over-generalizing assumptions about the quality of the production process. Of course, there are aspects of this industry, its production and development activities that can, and should, be defined as creative – but there are also parts which are stifled by an inability to change normative patterns. Some aspects of the industry have become institutionalized and inflexible, and prevent change that true creative acts could bring. I shall argue that the creative aspect can be found in most parts of the indus-try's value chain, just as creativity can be found in many other industries which are not included in the creative industry category as defined above. This means that there are games developers who are very creative, but this also goes for publishers, distributors, sales and games consumers (gamers). This creativity is manifest in, for instance, new business models, the utilization of new technologies for new gaming experiences, and the constant renegotiation of gaming. Thus, the content of a game is not by definition the result of a creative process, but the result of a complex process including technical, functional and commercial decisions. Nor is the content of a game creative just because it is the result of an artistic process. We have to separate artistic work and creative work: artistic work generates cultural products (Hesmondhalgh, 2007), but does not neces-sarily have to be creative. An artist painting his or her Nth version of the same theme is not (necessarily) creative, just as a games developer creating the Nth version of the same intellectual property (IP) is not creative. In both cases, it is business as usual. For an action to be defined as creative, it would have to challenge the field of cultural production in which it is situated and which is defined by existing power struggles (Bourdieu, 1993); it would have to challenge what is taken for granted and deemed acceptable in that field. Video games are cultural products that have the ability to bring forth creative aspects in their production, distribution and use. The purpose of this chapter is to discuss the meaning of creativity in the context of an industry and a medium that are set to define notions of future cultural activity with an immense potential to affect our lives.

The ability to be creative, or become part of a process that could be defined as creative, is possible in many other industries, not just in the creative industries as currently defined. Koivunen and Rehn argue that 'while some might still connect creativity strictly with the fields of art and culture, a contemporary theory must adopt a broader approach and envision creativity as existing in all areas involving knowledge work and idea generation' (2009: 7). The implication is that creativity in the creative industries, including the video games industry, cannot be taken for granted. Nor should we assume that these industries are the only places where creative acts play a role. Creativity is not a mysterious act of inspiration, but the outcome of complex mental processes in the course of which individuals relate to their knowledge and experience, and combine ideas, experiences, problems resulting in novel outcomes that question or challenge current thinking or practice, and may, in an industry, bring new products and services to market – an innovation.

But surely, there is creativity in the video games industry?

Piñero, in a study for his doctoral dissertation (2003), explored how programmers defined and valued their work, concluding that they considered themselves to be artists, defining the code they produced as having artistic value. By that token, the video games industry employs a large number of artists, most of who work in games development. But this does not mean that all of these individuals are creative. There are also a large number of people working in the video games industry who do not have artistic jobs, but are instead performing routine work that still needs to be done in order to create, produce and publish games. Most of these individuals, artists or not, probably have the capacity for creative action; and on occasion they will have shown the capacity to innovate in this industry, both through creating innovative games, and through innovation in other parts of the value chain. Indeed, the rather short history of this industry offers numerous examples from the areas of games, publishing, distribution and gaming that could be considered to be the result of creativity.

One could argue that the development of one of the first video games, *Spacewar!*, showed what creative thinking could lead to. When Steve Russell, Martin Graetz and Wayne Wiitanen, students at the time, faced the challenge of demonstrating the power of the new PDP-1 computer at MIT in 1961, they decided that a video game would be the best means to do so (Kent, 2002). Although demonstrating that they could solve a task creatively by building a game, they did not have the creativity to exploit their idea for business purposes and turn this game into a profitable product. Steve Russell later said in an interview that 'we thought about trying to make money off it [*Spacewar!*] for two or three days but concluded that there wasn't a way that it could be done' (Kent, 2002: 20). We may no longer see the content of *Spacewar!* as particularly creative, but at the time when it was produced, namely during the Cold War, it was received as a skilful play on the fear of space invasion, nuclear arms and nuclear conflicts. Today we are witnessing how the video game genre has been diversified to incorporate all sorts of games. When Will Wright of Maxis created *SimCity* in the late 1980s, it was basically the start of a new genre of games. Although simulations had been used previously, the genre only now found its way into most gamers' computers. The same happened when Richard Garriott, ten years later, developed *Ultima Online* and made the massive multiplayer online role-playing game genre, normally referred to as MMORPG, one of the most popular genres of the time. And in 2012 the most creative games are developed for the iOS and Android platforms, but they do not aim to be seen as AAA titles.

Creative thinking is reflected not only in the content of games. The physical act of playing video games has for a long time been hampered by the controls used in home environments. Whereas gaming parlours can offer gamers a number of different ways to interact – sitting in a race car, standing on a pair of skis or holding a rifle – playing a game in our living rooms imposes constraints: we have to limit our movements to the control in our hands. Until Nintendo developed the Wii-remote in late 2006, no other control designed for home gaming had really taken off. Nintendo changed the rules of the game: instead of controlling a game with your thumbs, you could now simulate the movements corresponding to the actual movements in the game by holding a motion sensor in your hand(s). This was later followed by Microsoft, which launched Kinect for Xbox 360, an accessory which made it possible for the gamer to interact with a game using only his or her body. By 2010 the handheld control had become unnecessary: such technological breakthroughs are an expression of creative problem solving.

While video games used to be acquired through physical stores, today's business models display a large number of creative solutions to engage with consumers in transactions that go beyond the original publisher-to-consumer model. First, the development of the Internet made it possible to sell games through online stores, allowing physical stores to expand into this new distribution. More importantly, the Internet made it possible for developers to distribute their games themselves through a direct route to the customer. Second, the Internet has changed how gamers are charged. Today several games are using a business model that charges gamers not for the game, but for content in the game. The possibility to handle micro transactions (defined by PayPal as less than $12) over the Internet, has made this type of business model possible, and added new dimensions to the game. If playing a game is free, but accessing better (more exciting, complex or challenging) areas in the game comes at a premium price, the design of a game and the development of its content become, inescapably, affected by the way revenue can be generated. Indeed, as many game developers have confirmed in interviews with the author, finding new business models, or exploiting existing business models differently, has, at this point in time, been defined as the major challenge in the industry, and a challenge for which ever new creative solutions need to be found.

A final example to illustrate the different forms of creativity in the games industry relates to the use of Alternative Reality Games (ARGs) for promotional purposes (Zackariasson and Wilson, 2010). Usually, promotional activities in the industry use traditional channels: trailers, posters and industry fairs. ARG is a genre that aims to dissolve the boundaries between play and non-play, online and offline spheres. An ARG is played in real time, involving a 'puppet master' and other individuals in charge of running the game. In transcending the online–offline boundary it takes place in both the digital and physical spaces; and at a certain level it is also designed to lead participants into doubt as to the authenticity of the game. In 2004 the ARG *The Haunted Apiary, or I Love Bees*, was launched by 42 Entertainment (McGonigal, 2007). This game was designed to promote the video game *Halo 2*, produced by Bungie Studios and scheduled to be released later that same year. The later success of *I Love Bees* is associated with subsequent sales of *Halo 2*. Within hours after its launch, *Halo 2* sold 2.4 million copies, reaping

$125 million in sales. Even if the ARG was only one among numerous promotion activities, the novelty and interactive aspect, and the buzz created, made this an important part of the success of *Halo 2*. Those who participated in the ARG before the launch of *Halo 2* had the opportunity to experience the story of that game in a first-hand encounter and be part of the buzz that surrounded that game.

One can thus conclude that creativity is indeed thriving in the video games industry, and not just with regard to content generation of a game. But this is not without problems, as there are structural challenges in this industry that constrain creative and innovative actions. Tschang (2007), for instance, argued that creativity in the games industry risks becoming marginalized as business and production interests move to the forefront. As consumers continue to expect innovative and immersive games, this presents developers with the challenge of finding ways to balance the tension between business interests and creativity – as if these were opposites, and thus mutually exclusive. The issue that needs to be addressed is thus *not* whether creativity exists in the video games industry. The preceding sections have indeed demonstrated the different levels at which creativity manifests itself beyond the confines of the game and its content. The true issue concerns the relative importance of creativity in the industry, the levels where it resides, and the possibilities of creativity as a major driving force in the industry. Instead of making the assumption that the video games industry is creative by definition, we have to look at how creativity can be fostered in this specific industry, in order to ensure its potential.

What is creativity?

Creativity has become a widely used concept that promises grand outcomes and hope for whatever field we may wish to apply it in. Creativity is the spark that promises a different and better future – and in this promise lies, seemingly, the justification for engaging in creative activities. Yet what precisely we mean by creativity has remained somewhat elusive, and the creative process is consequently mystified and glorified.

The meaning of creativity, and creative behaviour and thinking, is a topic that seems to vex both academia and practice. But despite some conceptual vagueness, there is a widely held agreement that the value of being creative is immense, no matter which field it is enacted in. Browsing in bookstores, we are confronted with a never-ending flood of titles suggesting creativity: creative cooking, creative advertising, creative writing, creative leadership, creative family, creative ministry and so forth. The conclusion to be drawn from this abundance of offerings is that the possibilities for being creative are endless and figure in almost any domain of human life. By that token, there must be possibilities to be creative in the video games industry, no matter what one does, just as there are possibilities to be creative in any other industry. And this, of course, merely leads us back to the central question: what, precisely, does it mean to be creative?

Most definitions of creativity include reference to the novel ways of one person's relation to a concept, a product, or a situation, and his or her actions in relation to this object or situation. The results of creative thinking and behaviour replace something old, or existing, with something new. Amabile (1996), for instance, defines a creative task as one that is heuristic in nature (with no predetermined path to a solution), and a creative outcome as a novel and appropriate (for instance useful) response to such a task. Creativity thus seems to relate to the ability to respond adaptively to the need for new approaches, solutions, products, resulting from a process initiated by an individual or group of individuals (Barron, 1988).

Studies of creative thinking have identified a number of different sources that enable a creative act. These include individual cognitive abilities and thinking styles (Torrance, 1988; Sternberg and Lubart, 1995), personality traits (Feist, 1998), affect (Shaw and Runco, 1994), and motivation (Amabile, 1996). According to these authors, it is thus a set of individual capabilities that enable a person to perform a creative act. The creativity debate is also manifest in the world of business where some individuals and entire professions are described as being creative (for instance game developers) while others, such as accountants, are (almost) accused of being uncreative. Indeed, educationalists and curriculum designers today, at least in the Western world, see creative thinking as an integral part of a student's learner journey, and a desirable outcome of any education process. The creativity debate shares some similarities with the by now ubiquitous leadership debate, to the extent that in both areas the nurture–nature issue seems as yet unresolved. Are we born to be creative, or to be leaders – or can we learn creativity or leadership, and how significant is the context in which we lead, or aim to be creative? Many still seem to side with nature – and this explains, in part, why games studios are trying to identify and hire the most creative people to develop the next generation of games.

A significant contribution to the discussion of creativity and its source, and one that has the potential to develop a better understanding of how creativity in the video games industry might be fostered, comes from Bourdieu. While the main part of Bourdieu's ideas and concepts relate to culture and power rather than explicitly to creativity, his notions of habitus and field offer an interesting, and for our purposes useful, way of understanding creativity in general, and specifically in the video games industry (Swartz, 1997; Jenkins, 2002). For Bourdieu, habitus and field are concepts that help us understand power in society: 'a field consists of a set of objective, historical relations between positions anchored in certain forms of power (or capital), while habitus consist of a set of historical relations "deposited" within individual bodies in the form of mental and corporeal schemata of perception, appreciation, and action' (Bourdieu and Wacquant, 1992: 16).

For Bourdieu, habitus is thus 'the social embodied' (Bourdieu and Wacquant, 1992: 128) and 'a structuring mechanism that operates from within agents' (Bourdieu and Wacquant, 1992: 18) while a field, using the analogy of a battlefield, is a space of conflict and competition. The relations between field and habitus are embodied in the individual, with different dispositions that have been learned over time, existing in a structured social space with its own laws and rules. The understanding of any social space thus presumes an understanding of the habitus and field it is positioned in. As examples, Bourdieu cites education, the arts, economy and law. There are a large number of fields, some overlapping each other, and each has formed its own logic. Indeed, most situations would incorporate a number of different fields that define relations between individuals and what is expected of those present in the field. Applying this to the video games industry, it is possible to distinguish the whole industry as a field, but also parts of this industry as fields in themselves, for example, game development, game publishing, independent game development. Within these fields, and the spaces where they overlap, large numbers of people are working, all with different schemata for actions and sense making.

Bourdieu argues that while psychological qualities might play a part in creativity, these can in no way explain the whole phenomenon of creative acts and their sources. Instead he proposes that creativity is the result of a habitus of an agent in a field, and the relationship of this agent to other agents in a field consisting of continuous power struggles: 'The source of "creative" power, the ineffable mana or charisma celebrated by the tradition, need not be sought anywhere other than in the field, i.e. in the system of objective relations which constitute it, in the struggle of which it is the site and in the specific form of energy or capital which is generated there.' (Bourdieu, 1993: 81)

Creativity can thus be seen as the capability to challenge what is taken for granted in any specific field in order to challenge power relations and power positions within this, the possibilities of an agent to affect the field, and to push the boundaries of the field (Zackariasson and Styhre, 2011). This notion also presents us with an alternative framework for understanding the concept of creativity in the video games industry. The possibilities for individual creative acts should be understood in relation to power positions in the field of game development, making creativity a relational concept instead of a static one. The result is that one has to consider the field of games development and agents within this field in order to understand the limitations and future possibilities of creativity.

A homogeneous field?

Most people who have worked in the video games industry, or have come into contact with it for any reason, share the feeling that there is a specific culture amongst those who develop games. There is a special feeling of going into a games development studio, both visually and in relation to the sound that prevails in these spaces. Despite the fact that the video games industry is becoming ever more professionalized, implementing regular working hours and work processes that are similar to those in other industries, those working in the industry continue to express their love for working in games, and nurture the idea of its uniqueness. The idea of games development not being a nine-to-five job, or, even better, not a job at all but a place to exercise one's passion, is a much cherished and frequently reiterated one.

Dovey and Kennedy (2006) argue that games are the result of the culture of those working in the industry, combined with technological and economic aspects, and they refer to the notion of male technicity in describing the games environments. Quoting from an interview conducted in 2003 with an individual defined as a 'creative driver' in the games development studio Pivotal Games (UK), the authors present an agent in this field who will have a major impact on the games that are being developed:

> I always played toy soldiers, still do, and role playing games, make believe. I actually read a lot of history. I think for me it was a classic time growing up, you had Robin Hood on TV, Richard the Lion Heart, Lancelot, you know. I remember them as being great ... I was an avid history reader, I went on to do an Economics and Social

History degree as well. After that I was a Role Playing Games Designer and Board Game Designer for major products, *Dungeon and Dragons*, *Games* Workshop's *Warhammer games* and various other companies. (Dovey and Kennedy, 2006: 60)

In one of his first encounters with the industry, the author of this chapter was introduced to employees by the CEO of Massive Entertainment in Sweden as a person who 'is not dangerous, he has no tie' (Zackariasson, 2003: 36 [author's translation]). This personal anecdote matches the experiences of others conducting research in similar environments: the hackers' culture (Ullman, 1997), the coders at Atari's research laboratory (Stone, 1995), or the computer construction environment in Data General (Kidder, 1981). These experiences are also confirmed by more recent observations from the video games industry specifically (Dovey and Kennedy, 2006; Deuze *et al.*, 2007). One could argue that the culture dominating the video games industry – specifically the field of games development – is of a young, male and highly technical one, a culture that, for example, thrives on long working hours, especially during crunch time periods, a work arrangement many women are reported to find problematic (Consalvo, 2008).

When considering the demographics of games developers a picture of a homogeneous group of workers emerges. A survey conducted by IGDA and involving over 6000 participants resulted in the following overview (Gourdin, 2005):

- Male = 88.5%, Female = 11.5%
- White = 83.3%, Black = 2.0%, Hispanic/Latino = 2.5%, Asian = 7.5%, Other = 4.7%
- Heterosexual = 92%, Lesbian/Gay = 2.7%, Bisexual = 2.7%; Other = 2.6%
- Average age = 31 years
- Average years in the industry = 5.4 years
- Percentage of people with disabilities = 13% (such as cognitive, mobility, sight)
- More than 80% have a university level education or higher

If we go with these statistics, the games industry is dominated by White Caucasian males just over 30 and displays a significant underrepresentation of society's diversity.

Most, if not all, of those working in the industry are also gamers. In an interview conducted by the author of this chapter in 2003 in one of the major Swedish games developing studies, the CEO stated that he would rather hire a person who is a gamer then someone who has superior technical capability. The interview reported by Dovey and Kennedy (2006) is, by all accounts, fairly representative for games developers: they share the same taste and have similar experiences and backgrounds, resulting in similar views on games, society and life in general – a structuring mechanism that frames, channels and standardizes behaviours and actions (Bourdieu and Wacquant, 1992). Admittedly, most such surveys in the industry are directed towards developers and there is relatively limited knowledge about other groups in the industry who may well display more heterogeneous features. However, the games developers are the core group of workers in the industry most closely associated with the notion of creativity.

The question that surfaces is, consequently, this: what are the possibilities of creative acts in a field where the agents present such similarities in habitus? Having taught on university programmes in games development, the author has often encountered students with rather limited terms of reference or width of horizon. Most students seem to share the same outlook on games. When challenged to produce new ideas, students produce few references beyond those to other games. If references are made to other media, such as films or books, these are mostly drawn from the fantasy or science fiction genres. If such limitations take deeper roots, or are further institutionalized in university programmes, the boundaries of the field in which games are developed will be narrow and rigid. Indeed, despite what the Queen of Hearts suggested to Alice in Lewis Carroll's *Alice in Wonderland* (1865), it is quite hard for one person to imagine what is unimaginable:

There is no use trying; one can't believe impossible things. (Alice)

I dare say you haven't had much practice. When I was your age, [...] I always did it for half an hour a day. Why, sometimes I've believed as many as six impossible things before breakfast. (Queen of Hearts)

The consequence of this homogeneity is that when games concepts are developed and new games ideas are presented, these often reflect the taste and preferences of the game developers (Hagen, 2010), and not those of the potential consumers: 'Game designers prefer [to] tap into their (self-perceived) unlimited creativity and come up with their own ideas' (Abeele and Van Rompaey, 2006: 1470). This argument is in line with Hesmondhalgh who argues that the 'romantic conception of art in Western societies established the idea that art is at its most special when it represents the original self-expression of a particular author' (2007: 20). This romantic concept of art presents creativity as being fundamentally opposite to commerce and pragmatic functionality, and has had a major impact on cultural industries. It defines the product of culture industries in terms of what Akrich (1992, 1995) describes as the I-methodology, a notion of culture production shaped by personal tastes and preferences where the artist or designer inscribes himself (and indeed, in the video games industry the majority of artists *is* male) into the product, in our case into the game: 'Designers thus define actors with specific tastes, competences, motives, aspirations, political prejudices, and the rest, and they assume that morality, technology, science, and economy will evolve in particular ways. A large part of the work of innovation is that of '*inscribing*' this vision of (or prediction about) the world in the technical content of the new object' (Akrich, 1992: 208).

Thus, in the video games industry, creativity is defined, and evaluated, by agents exhibiting a fairly homogeneous habitus in a narrow field. These agents define both what a game is, and also what qualifies as a good or a bad game. Any creative offerings, in whatever area, that have the potential of bringing new games ideas into the arena and to the consumers are evaluated in relation to the field, dismissed if they stray too far from what is considered a good game, and accepted if they can be seen as having a firm root within the field, as accepted. Games (or actions) that push the boundaries of the field, as defined by its dominant agents, are judged as creative. But if these actions stray too far beyond the accepted boundaries, they are defined as beyond games, and beyond creativity.

Creative possibilities

While many of those working in the field of the video games industry are aware of the need to foster enabling environments in which creativity can flourish, few seem to realize the problems that the homogeneous industry presents. This has resulted in a field where those holding positions of power are able to define both content and borders of the field. Although the power relations today may offer a few possibilities to challenge the status quo of prevailing modes of thinking and operating in the industry, it is hard to argue that the games of the twenty-first century are that much different from those of the 1970s and 1980s. Further, if the homogeneity of the field makes the provision of a more diverse and enabling environment particularly urgent, this is only the first step. It needs to be complemented by a second step, namely the expansion of the field, and the encouragement of a field population that is diverse and significantly challenges the current demographics of the industry, as summarized above.

One example of how games developers try to foster creativity is by using a work process based on Agile project management methods such as SCRUM. The Agile development process makes it possible to develop a game through incremental improvements (Walfisz *et al.*, 2006; Zackariasson *et al.*, 2006a, 2006b). A traditional project follows a waterfall model where all activities are planned at the start, in, for example, a Gantt chart, and the execution phase is a matter of implementing what has been planned previously. Using this kind of work process in developing a game would require designers to have all the content of the game fully planned at the start. But as it is impossible to know with certainty what content will create a fun and immersive game, it is not possible to plan the whole game at the start. When using Agile methods, only the base structures of the game are planned at the beginning of the project. These are then implemented in cycles, the game is tested throughout the whole development period, and further content is added, based on the experience of playing the game during the test phases. This work method allows for decisions to be made and content to be created throughout the project, just as it pushes the initiative lower down onto those actually building the game. Therefore it is likely that this method will provide extended opportunities to encourage and foster creative actions in games development – but it does not generate a diversity of populations.

The field of the video games industry creates structural limitations which constrain creativity. The power to define games lies in the hands of place holders who hold power positions, and traditionally these were the publishers. One way to challenge the structures of the field is to circumvent it, or at least a major part of what has been defined as the value chain of video games development (Zackariasson and Wilson, 2012). The introduction of distribution channels that enabled games developers to sell games directly to consumers presented a possibility to avoid one major part of the field. No one other than the developer had to approve the game, or game idea, in order for it to be produced and distributed. Company web pages became a major tool to communicate directly with the consumer and take the product to market. Recently the opportunities have increased immensely with distribution channels like Apple's Appstore and the Android store. These stores offer distribution and micro payment opportunities that enable both established and independent games developers to reach consumers directly. Independent studios are of course part of the established field, but they have possibilities to circumvent this same field as their dependency on publishers, and thus on established powers in the field, diminishes.

There are numerous examples of independent games developers who succeeded in developing games outside the field, only to be incorporated into the field later as an example of success. One of these is Mojang's game *Minecraft*, developed by Markus 'Notch' Persson from 2009 onwards, initially as a solo project. It is unlikely that Persson would have received any funding for the initial game development phase. Many games publishers admit that if they had been asked in 2009 to fund the game they would have declined. By making himself independent, Persson could merge game genres creatively without any interference from established power holders such as investors and publishers. This enabled him to realize his creative ideas and incorporate them into a game. Another example is the game *Fret Nice*, issued by Pieces Interactive in 2010, which was developed primarily by a student at the University of Skövde, Sweden. In this case, the university constituted a space outside the field that enabled the student to develop a traditional platform game, but with a non-traditional game control: a guitar. Both examples suggest that creative actions outside the field have the potential of being sustained without the limitations present in the field. Ultimately, however, the appreciation of the creative efforts put into the game, and thereby its success, are defined by the consumer: *Minecraft* has gained great exposure in the media and earned large revenues while *Fret Nice* has remained unknown to most gamers.

Concluding comments

Having the opportunity to be creative is of great importance to all working in the video games industry, not only in the development of games but in the industry in whole. One can argue that creativity is important for many industries, but as games are part of the culture industry it has characteristics that make creativity all the more important. If this industry wants to remain capable of developing games that meet, or exceed, the expectations of a growing number of (diverse) consumers the industry will have to reinvent itself. This relates not only to the content of games, but also to the ways in which games are published and distributed – and by whom.

Creativity is a structural concept. In order to foster an environment where creativity can flourish, games developers need to break the status quo when it comes to demographics. These have a major impact on what ideas are generated and are allowed to exist in this field, and how they are acted upon. In order to enable new types of games that are a result of a different creativity, one that goes beyond the field as it is defined today, there have to be people working in the industry who can go beyond the accepted boundaries of the field. Using Bourdieu's concepts of habitus and field, it is possible to map out creative possibilities in the industry, and to identify where such possibilities might be hampered by existing power relations prevalent in the field.

But creativity should be facilitated to ensure that it pervades the entire video games industry. It might be the case that video games publishers today feel forced to focus on repetitive, overly standardized genres, game content, and sequels, to recoup losses from games that did not reach expected sales. There is a sense among games developers that publishers dampen creativity. Being the funding agent, it is their responsibility to secure the success of games in their portfolio. While there will thus always be a tendency to play safe and invest in what is predictably successful, there should also be some wild cards – question marks in the portfolio that can grow into stars with the right support and nurture. The video games publisher has a pivotal role to play in negotiating game content between developer and consumer. The publisher, still, has the power in the field to facilitate breaks from the taken for granted norms prevailing in the industry.

References

Abeele, V. and Van Rompaey, V. (2006) *Introducing Human-Centered Research to Game Design: Designing Game Concepts for and with Senior Citizens*. Work in progress. CHI Conference, Montreal, Canada, 22–27 April, Extended Abstracts.

Akrich, M. (1992) The de-scription of technical objects, in W.E. Bijker and J. Law (eds), *Shaping Technology/Building Society: Studies in Sociotechnical Change*, Cambridge, MA: MIT Press, pp. 205–24.

Akrich, M. (1995) User representations: practices, methods and sociology, in A. Rip, T.J. Misa and J. Schot (eds), *Managing Technology in Society: The Approach of Constructive Technology Assessment*, London: Pinter Publishers, pp. 167–84.

Amabile, T.M. (1996) *Creativity in Context*, Boulder, CO: Westview.

Barron, F. (1988) Putting creativity to work, in R.J. Sternberg (ed.), *The Nature of Creativity*, Cambridge, MA: Cambridge University Press, pp. 76–98.

Beck, J.C. and Wade, M. (2004) *Got Game: How the Gamer Generation Is Reshaping Business Forever*, Boston, MA: Harvard Business School Press.

Bourdieu, P. (1993) *The Field of Cultural Production*, Columbia: Columbia University Press.

Bourdieu, P. and Wacquant, L.J. (1992) *An Invitation to Reflexive Sociology*, Cambridge: Polity Press.

Carroll, L. (1865) *Through the Looking Glass,* Chapter 5: Wool and Water, http://www.alice-in-wonderland.net/books/2chpt5.html.

Caves, R.E. (2000) *Creative Industries: Contracts between Art and Commerce,* Cambridge, MA: Harvard University Press.

Chatfield, T. (2010) *Fun Inc.: Why Games Are the 21st Century's Most Serious Business,* London: Virgin Books.

Consalvo, M. (2008) Crunched by passion: women game developers and workplace challenges, in Y.B. Kafai, C. Heeter, J. Denner and J.Y. Sun (eds), *Beyond Barbie and Mortal Kombat: New Perspectives on Gender and Gaming,* Cambridge, MA: MIT Press, pp. 177–92.

Demaria, R. and Wilson, J.L. (2004) *High Score: The Illustrated History of Electronic Games,* New York: McGraw-Hill/Osborne.

Deuze, M., Martin, C.B. and Allen, C. (2007) The professional identity of game workers, *Convergence: The International Journal of Research into New Media Technologies,* 13(4): 335–53.

Donovan T. (2010) *Replay: The History of Video Games,* Lewes: Yellow Ant.

Dovey, J. and Kennedy, H.W. (2006) *Game Cultures: Computer Games as New Media,* Berkshire: Open University Press.

Feist, G.J. (1998) A meta-analysis of personality in scientific and artistic creativity, *Personality and Social Psychology Review,* 2: 290–309.

Gourdin, A. (2005) *Game Developer Demographics: An Exploration of Workforce Diversity,* International Game Developers Association, http://www.igda.org/game-developer-demographics-report.

Hagen, U. (2010) Designing for player experience: how professional game developers communicate design visions, Paper presented at the Nordic DiGRA Conference, Stockholm, Sweden, 16–17 August 2010.

Herz, J.C. (1997) *Joystick Nation: How Video Games Ate Our Quarters, Won Our Hearts, and Rewired Our Minds,* Boston: Little, Brown and Company.

Hesmondhalgh, D. (2007) *The Cultural Industries,* London: Sage.

Jenkins, R. (2002) *Pierre Bourdieu,* London: Routledge.

Kent, S.L. (2002) *The Ultimate History of Video Games: The Story Behind the Craze that Touched Our Lives and Changed the World,* Rocklin, CA: Prima Life.

Kidder, T. (1981) *The Soul of a New Machine,* New York: Little, Brown and Company.

Koivunen, N. and Rehn, A. (eds) (2009) *Creativity and the Contemporary Economy,* Lund: Liber.

McGonigal, J. (2007) Why I love bees: a case study in collective intelligence gaming, in K. Salen (ed.), *The Ecology of Games: Connecting Youth, Games, and Learning,* Cambridge, MA: MIT Press, pp. 199–228.

Mollick, E. and Edery, D. (2009) *Changing the Game: How Video Games Are Transforming the Future of Business,* New Jersey: FT Press.

O'Donnell, C. (2012) This is now a software industry, in P. Zackariasson and T.L. Wilson (eds), *The Video Game Industry: Formation, Present State and Future,* New York: Routledge, pp. 17–33.

Piñero, E. (2003) *The Aesthetics of Code: On Excellence in Instrumental Action,* Doctoral Thesis, Royal Institute of Technology, Stockholm, Sweden.

Poole, S. (2000) *Trigger Happy: Videogames and the Entertainment Revolution,* London: Fourth Estate.

PricewaterhouseCoopers (2011) *Global Entertainment and Media Outlook 2011–2015: Events and Trends*, ed. by D. Gilhawley, www.pwc.com/en_TW/tw/publications/events-and.../e250.pdf.

Shaw, M.P., and Runco, M.A. (1994) *Creativity and Affect*, Westport, CT: Ablex.

Simonton, D.K. (1997) Creative productivity: a predictive and explanatory model of career trajectories and landmarks, *Psychological Review*, 104: 66–89.

Sternberg, R.J., and Lubart, T.I. (1995) *Defying the Crowd: Cultivating Creativity in a Culture of Conformity*, New York: Free Press.

Stone, A.R. (1995) *The War of Desire and Technology at the Close of the Mechanical Age*, Cambridge, MA: MIT Press.

Swartz, D. (1997) *Culture & Power: The Sociology of Pierre Bourdieu*, Chicago: University of Chicago Press.

Torrance, E.P. (1988) The nature of creativity as manifest in its testing, in R.J. Sternberg (ed.), *The Nature of Creativity*, Cambridge, MA: Cambridge University Press, pp. 43–75.

Tschang, F.T. (2007) Balancing the tensions between rationalization and creativity in the video games industry, *Organization Science*, 18(6): 989–1005.

UK SIC (Standard Industrial Classification) (2007) Ready-made interactive leisure and entertainment software development, http://www.econstats.com/uk2012on/OutFile_030.htm.

Ullman, E. (1997) *Close to the Machine*, San Francisco, CA: City Lights Books.

Walfisz, M., Zackariasson, P. and Wilson, T.L. (2006) Real-time strategy: evolutionary game development, *Business Horizons*, 49(6), 487–98.

Zackariasson, P. (2003) *Cyborg Leadership: Including Nonhuman Actors in Leadership*, Licentiate Thesis, Umeå University, School of Business.

Zackariasson, P. and Styhre, A. (2011) Carry on! Understanding creativity through popular culture, Paper presented at the Standing Conference of Organizational Symbolism, Istanbul.

Zackariasson, P., Styhre, A. and Wilson, T.L. (2006a) Phronesis and creativity: knowledge work in video game development, *Creativity and Innovation Management*, 15(4): 419–29.

Zackariasson, P., Walfisz, M. and Wilson, T.L. (2006b) Management of creativity in video game development: a case study, *Services Marketing Quarterly*, 27(4): 73–97.

Zackariasson, P. and Wilson, T.L. (2010) Alternative reality games explorations, in *Proceedings of the EURAM Conference*, Rome, May 2010.

Zackariasson, P. and Wilson, T.L. (2012) Marketing in the video game industry, in P. Zackariasson and T.L. Wilson (eds), *The Video Game Industry: Formation, Present State and Future*, New York: Routledge, pp. 57–75.

7
HR Issues in the Computer Games Industry: Survival at a Price

Sue Shaw and Gill Homan

Introduction

Human resource management (HRM) in the computer games sector needs to be seen within its industry context. The structure of this part of the creative media industry, the way it is geographically clustered and networked, the extent to which it is largely project based, and its use of a core and periphery workforce are important influences on its human resource (HR) policies and practices. The sector is dominated by a small number of transnational corporations, Sony, Nintendo and Microsoft, but primarily populated by small to medium-sized companies with a staff strength of 35–60 (Kerr and Flynn, 2003). In the United Kingdom, these constitute 75 per cent of the sector. This is a global industry and predicted to be worth some $68.4 billion in 2012 and $86.7 billion in 2014, an annual growth rate of over 10 per cent. In 2009 it employed 7,000 people in the United Kingdom down from 9400 in 2004. Eighty-nine per cent worked in development, the remainder working in functional support; 77 per cent of organizations used freelancers while 29 per cent expected to increase their usage in the near future (Skillset, 2011). Traditionally companies of this size do not employ HR professionals. The workforce is heavily gendered: women constitute 6 per cent (12 per cent in 2006) of the workforce compared with 47 per cent nationally. Similarly, 3 per cent come from minority ethnic backgrounds (4 per cent in 2006) compared with 9 per cent nationally (Skillset, 2011). The operation of social and economic networks, which are a feature of both job access and knowledge exchange, may militate against diversity and reinforce gender and racial segmentation (Christopherson, 2008). The industry has a young workforce with 61 per cent younger than 35, compared to 35 per cent in the wider economy. In 2005 the figure was 76 per cent, suggesting a shifting age profile (Skillset, 2011). These statistics frame the industry's employment context.

Games organizations are in the business of creating or extending knowledge in an emerging industry with rapidly changing technology, complex industry and financial structures and products with a short shelf life. The industry is seen as one of the drivers of cultural globalization but facing major challenges which determine the success of its key players. These include the management of highly skilled creative labour 'working under artisanal conditions' and the uncertainty of demand created by a product that requires constant renewal (Kerr and Flynn, 2003: 96). While it is generally accepted that creative output is the product of the creative individual working within an enabling environment, the dynamic nature of the industry presents those people that work in it with 'new forms and levels of risk that also have to be managed' (Christopherson, 2008: 91). These factors have implications for HR within the sector. This chapter firstly examines different aspects of HRM practice within the sector and then goes on to explore the environment in which HR practices are enacted. The chapter concludes by reflecting on the emerging discourses and discusses implications for the future.

HRM in the games sector: the employment of creative individuals

Resourcing

Issues facing HR include sourcing the appropriate creative individuals, retaining them in a highly competitive environment and ensuring they retain their currency in a rapidly developing field. Rewarding and motivating creative workers means understanding what they value, which may challenge traditional HR doctrine. Ensuring a work environment that enables creativity provides specific management challenges, given the context outlined above. These include balancing individual needs with the realities of objectives and acting as the architect of creative space while operating in a flexible workforce model.

Sourcing creative workers requires an understanding of what constitutes a creative individual in this industry. Defining the boundaries of the creative workforce within the games sector is not unproblematic given its diverse communities of specialists which include script writers, game designers, graphic artists, sound designers and software engineers (Cohendet and Simon, 2007: 588), or what Townley *et al.* call 'the motley crew' (2009: 939). The sector's relative youth and reliance on information and communication technology (ICT) account for the difficulty in understanding the identity of the games creator and whether it is embodied in technical or creative expertise (Cadin and Guérin, 2006).

A further question is how creativity is identified. Is it some innate intellectual ability or personality characteristic identifiable through psychometric tests? Alternatively, as will be explored later, is it dependent upon environmental stimuli in terms of group and organizational factors and processes? Thompson *et al.* assert that the 'distinctive characteristics of creative labour are best understood within particular sector and market contexts' (2007: 636) while Mumford argues that 'it is the individual who is the source of a new idea' (2000: 314). Many studies have examined the personal qualities, characteristics, attitudes, preferences and styles that differentiate a creative person (see Selby *et al.*, 2005, for a review of creative personality research). Mumford (2000) suggests that individual creativity incorporates knowledge, process and work styles. Implicit in this concept of creativity are independent thinking, self-confidence, strong achievement orientation, ability to tolerate ambiguity, capacity for learning and problem-solving styles ranging from adaptation to innovation. Studies also indicate that creatives develop a high level of tacit knowledge through their ability to utilize complex and interrelated activities and concepts in a disciplined and focused way. It is these characteristics which lead Mumford (2000) to suggest that roles be defined in terms of broad core duties and selection be based on breadth and depth of expertise, and skill in working with that expertise. Townley *et al.* (2009) highlight the importance of social capital and the ability of the individual to gain and disseminate ideas, information and knowledge through membership of social networks and consequently speak of the myth of the lone genius. Therefore should ability to work in a team, communication and networking skills be added to the already substantial list of desirable characteristics?

Having established the characteristics of a successful creative individual, the issue from the HR perspective becomes one of sourcing talent. In such a young industry, one might expect further and higher education to be the primary talent pipeline; however, just 48 per cent of UK employers recruited from higher education whilst 29 per cent recruited from within and 38 per cent from outside the industry. In fact, 58 per cent of employers specifically reported difficulties in recruiting from the education sector (Skillset, 2011). There is evidence that firms systematically seek out new talent and individuals of high potential through recruitment networks (Mumford, 2000) and according to Skillset (2011) 42 per cent of new hires did so via some form of personal or networked contact as opposed to 18 per cent who used advertisements. However, these kinds of informal approaches are not conducive to employment equality and may even reinforce labour segmentation (Christopherson, 2008).

Educational provision, still in its infancy in this field, does not yet satisfy industry needs either numerically or in terms of the skill set. One can question whether higher education can ever supply the specific needs of this industry given the constantly growing, shifting and transient nature of its body of knowledge and resulting technology (Teipen, 2008). In their review of the UK games industry, undertaken for NESTA (National Endowment for Science, Technology and the Arts), Livingstone and Hope state that 'there are severe misalignments between the educational system and what the video games and visual effects industries need', a situation that 'starts with schools [...] and is compounded by poor university courses' (2011: 5). This impacts negatively on the United Kingdom's competitive position in the global industry resulting in many employers recruiting overseas.

The games industry does not have the recognized entry routes and career paths supported by well established vocationally oriented education that characterize more established industries. Various countries have sought to address this issue differently. Teipen (2008) refers to the well-established training for games designers supported by Nintendo in Japan, and Ubisoft in France, and the 50 or so educational organizations specifically focused on the video games industry in the United States. In Europe, the position is patchier, and in her study of Sweden, Germany and Poland, Teipen (2008) found that of the three, Sweden had the best developed, albeit embryonic, educational environment supporting industry needs.

Postgraduate courses, more flexible and responsive than undergraduate degrees, together with employer training may be the way forward. In the United Kingdom, Livingstone and Hope (2011) assert that the industry needs those hard skills developed by a science degree (currently held by 20 per cent of the sector) rather than the softer skills promoted by many of the games degrees on offer currently. Moreover, the value and importance of a formal degree seems to vary across jobs, with a game designer's reputation and track record being more important than a degree (Teipen, 2008). This, of course, may be more difficult to argue at the career entry stage and also in view of the ever-increasing sophistication and complexity of games technology.

Performance management

It is important to manage the creative individual to enhance and capitalize on their abilities – yet conflicting interests create tensions in a traditional performance management system. It is, for instance, acknowledged that creative people generally have high levels of intrinsic motivation which can easily be diminished by premature judgement during the ideas phase of the creative process. They need to know that even in failure their input will be valued despite the fact that they may challenge the existing paradigm or destroy established ideas and practices. This is particularly true in the games industry where there might be many costly failures before achieving a financially success-ful product (Mumford, 2000). Developing performance indicators that reflect the complex nature of the knowledge, skills and output charac-teristic of creative work can also be problematic, particularly where the reviewer may be someone without the same level of technical expertise as the reviewee. Mumford (2000), drawing on previous research (Scott, 1995; Mehr and Schaver, 1996; Amabile, 1997), argues that specific objectives may limit innovation as they may inhibit creativity and reduce intrinsic motivation. In contrast, positive formative feedback and high levels of personal autonomy enhance creativity (Zhou, 1998). Thus, bespoke systems may be necessary with performance objectives which are defined more broadly to enable variable approaches to working and outcomes, and which are reviewed more frequently than the traditional annual cycle. Such an approach acknowledges and values the apparently fruitless dead-ends that add to the repository of accumulated knowledge from which new creativity emerges. This is an aspect of what Cohendet and Simon call 'creative slacks' (2007: 588), which we discuss in the later section on creative space.

Collaborative peer review is advocated in the industry to evaluate the direction of the creatives' work and the strategies employed. This is seen as both a more informed and sympathetic approach, less likely to focus on general organizational requirements such as conformity with administrative processes and contribution to short term goals. Timeframes are also a significant factor in evaluating the work of video games developers. It takes about two years to create a console game (Cadin and Guérin, 2006), but the publication and sales of games are highly seasonal or linked to book or film releases; thus timeframes for delivery need to be tightly managed and are a key performance issue. A key feature of the industry is that creative endeavour is firmly embed-ded within a complex and tightly framed context of profit-driven activity (Eikhof and Haunschild, 2007), supporting our earlier assertion that the annual appraisal may be too rigid and poorly focused, and above all insufficiently proactive for this industry.

Motivation and reward

Performance management and evaluation are traditionally linked to employee reward at a number of levels including the individual via performance-related pay, teams and groups through bonus schemes and profit-related pay and share option schemes that link organizational or divisional performance to employee reward. In 2010, an employee in the UK computer games industry averaged £30,800 in salary, within a range of just below £20,000 to £47,000 (Skillset, 2011). Despite a standard week of 42 hours, there is an accepted culture of generally unpaid long hours, particularly at crucial points in the development process, which raises the issue of work–life balance. Wage levels appear, at least within small organizations, to be individually negotiated allowing for pay differentiation within the same role. Pay differentiation between levels, for example between games developers and project managers, differs between small and large firms, ranging from up to 20 to 70 per cent and more (Teipen, 2008: 324).

A number of points emerge from the creativity literature which are significant to the area of reward, firstly the importance of intrinsic motivation in creative individuals, and secondly that the development of ideas must be rewarded. Teipen (2008) attributes intrinsic motivation in the case of games developers to their tendency to be gamers who have pursued a career that originated as a hobby. An organizational culture that provides less bureaucratic and hierarchical structures and that allows for self-organization within teams appeals to the games developer and the mostly young organizations largely staffed by young employees and managers reinforces this culture. There is evidence (Hotho and Champion, 2011) that organizational growth, combined with the development of more formal systems, can actually reduce intrinsic motivation. Highly valued intrinsic rewards appear to be autonomy both in work strategies and the fulfilment of the work contract in areas such as working hours; freedom to pursue creative interests; and support in skills development. Intrinsic rewards need to be designed into the work environment and development policies of the organizations.

Extrinsic rewards cannot be ignored and take the form of bonus payments related to both goal achievement and commercial success. Evidence (Teipen, 2008) suggests that these tend to be individually based and vary widely from organization to organization in terms of the percentage of total pay. Both small and large firms appear to make use of share option schemes. These have a number of advantages: they do not impact on the profit and loss accounts of the organization; they may make the recruitment package more attractive particularly for smaller organizations where the ability to offer competitive salaries may be limited; they offer the opportunity for high profit returns to the employee; they have motivational potential; and they link performance to company finance. Share option schemes appear to be more embedded in the United States but are also a successful feature of reward packages within Europe.

Employee development

Highly innovative and creative work requires the continuous acquiring of new skills and the refreshing of existing core skills. The opportunity to update and develop intellectual capital is key to intrinsic motivation for creative individuals and an area where the interests of the employee and the organization coincide. For the individual, the need for continuous development is driven by their raison d'être, but also defines their marketability; for the organization, this need is determined by their business imperative: to develop products that are leading edge.

Skillset's *Labour Market Intelligence Digest* (2011) reports on training and development activity for the United Kingdom. According to their findings, games firms are committed to training their staff and are even extending development to freelance workers on occasion. This is evidenced by the retention of training budgets during the current recession. Organizational commitment varies with size, with only 25 per cent of those employing less than five, but 80 per cent of those with over 25 employees offering learning opportunities. The two most popular reported forms of training are attendance at external courses and seminars (63 per cent) or in-house training using external providers. Of the surveyed organizations, 54 per cent use in-house methods such as coaching, mentoring, and ad hoc support on the job. Surprisingly, given the nature of the sector, Internet-based training is utilized by only 36 per cent of organizations and higher education by just 3 per cent. Areas of staff development include management and leadership development (36 per cent); art, design and creativity (28 per cent); general software development skills (24 per cent); specific software (14 per cent); copyright and intellectual property (IP) (11 per cent). Of those receiving training, 66 per cent are company funded and almost 30 per cent self-funded. While these figures show a commendable commitment to development by both employers and employees, there are barriers to training which mirror those voiced by small businesses as a whole, in particular, from the organization's point of view, insufficient time and cost. For individuals seeking to access learning and development, the chief barriers are lack of information, and lack of suitable courses and online materials (Skillset, 2011).

The emphasis on mentoring, coaching and other forms of internal development as well as the constant input from external sources reflects the importance of the nurturing, development and transfer of what Leonard and Swap (2004) call 'deep smarts'. 'Deep smarts' refer to the experience-based tacit knowledge and expertise repertoires individuals can build through deliberate practice. They include the ability to comprehend complex systems, and recognize patterns, combined with tacit understanding of the market and the customer, and with an awareness of how internal and external forces can affect the organization. Deep smarts grow organically, over time, and through diverse experiences. They cannot be taught, and they cannot be trained, but, as Leonard and Swap argue, they can and need to be cultivated because an organization's true competitive advantage and vitality reside in them. Harvesting the value of deep smarts is thus a management task, and one of the key reasons for striving to retain the expert work force. Building an organization that enables the development, leveraging and retention of deep smarts through investment in learning and development, the creation of a work environment that contains opportunities for networking and knowledge transfer and assignments that promote internal learning becomes a management responsibility that resonates particularly strongly with the requirements of creative businesses (Cadin *et al.*, 2006).

Careers in the games industry

There is evidence that leadership and management skills are seen as key areas of development by staff because they 'will have to manage a project team in the near future' (Skillset, 2011: 16). This is the first step on the career ladder for the creative employee and has to be balanced by the need to keep technical knowledge and skills current. Hotho and Champion (2011) highlight another tension, using the concepts of exploitation and exploration. Exploitation relates to those activities driven by the need for profit maximization and efficiency, both prerequisites for innovation. In the games context, exploitation relates to the work for hire (WFH) activities focusing on developing games to client specifications, or developing new generations of existing games. Exploration relates to the riskier activities normally associated with developing entirely new games, and the search for IP. Balancing often routine client work with opportunities for the creation of IP can be challenging for organizations and yet many recognize the need to do this for retention purposes, to maintain motivation and for career building for their creative individuals, apart from adding value to the business.

Creative careers in general are often seen as being without boundaries, influenced by stretch opportunities to extend experience and skills in different areas (Jones, 2010). This strategy is enabled by the exploitation of social capital and social networks and by association with genre-specific people, practices and objects. Managing their curriculum vitae for career progression is a complex process for the creative individual within the industry, not just a matter of undertaking a series of jobs or roles which combine to present a coherent progression of knowledge, skills and responsibilities. It is a strategic use of contacts, contracts and job opportunities which may, for example, trade pay for an IP development opportunity or trade creative opportunity for the experience of building and leading a project team. Working for specific companies or even with specific people can be seen as capital for a future career, sometimes even before that career has effectively started. This was confirmed, anecdotally, to one of the authors when an individual employed in the games industry stated: 'I was willing to work for nothing just to be able to say at future interviews that I had worked with [X].'

Informal contacts and social networks appear to have considerable currency within the sector, not only in terms of career information and as a source of future job opportunities but, in certain cases, also as a means of career entry. Career entry can be facilitated firstly through work placements or internships obtained through informal or personal contacts and secondly through the interaction of game players with games developers. In the latter instance, suggestions by games players resulting in the modification of the product have on occasion led to the player being offered a job. This reinforces the proposition expressed earlier that creative individuals are often those who have developed a hobby into a career. Networks are generally seen as positive structures for support and cooperation, leading to the idea of a knowledge-based community, but they can also be used for competitive advantage particularly in the area of individual career management (Townley *et al.*, 2009). However, as we argued earlier, they may also reinforce labour market segregation.

The predominance of small firms makes career management a challenging issue. The need to retain creative talent, particularly at crucial times in the development cycle, means that even when organizations cannot offer progression opportunities they must offer the building blocks of progression such as learning and development, stretch projects, access to social networks and information or mentor programmes, even though these may eventually enable the individual to move on.

This section has explored different areas of HR practice within the games industry particularly from the perspective of the creative staff that form the majority of the workforce. The next section examines the employment context in which creative staff flourish and the HR implications of this.

The employment context of creative workers within the games industry

Creativity, residing in individuals or in groups, leads to the formation of new knowledge or the application of existing knowledge to new applications. While current thinking does not deny the role of talent, imagination and disposition, it is now accepted that the environment has an important role to play in fostering creativity (DeFillippi *et al.*, 2007). Christopherson (2008) argues that in order to understand creative work fully we need to recognize the role that risk and uncertainty play, and the ways in which the political and economic context shapes that risk and changes it over time, with implications for workforce strategies and work processes. The tax break for video games companies, introduced by George Osborne in the March Budget in 2012, is a current example of this process.

Organizational culture and creativity

Research points to the important role played by the organization in providing an effective work environment for creative individuals (Mumford, 2000). Smith and Pacquette (2010: 119) assert that the 'creative process and creativity itself require an open ended environment in which experimentation can occur and where being unorthodox and defying the norm are encouraged'. This is almost diametrically opposed to the accepted doctrine of organization that has been fostered by management theorists since the time of Fayol, Follett and Taylor to the present day, and according to which organizations strive to reduce chaos and achieve predictability. Arguably, the provision of a work environment and a style of management which enable creativity presents particular HR challenges in relation to culture, structure and leadership. Consequently the focus moves to considering what kind of HRM strategies might enable and enhance creativity. These include multiple interventions that take into account the individual, the group, the organization and the strategic environment (Mumford, 2000).

To understand the role of the environment in enabling creativity, it is important to understand the psychology of the creative process and the creative individual. The key points that emerge from research in this field emphasize the contradictory nature of the creative personality. The environment must provide a safe psychological space for the creative individual to flourish, and simultaneously allow the freedom to challenge and take risks: therefore the culture must be one that stresses the value of innovation, enables risk taking while also tolerating a high degree of failure. This aspect of culture is easier to foster in small organizations, for the reasons mentioned earlier; nevertheless, Smith and Pacquette's (2010) study explains how the same balance has been achieved in two large creative organizations, Pixar and Google. Pixar Animation Studios promotes risk by allowing employees to undertake projects deemed impossible, based on the premise that giving employees the permission to explore the unknown can be highly motivating, even if the project, in the end, may lead nowhere. Similarly, Google has made great efforts to ensure that, as the company grows, employees retain the freedom they currently have to develop new ideas, or find creative solutions to seemingly insurmountable problems. The argument, again, is that this freedom will maintain the fascination with creative problem solving, and their motivation to invest their ideas in the company (Smith and Pacquette, 2010).

Organizational structure and creativity

It is not just culture that fosters creativity; HR specialists need to give consideration to organizational structures and physical layout. There is a belief that traditional hierarchical structures and practices are inappropriate because of the intangible nature of creative individuals' human capital (Thompson *et al.*, 2007). This is confirmed in practice, to some degree, for example in organizations such as Google, which has endeavoured to maintain flat, transparent and non-hierarchical structures despite its rapid growth and the consequent increase in more routine work (Smith and Pacquette, 2010). Work in the computer games industry is typically project based, albeit characterized by differing levels of standardization, due to the nature of games development which makes adherence to rigid plans difficult. This, too, mitigates against a hierarchically structured work flow. In reality, however, many of the larger organizations within the sector have the structures and hierarchies that one might expect of large companies and it tends to be the smaller ones that operate wholly on project-based structures.

Creative work is often ill-defined or poorly structured, particularly at the stage of ideas development, and individuals need the freedom to range widely through concepts and information that might seem irrelevant to the problem in hand, yet spark off the creative thought process that will result in new ideas, understandings and interpretations. These new insights, however, have to lead to new products and commercial results, and a constraining framework of delivery is therefore needed. Facilitating the creative thought process requires subtle management of the creative thinking space and an understanding of the strengths of individuals, some of whom may be more effective at different stages of the creative process. However, the intersection of 'commerce and art' (DeFillippi *et al.*, 2007: 515) can create tensions. One of the strategic decisions that may give rise to this tension is the balance between innovation and exploitation. Exploitation has, at least within the short term, less risk and quicker returns. However, innovation not only leads to new sources to exploit but also builds the intellectual capital of the organization. Integration is needed between the different and diverse creative groups which exist within a games company and the commercial requirement to maximize outcomes and bring a product to market within time, cost and market constraints. If the delicate balance is not achieved, the result is either a reduction in diversity and in creativity or chaos and inefficiency (Cohendet and Simon, 2007).

DeFillippi *et al.* (2004), cited in Jones *et al.* (2004: 138), describe the need to 'reconcile tensions between the work ethos and human resources activities in creative and more routinized activities' and the need to 'balance the advantages of flexible organization and temporary organization with the advantages of tight integration' as the paradoxes of managing and organizing creativity within the cultural economy. Referred to as the 'distance paradox' (DeFillippi *et al.*, 2007: 515), the 'coupling or decoupling of creative and routine activities' (Bilton and Leary, 2002: 49) and the 'exploration-exploitation dilemma' (Cadin and Guérin, 2006: 249), the extent to which creative work needs to be separated out from more routine activities is a contentious issue in larger and in smaller organizations. Given the tensions that exist between 'innovators' and operations, organizations and their HR practitioners can be faced with real challenges about how the business should be structured. For example, Cadin and Guérin (2006) argue that organizations that aim to embed innovation and exploration as standard have to address a range of questions. Should they create structures that are specifically dedicated to innovation and physically separate these from the operating structure? Should the resources tasked to undertake innovation be dedicated to one innovation project and then be reabsorbed? Should innovation/ exploration projects be subcontracted? Or can intrapreneurship and project teams be developed in house? Writers even go so far as to explain the physical nature of the working environment, emphasizing the importance of shared space and boundary objects (Cohendet and Simon, 2007). Pixar exemplifies this in the positioning of a large atrium in the middle of their facility. The atrium contains meeting rooms, cafeterias and mail boxes and creates a space that allows people to meet and interact during their normal office routines and tasks.

Most writers in the field agree that, notwithstanding the size of the organization, structures conducive to leveraging creativity for commercial use must be flexible and networked, utilizing self-managed and diverse project teams with devolved decision-making and democratic lines of communication (Hotho and Champion, 2011). These structures enable the autonomy, task complexity, work identity and ownership that are seen as essential to creative work and which, according to Hackman and Oldham (1980), provide the basis of job satisfaction. In addition, as noted by Mumford (2000), group working and projects provide opportunities for career planning and individual development.

Common to all organizations in the industry is the development and use of social networks for support, collaboration, information and ideas exchange; these are more easily sustained within small organizations but require additional support to sustain them within the constraints of larger business structures. Indeed, Mumford (2000) contends that the management and development of interactions is just as important as the effective management of creative work groups, and he stresses the importance, for creativity and innovation, of having a culture that values collaboration. There is strong evidence to suggest that social networks and information exchange play a central role in enabling creativity. Networks can be open or closed, but are generally vigorous, adaptive and inclusive and treat knowledge and expertise as a shared asset. They tend to be self-disciplining in terms of both rewards and sanctions and, because membership is voluntary, provide substantial sources of psychological satisfaction (Townley *et al.*, 2009). Research into the impact of network configurations in leveraging creativity points to the importance of weak ties, peripheral network positions that bridge diverse networks and small, tight networks (Burt, 2004; Perry-Smith, 2006; Uzzi and Spiro, 2005, quoted in De Fillippi *et al.*, 2007).

Alongside these network and project based structures, Cohendet and Simon (2007) suggest that management-imposed strict time lines and deadlines ensure that creativity is managed efficiently and effectively and in line with commercial necessity. Their study of VGC, Montreal, examines how this is achieved in practice through a form of hybrid project management whereby classical principles of project management are combined with other practices that foster creativity to establish a 'hard architecture of knowledge' (Cohendet and Simon, 2007: 595). This is underpinned by harnessing the creative potential of the communities of specialists (scriptwriters, game designers, graphic artists, sound designers, software programmers and testers) who, while assigned to a project, still remain connected to their community through work and social networks, both inside and outside the company. In this way 'micro creative ideas' that surface during a project can be retained as a 'creative slack' within the community and used at a later date. They argue that this 'dual identity' not only facilitates interactions between the communities and resolves the tensions between routine and creative work but also reinforces the company culture (Cohendet and Simon, 2007: 598–9).

Management and leadership

Central to any discussion of the work environment is the role of the manager and their style of leadership and management. The size of the organization affects how these roles are structured; however, there are clear responsibilities that approximate to different levels and/or functions. These include project managers, functional and commercial managers and, particular to many small organizations, the entrepreneur or owner-manager.

There is a strongly held view that creative workers' search for autonomy makes them difficult to manage (Bilton, 2007). As with any form of knowledge workers, management methods in the games industry need to be outcome focused and supportive of self-regulation and self-organization (Mumford, 2000; Teipen, 2008). Multifunctional teams working in the industry require strong project leadership with a positive attitude towards and a high tolerance of failure, and a management style which prioritizes innovation and change over stability and routine (Hotho and Champion, 2011). This role could be characterized as that of the architect who manages the boundaries between creative and commercial worlds, and maintains the creative space while also ensuring deadlines and objectives are met. In smaller companies this level of management would also be responsible for the implementation of HR policies and practices.

Managing the high degree of autonomy within creative work and the commercial activities involved in harnessing resources, and managing the product to market have implications for leadership at the organizational level. It is also about managing the inflows and outflows of a core and peripheral workforce. Work practices in the creative industries are shaped by artistic and economic logics, and the games industry is no different. Both logics pull in opposite directions, and careful brokering between the two is required to prevent the former from being at risk as the latter, strengthened and legitimized by the commercial imperative, seeks to dominate. For these reasons, it is suggested that it is inappropriate to adopt standardized management tools and best practice, and that managers should instead rely on more individualized approaches (Eikhof and Haunschild, 2007).

A common approach to managing the tensions between creative and commercial interests is to have dual leadership roles, one taking responsibility for the creative and one for the commercial side of the business (Townley *et al.*, 2009). Tensions built into this approach – the conflicting logics of creative and commercial interest, the conflict between product focus and market focus, to name but a few – may add to the reluctance manifest in many small development studios to grow, or even to the volatility of the industry structure itself. Mumford (2000) suggests that leadership has a marked impact on creative work in the way that it provides support, builds confidence and communicates a vision for the work. For these reasons, he advocates selecting leaders on the basis of managerial skill and not just technical competence and also providing training and development. However, the ability to balance commercial and artistic leadership is a challenge that is often underestimated (Hotho and Champion, 2011).

In nearly four decades, the computer games industry has spawned many small businesses that have withstood the test of time, and many that have not. From an HR perspective it is interesting to explore the key characteristics of these entrepreneurs and to ascertain whether they need additional, different or similar skills from those in other sectors. Entrepreneurial characteristics have been described variously as a high need for achievement, ability to absorb and take risks, high levels of self-efficacy, high levels of commitment and energy amongst others (Chaston, 2008).

The ability to manage innovation and growth has long been identified as a source of concern to governments, and is reflected in economic policies throughout the industrialized world. SMEs predominate in the United Kingdom's economic landscape as elsewhere, and are seen as the drivers of economic growth. The computer games industry is no different. Indeed, it is a hugely polarized industry, with only a small number of large companies and a plethora of small and micro firms. Entrepreneurs' levels of skills and relative reluctance to engage in management development have been identified as a major problem (Homan and Shaw, 2009). Specifically in the games industry, Teipen's (2008) study, which was based on companies in Poland and Sweden, identified the lack of professional knowledge and qualifications as a problem for the effective and growth-oriented management of development studios. Teipen highlights that such companies are likely to be founded by entrepreneurs 'with no formal educational degrees, who have little management knowledge' and 'no consistent business strategy' (2008: 327). An additional factor in the computer games industry is, of course, that where entrepreneurs possess formal qualifications, these will be technology-based qualifications, resulting in a focus on the product rather than the market logic.

Hodgetts and Kuratko (2001, quoted in Chaston, 2008: 824) emphasize that 'the ability to remain entrepreneurial while adopting administrative traits is vital to the venture's successful growth'. Entrepreneurs within the games industry appear to be reluctant to grow for a number of reasons which centre on the tensions between commercialization and artistic integrity. Hotho and Champion (2011) cite fear that growth will lead to compromise of artistic integrity, preference for maintaining a certain lifestyle rather than pursuing commercial aspirations, or concerns about the balance between the creative and commercial imperatives of growth as key factors resulting in a reluctance to grow the business.

Most entrepreneurs in SMEs have to develop meaningful and/or long-term business relationships within the supply chain. For entrepreneurs in the games sector these are complicated by the way in which the industry has traditionally been financed and the power that this deposits in the hands of international publishers who can exert unduly strong influence over the day-to-day operations of small development companies (Teipen, 2008). This is a difficult challenge for entrepreneurs who appear reluctant to cede power and control to others, sometimes even their own managers (Homan and Shaw, 2009), and may be one reason why they concede to the large organizations' strategy of acquisition (Kerr and Flynn, 2003). It would appear that while entrepreneurs within this sector face many of the problems of SMEs generally and require similar skill set, they face *additional* issues because of their creative roots as gamers and the financing and structure of the industry.

Conclusion

This chapter has examined the nature of HR within the computer games industry, focusing in particular on the employment issues of creative people within the sector and the management issues this poses. It has been argued that such creative people are highly individual and that their management is best understood within the context of the games sector itself. The predominance of small firms and the way games firms are geographically clustered and networked both internationally and within countries, are important influences on resourcing and talent management. The volatility and extreme competiveness of the market place, and the extent to which much of the work is project-based, not only demand a particular configuration of core and periphery workers including freelancers, but also raise questions about skills acquisition and development, reward, motivation and retention. At the heart of this are three questions: what constitutes a creative individual within the computer games sector; what skills and knowledge do they have or need to develop their careers, and the product; and what kind of environment ensures high levels of performance both for the individual and for the organization, particularly within an industry characterized by high levels of risk and uncertainty? The discussion has shown that skills still seem to be in short supply, and has highlighted the ongoing mismatch in the talent pipeline between educational provision and the sector. It has also suggested that what are deemed appropriate HR practices, in the context of the sector, may challenge conventional HR wisdom.

The sector is relatively young, but this exploration of HR issues has also highlighted a number of interesting discourses that are beginning to emerge in the literature in relation to HR in the games sector. A recurring theme is that of paradox and tension, and this has implications for people management. This is pre-eminent in the debates around creative and routinized activities, and it is here that the notion of space emerges through concepts such as the distance paradox, the notion of the intersection of commerce and art, and the practice of physical separation of creative activities (and the people who undertake those activities) from those undertaking more routinized work, the separation between WFH and IP, exploitation and exploration. Space is not only used to facilitate creativity. Industry practice also shows how it is used to enhance knowledge exchange through the networked nature of the business. The games industry requires not just communities of specialists working together but also the collaboration of cross-disciplinary specialists. But therein lies another tension, as games communities tend to be geographically concentrated and communities of specialists transcend organizational boundaries as they seek to enhance their intellectual and social capital. Indeed creative careers are often boundaryless, with individuals moving across organizations within the industry rather than within an organization. The question for gatekeepers of talent is how to strike a balance between giving individuals space and freedom and encouraging the enhancement of intellectual and social capital on the one hand, while on the other ensuring that they continue to retain people, particularly the boundaryless worker, at commercially sensitive stages of a project. The key to this may lie in the role of the manager, traditionally an agent of the owner delivering and enforcing the organization's systems, structures and practices in order to achieve the business objectives. Yet with creative workers this role has to encompass some very different facets in order to achieve the organization's goals: the facilitation of effort directed at tasks and projects in order to feed intellectual development from which the organization may not immediately benefit; encouragement of non-conformist ways of working and the ceding of the management prerogative while still holding responsibility for achieving commercial success in a highly competitive environment. This adds yet another layer to the already complex role of the manager in many small organizations with few resources to invest in their development. Another and as yet scarcely acknowledged discourse relates to the extent to which the networked nature of the business leads to and reinforces labour segmentation to the detriment of women and ethnic minorities and in doing so deprives the industry of their talent, and potentially of new markets.

Time is another theme which emerges within the context of managing people within the sector. This is not just about time flexibility within the nature of work contracts which is inherent in the very nature of games development with its contract slacks, peaks and troughs and strong project focus. It is also about the way in which time is perceived within the role of the creative individual and how the tension between 'freedom' and work intensification is justified and managed in terms of work life balance and the wider supporting workforce.

This assertion that creative staff are somehow different from other staff and need to be treated and managed differently is perhaps the most dominant discourse in the study of people management within the sector and with it the coining of new terms such as 'creative slacks' and 'deep smarts'. What is interesting is the way this group tend to get treated in the literature as a single entity whereas the reality is quite different. Video games projects depend on the in-depth collaboration and interface of a wide range of specialists representing a multiplicity of different types of creativity that have their origins in various disciplines from art to engineering. If they wish to maximize organizational performance then the onus on HR practitioners and people managers is to recognize this and reflect it in HR practices. The idea that conventional HR wisdom is somehow inappropriate in the games sector has been a pervasive thread throughout this chapter. However, it may be that as the demand for knowledge workers and creative and innovative employees increases, conventional HR practice can learn lessons equally from emerging practice in the games sector in the design of HR systems that reflect staff needs and not simply those of the organization. This may be a further challenge to the 'one size fits all' debate and may address some of the issues of small businesses who balk at the examples of best practice from large organizations that they are constantly urged to adopt. After all if these approaches can work in both small development companies and the UBisofts and VGCs of this world they may have something to offer HR in other industries.

References

Amabile, T.M. (1997) Entrepreneurial creativity through motivational synergy, *Journal of Creative Behavior*, 31: 18–26.

Bilton, C. (2007) *Management and Creativity: From Creative Industries to Creative Management*, Oxford: Blackwell.

Bilton, C. and Leary, R. (2002) What can managers do for creativity? Brokering creativity in the creative industries, *International Journal of Cultural Policy*, 8(1): 49–64.

Burt, R.S. (2004) Structural holes and good ideas, *American Journal of Sociology*, 110: 349–99.

Cadin, L. and Guérin, F. (2006) What can we learn from the video games industry? *European Management Journal*, 24(4): 248–55.

Cadin, L., Guérin, F. and DeFillippi, R. (2006) HRM practices in the video game industry: industry or country contingent? *European Management Journal*, 24(4): 288–98.

Chaston, I. (2008) Small creative industry firms: a development dilemma, *Management Decision*, 46 (6): 819–31.

Christopherson, S. (2008) Beyond the self-expressive creative worker: an industry perspective on entertainment media, *Theory, Culture and Society*, 25: 73–95.

Cohendet, P. and Simon, L. (2007) Playing across the playground: paradoxes of knowledge creation in the videogame firm, *Journal of Organizational Behavior*, 28: 587–605.

DeFillippi, R., Grabher, G. and Jones, C. (2004) Call for papers: paradoxes of creativity: managerial and organizational challenges of the cultural economy, *Special Issue of Journal of Organizational Behavior*, http://www.job-journal.org/authors/calls/creativity.htm.

DeFillippi, R., Grabher, G. and Jones, C. (2007) Introduction to paradoxes of creativity: managerial and organizational challenges in the cultural economy, *Journal of Organizational Behavior*, 28: 511–21.

Eikhof, D.R. and Haunschild, A. (2007) For art's sake! Artistic and economic logics in creative production, *Journal of Organizational Behavior*, 28: 523–38.

Hackman, R.J. and Oldham, G.R. (1980) *Work Redesign*, Reading, MA: Addison-Wesley.

Hodgetts, R.M. and Kuratko, D.F. (2001) *Effective Small Business Management*, Orlando, FL: Harcourt College Publishers.

Homan, G. and Shaw, S. (2009) Using HR to leverage growth in SMEs in the new media sector, Paper presented at the conference on 'Managing for Success in the New Creative Industries: Knowledge into Practice Initiative Conference', University of Abertay Dundee, in association with CIPD, October 2009.

Hotho, S. and Champion, K. (2011) Small businesses in the new creative industries: innovation as a people management challenge, *Management Decision*, 49(1): 29–54.

Jones, C. (2010) Finding a place in history: symbolic and social networks in creative careers and collective memory, *Journal of Organizational Behavior*, 31: 726–48.

Jones, P., Comfort, D., Eastwood, I. and Hillier, D. (2004) Creative industries: economic contributions, management challenges and support initiatives, *Management Research News*, 27(11/12): 134–45.

Kerr, A. and Flynn, R. (2003) Revisiting globalization through the movie and digital games industries, *Convergence*, 9(1): 91–113.

Leonard, D. and Swap, W. (2004) Deep smarts, *Harvard Business Review*, 82(9): 88–97.

Livingstone, I. and Hope, A. (2011) Next Gen. Transforming the UK into the World's Leading Talent Hub for the Video Games and Visual Effects Industry, NESTA: http://www.nesta.org.uk/areas_of_work/creative_economy/skills_review/assets/features/next_gen.

Mehr, D.G. and Schaver, P.R. (1996) Goal structures in creating motivation, *Journal of Creative Behavior*, 30: 77–104.

Mumford, M. (2000) Managing creative people: strategies and tactics for innovation, *Human Resource Management Review*, 10(3): 313–51.

Perry-Smith, J.E. (2006) Social yet creative: the role of social relationships in facilitating individual creativity, *Academy of Management Journal*, 49: 85–101.

Scott, R.K. (1995) Creative employees: a challenge to managers, *Journal of Creative Behavior*, 29: 64–71.

Selby, E.C., Shaw, E.J. and Houtz, J.C. (2005) The creative personality, *Gifted Child Quarterly*, 49: 300–14.

Skillset (2011) *Computer Games Sector: Labour Market Intelligence Digest*, http://www.creativeskillset.org/games/industry/article_6918_1.asp.

Smith, S. and Pacquette, S. (2010) Creativity, chaos and knowledge management, *Business Information Review*, 27(2): 118–23.

Teipen, C. (2008) Work and employment in creative industries: the video games industry in Germany, Sweden and Poland, *Economic and Industrial Democracy*, 29(3): 309–35.

Thompson, P., Jones, M. and Warhurst, C. (2007) From conception to consumption: creativity and the missing managerial link, *Journal of Organizational Behavior*, 28: 625–40.

Townley, B., Beech, N. and McKinlay, A. (2009) Managing in the creative industries: managing the motley crew, *Human Relations*, 62: 939–62.

Uzzi, B. and Spiro, J. (2005) Collaboration and creativity: the small world problem, *American Journal of Sociology*, 111: 447–504.

Zhou, J. (1998) Feedback valence, feedback style, task autonomy, and achievement orientation: interactive effects on creative performance, *Journal of Applied Psychology*, 83: 261–76.

8
How Funny Are Games?
Violent Games Content and
Studio Well-Being

Patrick Stacey, David Thomas and Joe Nandhakumar

Introduction

This chapter focuses on the twin responsibilities of game studios for the social groups they create content for and employ. Through two nascent and ongoing studies we investigate the contextual forces of violent game development and gamework well-being. Our analysis of both studies draws on the theory of interpretive schemes (for instance, Bartunek, 1984; Ranson *et al.*, 1980) as an analytical lens (Walsham, 2003), which theorizes about the systems of meaning that people draw on in order to make collective sense of phenomena and conduct. This chapter is organized as follows: first, key motivations, prior literature, a theoretical framework, the research approach and methods used are introduced. We then present two empirical studies regarding violent game development and gamework well-being; each contains a case study, analysis and conceptualization. These sections are followed by a synthesized discussion and conclusion.

Motivations

Death Race, released in 1976 featuring black and white graphics, is known as one of the first violent computer games. In it 'blocky' avatars turn into gravestone crosses when they collide with racing cars. The more familiar game *Tomb Raider* features much more graphic violence at the hands of game character Lara Croft. Yet violence is not an impediment to featuring in a governmental agenda; the British government once hailed *Tomb Raider* as exemplary of the role of innovative design in the United Kingdom's knowledge-driven economy (Sainsbury, 1998). It is a paradox that a seemingly laudable enterprise could be equally lambastable. This has often swept through the media, sticking to the games industry like a terrier that will not let go of a trouser leg. In 2007 *Manhunt 2, Law and Order: Double or Nothing* and *Resistance: Fall of Man* were all accused of wanton violence. *Resistance: Fall of Man* was heavily criticized by the Bishop of Manchester for depicting a desecration of Manchester Cathedral. The United Kingdom's British Board of Film Classification (BBFC) banned *Manhunt 2* on account of its brutality. This decision coincided with a call by the United Kingdom's former Leader of the House of Commons, Jack Straw, for game publishers to be more responsible for their content. Such appeals find support in academia, including studies of the effects of violent games on children (Subrahmanyam *et al.*, 2000). Indeed, the media, religious, governmental and academic institutions have participated in creating the video game nasty, conjuring up images of game developers as insensitive and even sociopathic. But what is it like in a game studio that produces violent games? Our research question here is: what processes are involved that lead to the creation of violent games? While academic journals are awash with articles regarding the effects of violent games, they are arid with regard to their development processes. A specific motivation for this aspect of the current chapter then is the paucity of knowledge regarding the conception and development of violent games. Perhaps by understanding these processes we can suggest strategies for limiting violent content.

A key concern in this chapter is the nature of game studio responsibilities for the social groups they employ, namely the artists, engineers, designers, musicians and so forth. There have been reports in the media of poor worksite well-being in these organizations, notably with reference to the EA spouse incident of 11 October 2004 (see Krotoski, 2009), in which the disgruntled spouse of a game developer working for Electronic Arts (EA) highlighted malpractices there. A follow-up piece in 2009, published by *The Guardian* (Krotoski, 2009), suggests that this issue has all but been swept under the carpet. Recently Codemasters, ranked 69th on the *Develop 100* list (*Develop*, 2011), was embarrassed when one of its developers exposed the poor working conditions there during the development of the 2011 title *Bodycount*. Semi Essessi claimed that he had not been compensated for over 400 hours of overtime leading up to the game's launch (Oshry, 2012). Similar concerns have been leveled at Apple Inc. While Apple products evoke gushes of delight in the users of its iPhones and iPads, the company has generated shock and shame over its manufacturing practices. According to media reports, a number of employees at Foxconn, Apple's manufacturer, have committed suicide, apparently as a result of intense pressure to supply the market with sufficient devices to meet demand. Putatively well-loved and admired products, just like the *Tomb Raider* game, thus at times cast a dark consequential shadow. Again, computer games are in the dock.

This situation is alarming given that creative industry sectors such as computer games are a major source of the United Kingdom's competitive advantage and economic growth (Oakley *et al.*, 2008). This is highlighted by industry forecasts produced by PricewaterhouseCoopers (PwC) and reported in the *Financial Times* (Palmer, 2012), suggesting that the global market for video games was set to grow from $52.5 billion in 2009 to $86.8 billion in 2014. Even more alarming is the initial finding from a study undertaken by TIGA (2012) describing a significant brain drain from the United Kingdom and claiming that the industry's workforce shrank by 10 per cent between 2008 and 2011. Furthermore, it is widely held that there is a direct relationship between emotional well-being and creativity (Amabile *et al.*, 2005). This means that until we address and understand well-being in this particular setting the dire consequences for creativity and output at the more macro-levels will remain (Oswald *et al.*, 2003). Currently, there is little scholarly knowledge of the forces of worksite well-being amongst game developers and, therefore, little understanding of how to transform them. Framed as a research question: what are the forces and dynamics of worksite well-being in game development studios? This is a second major motivation for the subject matter of this chapter.

Perhaps violence and well-being seem odd bed-fellows in a chapter that has a deliberately ironic title. As we have alluded to above, however, they can both sleep in the bed of studio responsibility quite comfortably. But in some ways they are concepts of the same nature; both are emotional (Gray, 1970; Stacey *et al.*, 2011). Later in this chapter we expand on this theoretical convergence, demonstrating the salience of an interpretive perspective in furthering our understanding of these related phenomena. First, we will review the prior research that has been undertaken in this area.

Prior research

Violent game play

One stream of computer game research is indeed interested in user/player behaviour issues, such as social acceptance (Hsu and Lu, 2004), virtual social conflict (Lastowka and Hunter, 2004), real-life mimicry (Nutt and Railton, 2003), obsession (Rehak, 2003), and, fittingly, aggression (Williams and Clippinger, 2002). This stream of research investigates the violent and aggressive games notably with regard to their effect on child behavior and development. Subrahmanyam *et al.* (2000: 123) found that 'playing violent computer games may increase aggressiveness and desensitize a child to suffering, and that the use of computers may blur a child's ability to distinguish real life from simulation'.

Building on the desensitizing effects, Gentile and Anderson (2003) found that violent games propagated anti-social behaviour, and that this was particularly associated with the realism that video games have today: 'There are many theoretical reasons why one would expect violent video games to have a greater effect than violent television, and most of the reasons why one would expect them to have a lesser effect are no longer true because violent video games have become so realistic, particularly since the late 1990s' (Gentile and Anderson, 2003: 151). The same authors also point to increases in aggressive thoughts and feelings, as well as physiological arousal. Reasons for violent game 'potency', according to the same authors, include identification, participation, practice, continuity or flow, repetition and reward. We present these in detail in Table 8.1.

However, Farrer *et al.* (2006) suggest that players of violent games are more engrossed when they play from a third-person rather than a first-person perspective. So, play perspective may not be as strong a factor as suggested by Gentile and Anderson (2003). Rather the degree of blood seems to be a factor, as is considered by Farrer *et al.*'s (2006) experiment, which revealed that the participants perceived greater gore when there was greater blood violence.

Put differently, the more blood that was shed through the actions of the player, the more violent the game was perceived to be. Indeed, there are several studies that produce similar findings, with agreement and disagreement to different degrees (for instance, Anderson and Bushman,

Table 8.1 Potent forces in violent games

1	Identification with an aggressor increases imitation of the aggressor
2	Active participation increases learning
3	Practicing an entire behavioural sequence is more effective than practicing only a part
4	Violence is continuous
5	Repetition increases learning
6	Rewards increase imitation

Source: Gentile and Anderson, 2003.

2001; Anderson, 2004; Olson, 2010). The primary concern, however, is very much focused on child learning and development. In response to such anxieties, law-makers in California have attempted to ban the sale of violent video games to children. In the United Kingdom, the 2008 Byron Review of computer games (Byron, 2008) was a similar response to the 'summer of gore' in 2007. It resulted in suggestions for adapting the rating of games, but produced little in the way of cross-boundary understanding between players, parents and developers. Primarily, we still have an insufficient understanding of the process by which violent games are developed, whether responsibly or not. However, research into well-being in the games industry, and the implications for employer responsibility, may further our understanding of this process.

Studies of well-being

According to Tschang (2005: 993), 'starting in the 1990s and going into the 2000s, several factors dictated a more professional and corporate image of games: large publishers emerged, IP became increasingly important, and project and team sizes increased.' Aligned with this industrialization process is the accelerating intensity of game development work. Exemplary of the consequences is the EA Spouse incident, discussed previously in this chapter. Consequently, the International Game Developers Association (IGDA) conducted global quality of life (QoL) surveys in 2004 and 2009. The IGDA (2004) study found much evidence for poor QoL triggered by impossible deadlines, peer pressure and lack of concern and support for the family unit, leading to early departures to rival industries. Notably the lack of meaning attached to the family unit and pressure from peers and management indicate the presence of structures of meaning that were toxic to many developers. Reinforcing the view that some studios may lack concern for their employees and the content of their games, our survey of the top UK and Irish game developers' websites found only one that mentioned any form of corporate social responsibility policy (see Table 8.2).

In April 2009 *Develop Magazine* conducted a survey, the results of which supported the 'impossible deadlines' finding of the IGDA (2004) study (*Develop Magazine*, 2009). Furthermore, managers' 'sociopathy' was highlighted, that is to say they exhibited anti-social behaviour and little or no regard for the feelings or well-being of their employees. This industry magazine also ran a survey of salaries in the games industry in 2010, revealing satisfaction with salary levels across a range of disciplines. This is perhaps surprising in light of their 2009 survey, but commensurate with the general observation that, while wealth in

Table 8.2 Top 12 UK game studios (develop100.com) and CSR mention

Studio	Rank	Location	Platforms	CSR mention
Rockstar Leeds	9	Leeds	Mobile	No
Rockstar North	28	Dundee	Multiplatform	No
Freestyle Games	32	L Spa	Multiplatform	No
YoYo Games	40	Dundee	iOS	No
Curve Studios	41	London	PSN/PSP/WiiWare	Yes
Johnny Two Shoes	44	London	iOS	No
Hello Games	46	Guildford	PSN	No
Revolution	48	York	iOS/Wii/DS	No
Strand Looper	54	Virtual	iOS	No
Fallen Tree Games	60	Nottingham	iOS	No
Codemasters	69	Leamington Spa	Multiplatform	No
Big Pixel Studios	73	London	iOS	No

the UK has increased since World War II, well-being has remained flat (Blanchflower and Oswald, 2004). So a logical question here is whether the 'pain' associated with the detrimental employment practices, is worth it? It would seem on the surface that the 'pain' is adequately compensated for. But what of the United Kingdom's focus on innovation? A direct relationship between well-being and creativity has long been accepted (Amabile *et al.*, 2005); being well is important to the creative aspect of the innovation process. Despite evidence of some salary satisfaction this is inadequate when framed within an innovation imperative. An understanding of the dynamics of well-being is needed in the games industry.

There have been relatively few studies of well-being in game studios. Stacey has previously conducted a study of game studios concerned with their quality of life and other facets (Stacey, 2009). This work generated 1664 pages of interviews with developers. The findings of that study indicated that interdisciplinary tension, design ambiguity and staff turnover were triggers of negative impacts on well-being. This led to reduced team cohesion, and a variety of negative emotions such as irritation, frustration, desperation, loss of enjoyment, stress and dismay, as well as loss of a sense of community generally. In this scenario it was less the case that the meaning structures were 'toxic', but more so that they were too immature, such that shared understanding was hard fought. This was primarily because the company was a start-up only a few years old.

Piecing these various studies together, as summarized in Table 8.3, presents us with an image of an industry that has serious issues with its development and management practices. Meanwhile well-being

Table 8.3   Summary of game studio QOL findings from a variety of studies

Study	Key triggers of poor QoL
IGDA (2004)	Impossible deadlines
	Peer pressures
	Lack of concern and support for the family unit
Develop Magazine (2009)	Impossible deadlines
	Management sociopathy
Stacey (2010)	Interdisciplinary tension
	Design ambiguity
	Staff turnover

research in other settings has been voluminous, notably relating to developing countries (Ehigie *et al.*, 2006), caring for the elderly (Selai and Trimble, 1999; Tester *et al.*, 2004), health such as cancer, heart-related conditions, habitat, or childbearing (Aassve *et al.*, 2006) and schools (Ollerenshaw and McDonald, 2006). What comes out of much of this research is a focus on subjective well-being (SWB), to which we turn in the following section where we present our theoretical framework.

Theoretical framework

In much of the well-being research discussed above, scholars agree that there are three dimensions to SWB: physical (fitness, environment, artefacts), psychological (cognitive functioning and mood), and social (for instance sense of community). There are many studies that particularly attest to the primacy of social relations as a dimension of subjective well-being (Selai and Trimble, 1999; Myers, 1999; Diener and Seligman, 2002). But these dimensions are interacting, particularly the psychological and social dimensions (Ryan and Deci, 2001). This interactive relationship is important to the creative aspects of innovation. Taylor and Brown (1988) suggest that the capacity for creative, productive work is fostered both by enhanced intellectual functioning, which may be an outgrowth of positive illusions, and by the increased motivation, activity level, and persistence that are clearly fostered by a positive sense of self, a sense of control, and optimism (see Taylor and Brown, 1988: 198–9).

The sense one gets from this view is that the agent has the capacity to interpret events in a positive manner and thereby to contribute to feeling positive. This is echoed in appraisal theories of SWB: 'our emotional reactions depend not on the specific characteristics of stimulus events, but rather on the way that we interpret and evaluate what is happening to us (appraisal)' (Parkinson and Fischer, 2005: 6). The appraisal

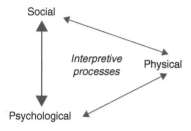

Figure 8.1   Interpretive model of SWB

or interpretive process is, therefore, a central concept in models of SWB (Lazarus, 1968, 1991; Scherer, 2005). We depict this dynamic in Figure 8.1. In order to research and understand well-being, we need to focus further on the social dynamics of interpretation. To aid us in this respect, we draw on the theory of interpretive schemes (Ranson *et al.*, 1980; Bartunek, 1984; Giddens, 1984), which we delineate in the following section.

Interpretive schemes

Interpretive schemes are domain assumptions (Gouldner, 1971) that form part of the background condition of human interactions (Ranson *et al.*, 1980). They help guide and collectivize people's understandings and action (Bartunek, 1984; Ranson *et al.*, 1980). For instance, the cover design of the violent *Manhunt 2* game is an interpretive scheme since its horror helps guide people in deciding whether they want to purchase it. Indeed, the Pan European Game Information (PEGI) rating scheme is an interpretive scheme for game content, which includes the age ratings 3, 7, 12, 16 and 18. The 18-rated games are accompanied by black and white symbols that help further interpret the content, and include violence, bad language, fear and drugs. This connects to the appraisal view of SWB since people draw on such interpretive schemes to help them make sense of and *feel* their circumstances (Shweder and Haidt, 2000). For example, a PEGI rating on a computer game product informs players of the expected (emotional) content of the game which they draw on in order to produce their own interpretations and make their own decisions about how to act. Interpretive schemes encompass possible or available meanings, which individuals draw on as they socially construct their SWB. In order to complete the meaning of Figure 8.1 above, intepretive processes involve an interaction between interpretive schemes (structural level) and the act of interpretation (agent level). This articulation of our interpretive schemes is also important for our study of violent game development, since violence is also an emotional concept (Gray, 1970). We therefore draw on interpretive schemes as a central analytical device that links the empirical studies presented here. In the next section we describe our research approach to these studies.

Research approach and methods

This chapter reports on the interim results of two ongoing UK-based empirical studies into the meaning structures that shape and are shaped by processes of 'crunch' and violent content development. Firstly, in 2007 we conducted an on-site field study of game studio Goo (a pseudonym) that develops violent games for mobile devices. We conducted 20 formal interviews with designers, producers, artists, programmers and project managers. Goo is one of the world's largest developers of mobile games. To honour confidentiality agreements we use pseudonyms to protect the name of the company, their employees and products. Secondly, we surveyed a sample of game developers, during 2011 and 2012, from the Dundee and Coventry game hubs enquiring about several aspects of their work and well-being. We asked questions pertaining to respondent attitudes regarding statements relating to social, psychological and physical dimensions of subjective well-being (see Figure 8.1). For example, survey statements included: 'I am given a lot of freedom to decide how to do my own work'; 'I have a lot to say about what happens in my job'; and 'My workspace is configurable'. Altogether we asked questions relating to 52 statements. We emailed and called the participating companies to explain our research, after which they were given a link to our online questionnaire; we used *Limesurvey*. At the time of writing we had 34 responses from the participants. We emphasize that this survey is ongoing and nascent.

We used a combination of distanced and engaged means of collecting data. The survey was deployed as a first-contact method, which we intend to follow up with interviews to help understand further the results we discerned. We did not generate any hypotheses, since the survey was used in an investigative manner, to stimulate a more in-depth case study. A limitation is that we imposed an interpretive scheme, expressed in the survey items, on the respondents, which limits the richness of their responses. However, respondents were at liberty to decide what to answer and how to weight their responses on a Likert scale. The meanings may be considered as being implicit in the numerical data collected, since the way the published data was classified and presented relied upon researchers and participants making a decision about their significance (Nandhakumar and Jones, 1997). We, too, were at liberty to interpret the data in a manner consistent with our theoretical perspective, namely that of interpretive schemes. Given our focus on meanings, as well as an interest in producing an orderly set of understandings pertaining to the inchoate phenomena of violent game content and gamework well-being, we adopted an interpretive stance (Orlikowski and Baroudi, 1991; Walsham, 1993).

In order to analyze the qualitative data elicited in the violent game study, we employed Miles and Huberman's three-tier coding approach (Miles and Huberman, 1994). In the first tier, we performed descriptive coding in order to identify references to violence and related phenomena by the interviewees. Secondly, we performed interpretive coding which involved drawing on previous literature and concepts suggested by the themes identified during the first-tier descriptive coding (Strauss and Corbin, 1998). As the dynamics of interpretation were particularly strong, we adopted an interpretive schemes lens on the basis of which we then developed a simple notation to tag words, phrases and lines in the transcripts. In this way we teased out stimuli, interpretations and the interpretive schemes that helped shape them. Thirdly, we performed pattern analysis in which we drew together the findings from the interpretive coding across the transcripts and observations to create a rich picture of violent game development.

While the field study analysis was largely inductive, the survey analysis had an element of a priori theory; we grouped the questions according to the social, psychological and physical dimensions of subjective well-being (Figure 8.1). However, we did not set out with the goal of simply confirming the dimensions of that model. We were more interested in the dynamics at play not yet explored in that model, namely the interpretative dynamics. To this end we also applied the theoretical lens of interpretive schemes to the significant statistical results. This abstraction process produced interesting, though tentative, insights. Further, according to Walsham (1993), where micro-level studies have been conducted, analyzing data by drawing on macro-theory is a way of transcending the particular case settings.

With regard to the statistical analysis for the well-being study we used SPSS Version 19. According to Cornford and Smithson (2006) and Siegel (1956), the most important factor in selecting a statistical test is the type of measurement scale used. In our case we have a mixture of nominal and ordinal measures. The majority of our data is ordinal but some of the data, particularly demographic data such as age, is nominal. Cornford and Smithson (2006) recommend that in the case of mixed data a conservative approach should be taken. Siegel (1956) suggests that the most appropriate non-parametric statistical test for nominal data is the chi-squared test. We have described above how we operationalized our two research questions: (a) what processes are involved that lead to the creation of violent games? and (b) what are the (interpretative) forces and dynamics of worksite well-being in game development studios? We now present the results of our two empirical studies, along with their respective analysis and conceptualizations.

Case study 1: the development of a violent game

Case description

The study investigated how developers at Goo conceived and developed violent content in a recent game project. Their project was a historical warfare game called *Age of Empires for Mobile*. The empirical results are presented to illustrate how, according to the interviewees, the violent game mechanics were conceived and designed, and the contextual aspects that shaped this process. Violent game mechanics tended to be designed and developed through reference to the reproduction of schemes of meaning and legitimation, as well as artefacts. The violence design practices are presented in the following sections: schemes of meaning, schemes of legitimation and artefacts of violence.

Short story of development: *Age of Empires*

Age of Empires for Mobile was a licensed real-time-strategy game with a somewhat pre-ordained specification; the original PC game had been certificated '12', denoting that it contained minor violence. The first month of the game's development involved mostly design and proto-typing, and while there was an initial specification, Goo still had their own ideas. Initial talks with the licensor drew scepticism, since they wanted to create a prequel to the original PC game. In the PC game there were six factions of armies, but Goo thought this too cumbersome for mobile. They wanted to do a 'good job', to 'build some character' into the game, so decided to have only two armies in the campaign. They pitched that it should be the Knights Order from Britain versus the Ottomans in the battle for Malta, which drew on actual histori-cal events. In order to convince the licensor, a game design document was drafted, which proved effective. However, Goo were told to tone down the violence: 'there was talk whether there would be an extreme version, or not, that was depicting violence, but they didn't go for it, they said, if we have to have violence then make it as cartoony as possible' (Project Manager). In the second month, during the pre-alpha phase, coding began in earnest along with the development of certain tools. The third month saw the game move towards alpha stage; this featured low techno graphics. As the game edged towards beta, the full quality graphics replaced the low techno ones, making the game feel more saturated, less real and more 'cartoony'; the game had realistic elements but because the colors were bright it tended to tone down the graphic violence. In the fourth and final month, the game moved from beta to the final version, involving 'bug fixing', ensuring the levels were play-balanced and that the game's denouement felt 'nice' and satisfying. This featured an all-out climactic battle for the capital of Malta. We now turn our attention to the accounts given by the developers regarding such violent aspects of the game.

Violent content: *Age of Empires*

Specific user controlled acts and artefacts of violence were designed into the game, which were inspired by the historical events pertaining to the warfare endured during the Siege of Malta. Indeed, the developers were all keen to emphasize their rootedness in this historical battle, suggesting that they were simply trying to be faithful to history, and that none of the violence they programmed was wanton. For instance, one producer (Producer 2) said: 'it's a historic game so I think to some extent violence is more accepted in something historical just on the basis that, you know, history is violent' and continued: 'it's historical and it happened and you can't change the fact that it happened and start pretending that people are running round with bananas, they were ... running round with swords and cutting arms off with them and things, so you can't pretend that didn't happen.' He even pointed to a specific interpretation of the Siege of Malta, suggesting a genuine interest in it: 'the historians all kind of agree that the grandmaster of the Knights of St John went running out into the breach of the actual walls and was like firing away at them so the guys, he was fending off like about five guys at a time.' The latter served as inspiration for the game's climactic battle. Another producer (Producer 1) also referred to the rational and sane character of the game: 'so you can plan your attacks. I think any game where you can think about how I'm going to brutalize the enemy is instantly less violent. It's a campaign. I guess the best victory is the quickest one.' One of the designers (Designer 1) even recontextualized the game as a game of chess, an attempt to gloss over the violence: 'I mean, it's one of those where, conceptually, it's actually quite a violent game but in reality once you have sanitized it a bit and desensitized the player from the violent aspect, it's like, you know, it's like chess, in a way. You could argue that chess is technically a violent idea but it's sanitized in such a way as to be a mere game.'

There were other contextual facets at play beyond the game's historical connection, the developers' faithfulness to that connection and the emphasis on the strategic goals rather than the violent ones. Producer 1 said: 'And, when you set up a business you see things from a very, very different perspective and that's the politics and the money of it. And, it's funny, I don't think it's as people expect. It is in terms of, you know, the decisions we make when we design games, whether they are violent or something, the one thing we want to do, we want to pay everybody's wages, we want the company to flourish. We have a business and we have chosen to make a career out of it. I mean, I've been doing this for 17, 18 years.'

With regard to user-controlled violence, the developers claimed to have kept this very simple: 'Basically, as you are guiding your men into battle they will fight with each other. So, your command, your sort of input into the violence is limited to "go and attack that bloke over there". So, there is no sort of direct kind of violence element. I mean, but there ... it would be moderately graphic when you kill some-one' (Producer 2). However, this indirect control of violent acts was allowed to lapse in the final battle for Malta, almost like a release for the violence to finally express itself: 'I mean, this is a sort of concession to standard, direct control violent games insofar as you are this guy and I liked the idea of giving you control over this incredibly powerful grandmaster guy, lots of cannon fodder around you, and you just, if you click to attack he just goes one whack of his sword and they're dead. So, you are like... (*laughs*) you get that kind of heroic empowered feeling. You know, you are all powerful and you can just destroy them as if they are insects. So, yes, that was kind of like the climax for me' (Producer 2).

Analysis

The case description of *Age of Empires for Mobile* highlights potent shaping forces of violent game content at Goo. These arose out of individuals' interactions with established meaning structures, or interpretive schemes. These contributed to the shape and legitimation of the developers' understandings and reproduction of certain violent themes and actions.

We discovered five interpretive schemes: accepted historical accounts, rational warfare, business imperative, in-game commands, and popular violent games. We summarize these in Table 8.4. What struck us was the rational way in which violence was regarded and violent content developed, in a manner that was pure reproduction of acts of warfare in the context of a specific historical event, the Siege of Malta. The various interpretive schemes served to generate a legitimate structure around the project. Historical accounts of the siege, for example, were taken as self-justifying or taken for granted – there was no reflection on or probing of such established accounts and the shared sense of meaning they

Table 8.4 Interpretive schemes in use during violent game development

Interpretive scheme	Examples
Accepted historical accounts	*(i) General course of events, meanings regarding the Siege of Malta:* 'It's historical and it's... and it happened and you can't change the fact that it happened and start pretending that people are running round with bananas.' *(ii) Climactic battle for Malta:* 'Historians all kind of agree that the grandmaster of the Knights of St John went running out into the breach of the actual walls and was like firing away at them so the guys, he was fending off like about five guys at a time.'
Rational warfare	*(i) Adversarial attitude:* '... so you can plan your attacks. I think any game where you can think about how I'm going to brutalize the enemy is instantly less violent. It's a campaign.' *(ii) Warfare as strategy:* 'In reality once you have sanitized it a bit and desensitized the player from the violent aspect, it's like, you know, it's like chess, in a way.'
Business imperative	'When you set up a business you see things from a very, very different perspective and that's the politics and the money of it. And, it's funny, I don't think it's as people expect. It is in terms of, you know, the decisions we make when we design games, whether they are violent or something.'
In-game commands	'Basically as you are guiding your men into battle they will fight with each other. So, your command, your sort of input into the violence is limited to "go and attack that bloke over there".'
Popular violent games	'This is a sort of concession to standard, direct control violent games insofar as you are this guy and I liked the idea of giving you control over this incredibly powerful grandmaster guy, lots of cannon fodder around you.'

conveyed. This is indicative of Goo's processes of reasoning or vindication when it comes to choice and development of content genres. By establishing a seemingly cast iron context or back-story to the violence, this interaction between the context and the content generated an air of irrefutable acceptability. The reproduction of established meanings could be regarded as an innocent act, and therefore one that can be forgiven, as it resides largely in our practical consciousness (Giddens, 1984). The spark for the production of those meaning structures in this case was perhaps the Siege of Malta, or an event even further back. Those events are still exerting control over the actions and interpretations of people today, as illustrated in the case of the game developers. According to Giddens, control is 'the capability that some actors, groups or types of actors have of influencing the circumstances of action of others' (Giddens 1984: 283).

Conceptualization

Our conceptualization of violent content development in games is presented in Figure 8.2 based on the case analysis. It depicts the potent shaping effect of epic or emotive meaning structures, such as those connected to war, that often stir up passions. At the same time, developers choose to reproduce these structures and thereby establish legitimacy. There is a fine line between the shaping effects of the formative context, and their reproduction on the part of the actors or developers.

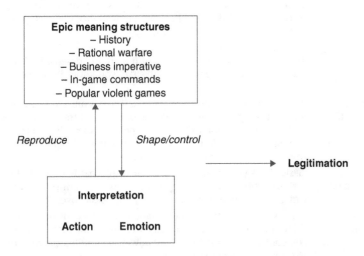

Figure 8.2 Conceptualization of epic meaning structures in violent games

Case study 2: gamework well-being

Survey description

Our survey collected 34 responses from game developers. An online survey was designed, the questions being based on a combination of IGDA's survey and the previous research findings from Stacey (2009). This survey follows the IGDA (2004) White Paper with respect to establishing a demographic baseline regarding age, gender and marital status. As illustrated in Table 8.5, despite a comparatively small sample size, the demographic profile of our study was very close to that presented by IGDA (2004).

In addition, the survey also included workload-related questions asking participants to comment on their average working week and on conditions during crunch, including their company's stance on crunch working arrangements. In order to evaluate subjective well-being, we posed 30 questions in total (of which 29 were multiple choice questions and one contained 28 Likert statements) to evaluate social, psychological and physical factors that could affect SWB. The weighting between these factors, across the items, was 3:2:1 for social, psychological and physical factors respectively.

Analysis

We organized the significant correlations in terms of the three dimensions of the SWB model (Figure 8.1), and a summary is contained in Table 8.6. The dependent variable was overall satisfaction, or happiness at work. A combination of psychological and social variables had a significance of 5 per cent. The questions relating to psychological aspects were: 'I have a say in helping set the way things are done on my job', 'I am proud to be working for my employer', and 'On my job, I know exactly what is expected of me'. There was only one social factor that occurred at this level of significance (10%): 'I trust the management at the place where I work'.

Table 8.5 Demographical comparison

	IGDA	This study
Gender	Male: 92.9% Female: 7.1%	Male: 84% Female: 16%
Age	33.8% between 25 and 29	38.7% between 25 and 29
Career	74.4% 8 years or less	70.4% 8 years or less
	2–5 years most common	2–5 years most common

Table 8.6   Psycho-social and physical well-being factors of significance

Factor	Label	Significance
I trust the management at the place where I work	*Social9*	5%
I have a say in helping set the way things are done on my job	*Psych17*	5%
I am proud to be working for my employer	*Psych12*	5%
On my job, I know exactly what is expected of me	*Psych6*	5%
The 'rules' in my office are relaxed	*Social31*	10%
I have enough information to get the job done	*Social21*	10%
When information is passed to me, I feel that it is properly formatted, i.e. in a form that I can understand	*Social22*	10%
In my job, I normally work as part of a team	*Social16*	10%
My workspace is configurable	*Physical30*	10%

Applying the theoretical lens

We now draw on our theoretical lens (Figure 8.1), in which interpretive schemes or meaning-laden guides for action (Bartunek, 1984) are a central concept, to interpret these preliminary statistical results. Firstly, we interpret the *Psych6* factor (Table 8.6) as indicative that effective collective sense-making is a feature in respondents' organizations and that this is an important aspect of their sense of well-being. Sense-making concerns how individuals and groups deal with ambiguity (Weick *et al.*, 2005) during processes of authoring and interpreting meaning. This entails drawing on interpretive schemes to help guide and coordinate collective understanding and action (Ranson *et al.*, 1980; Bartunek, 1984). Shared understanding, collective sense-making, or knowing exactly what is expected, infers the presence of meaning structures that have sedimented in the organization and have become part of the background condition for action (Ciborra and Lanzara, 1987). A contributing factor here is *Social16* (working as part of a team). This seems to be leading to a positive appraisal of organizational circumstances and contributing significantly to well-being.

This result is reinforced when considering associated factors *Social21* and *Social22* (see Table 8.6) which relate to information availability and formatting. The link between shared understanding and information processing has been made by a number of authors (Dearborn and Simon,

1958; Hedberg, 1981; Brown *et al.*, 2008). The results suggest that as information is made available and formatted in the social context, and then passed to the game developer, this contributes to (i) their ability to overcome ambiguity (Weick *et al.*, 2005), (ii) their understanding of what is expected of them and (iii) their sense of well-being. Further evidence of shared understanding is trust in management (for instance *Social9*).

Indicative of affordances in the workplace for the agentic shaping of meaning structures is factor *Psych17* (developers having a say in helping set the way things are done on their jobs). Having 'a say', co-designing the interpretive schemes of work, is another important part of enacting, of cultivating well-being in our case. This freedom to shape the conditions of action and for well-being is supported by factor *Physical30*, which places a premium on configurability, and *Social31* (the relaxation of the rules of work).

Conceptualization

Referring to our conceptualization of gamework well-being (see Figure 8.3), the factors of highest significance (5%) are placed inside the circle. The figure features well-being as a structurational process, involving mutualizing forces of trust, pride, having a say and known expectations. From an interpretive schemes perspective, however, we theorize that the link between known expectations and information availability and formatting is important for workplace well-being. In follow-up interviews we intend to explore further the nature of information availability and formatting (Boltanski and Thevenot, 1999) and its significance as a characteristic of interpretive schemes.

Having analyzed the studies separately, the following section will connect them, producing an understanding of the common theoretical ground linking the emotional concepts of violence and well-being.

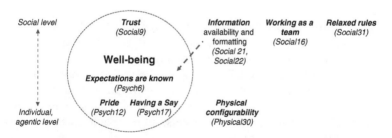

Figure 8.3 Conceptualization of the dynamics of gamework well-being

Discussion

Our studies have produced some new insights into two of the most controversial aspects of the computer games industry, their violent content and their workplace well-being. Indeed, the results suggest that positive well-being and violent games production can coexist in the same studio; negative well-being does not necessarily relate to putatively negative content. Regarding the latter, epic events or accounts of the Siege of Malta were the primary generators (Lawson, 2005) or contextual, interpretive forces that shaped the content of *Age of Empires*. An implication here, for limiting the development of violent content, is to focus on the primary generators of game design. As can be seen in the violent game case, this can be very potent once it has taken hold in a context and the developers start reproducing its significance. One strategy is to consider carefully the primary generators of game design and development processes. For example, can we find potent ones that are not violence-orientated, but still epic and enticing? A game studio manager also needs to be careful about initial conceptual suggestions he or she introduces into the context, being mindful of 'letting slip' a primary generator that some creatives may not be able to shake off. This insight challenges the effects-based research of violent games, which maintains that it is the level of realism in computer games that is so harmful and addictive to children (Gentile and Anderson, 2003). Rather, it could be the epic accounts or stories that are presented in the material that are the most captivating and compelling. Indeed, this was the most common form of interpretive schemes we found in the study, which was complemented by themes of rationality, business, issuing commands and connections to other popular violent games. It is hardly surprising that some of the bestselling games are war games such as the *Call of Duty* franchise. To this end, future research into violent game development could take a storytelling perspective (Brown *et al.*, 2008) in order to analyze further the way such epic meaning structures emerge.

Indeed, this approach could be useful for future well-being studies too, since we found indications of collective sense-making in the survey (known expectations and information availability). Stories and storytelling, in organizational settings, are the preferred sense-making currency (Polkinghorne, 1988). As Weick (1995) has suggested, stories are a key component of sense-making because they enable comprehension, implicate a causal order for events, allow people to talk about absent things, can act as mnemonics which may guide action and communicate shared values and meanings. They are a special form of interpretive schemes then. By seeking out the degree to which stories are shared and fragmented we could build up a richer picture of gamework well-being. Indeed, our ongoing and future work attempts to do so. This would indicate to what extent meaning structures are sedimented in a studio, which seems to be an indicator of well-being, particularly with regard to the information structural property. In light of this we could replace 'interpretive processes' in Figure 8.1 with 'storytelling processes'. An implication is that a sense of community or belonging (Selai and Trimble, 1999) is facilitated through shared stories and storytelling.

Conclusion

In this chapter we have provided an in-depth inquiry into two controversial areas of computer games and their development: violent content and studio well-being. We reviewed some of the key literature, used a theoretical lens that made sense across both studies, employed a mixture of research methods to operationalize the research questions, presented the nascent results of two empirical studies, along with conceptualizations and a synthesis of their key ideas. How funny is the world of games then? The alleged disastrous effects of violence and poor well-being that we find in the headline news are not funny. Yet, our results suggest that well-being is better than expected, with known expectations and information availability correlating significantly. It is encouraging for the UK industry in particular since it has been experiencing a brain drain of game development talent. With further study we envisage providing the industry with strategies and tactics to overcome the problem. We suggest a storytelling approach for further research to probe into this as yet rather opaque layer of game development.

References

Aassve, A., Mazzuco, S. and Mencarinii, L. (2006) An empirical investigation into the effect of childbearing on economic wellbeing in Europe, *Statistical Methods and Applications*, 15: 209–27.

Amabile, T.M., Barsade, S.G., Mueller, J.S. and Staw, B.M. (2005) Affect and creativity at work, *Administrative Science Quarterly*, 50(3): 367–403.

Anderson, C.A. (2004) An update on the effects of playing violent video games, *Journal of Adolescence*, 27: 113–22.

Anderson, C.A. and Bushman, B.J. (2001) Effects of violent video games on aggressive behaviour, aggressive cognition, aggressive affect, physiological

162   *Changing the Rules of the Game*

arousal, and prosocial behaviour: a meta-analytic review of the scientific literature, *Psychological Science*, 12(5): 353–9.

Bartunek, J. M. (1984) Changing interpretive schemes and organizational restructuring: the example of a religious order, *Administrative Science Quarterly*, 29: 355–72.

Blanchflower, D. and Oswald, A. (2004) Well-being over time in Britain and the USA, *Journal of Public Economics*, 88(7/8): 1359–86.

Boltanski, L. and Thevenot, L. (1999) *On Justification: Economies of Worth*, transl. by C. Porter, Princeton, NJ: Princeton University Press.

Brown, A.D., Stacey, P. and Nandhakumar, J. (2008) Making sense of sensemaking narratives, *Human Relations*, 61: 1035–62.

Byron, T. (2008) *The Report of the Byron Review: Safer Children in a Digital World*, http://media.education.gov.uk/assets/files/pdf/s/safer%20children%20in%20a%20digital%20world%20the%202008%20byron%20review.pdf.

Ciborra, C. and Lanzara, G.F. (1987) Change and formative contexts in information systems development, Paper presented at the IFIP Conference on Information Systems Development for Human Progress in Organizations, Atlanta, GA.

Cornford, T. and Smithson, S. (2006) *Project Research in Information Systems*, Basingstoke: Palgrave Macmillan.

Dearborn, D.C. and Simon, H.A. (1958) Selective perception: a note on the departmental identification of executives, *Sociometry*, 21: 140–4.

Develop Magazine (2009) The 2009 UK Games Development Salary Survey, http://www.develop-online.net/features/429/The-2009-UK-Games-Development-Salary-Survey.

Develop Magazine (2011) Develop 100: The Full List, http://www.develop-online.net/features/1230/DEVELOP-100-The-100-in-full.

Diener, E. and Seligman, M. (2002) Very happy people, *Psychological Science*, 13: 81–4.

Ehigie, B.O., Kolade, I.A. and Afolabi, A.O. (2006) Personality factors influencing politicians' attitudes towards well-being of citizens, *International Journal of Public Sector Management*, 19: 428–46.

Farrer, K.M., Krcmar, M. and Nowak, K.L. (2006) Contextual features of violent video games, mental models, and aggression, *Journal of Communication*, 56: 387–405.

Gentile, D.A. and Anderson, C.A. (2003) Violent video games: the newest media violence hazard, in D.A. Gentile (ed.) *Media Violence and Children*, Westport, CT: Praeger, pp. 131–52.

Giddens, A. (1984) *The Constitution of Society: Outline of the Theory of Structure*, Berkeley, CA: University of California Press.

Gouldner, A.W. (1971) *The Coming Crisis of Western Sociology*, London: Heinemann.

Gray, J.G. (1970) *On Understanding Violence Philosophically: And Other Essays*, New York: Harper and Row.

Hedberg, B. (1981) How organizations learn and unlearn, in P.C. Nystrom and W.H. Starbuck (eds) *Handbook of Organizational Design*, New York: Oxford University Press, pp. 3–27.

Hsu, C. and Lu, H. (2004) Why do people play on-line games? An extended TAM with social influences and flow experience, *Information & Management*, 41: 853–66.

IGDA (2004) *Quality of Life in the Game Industry: Challenges and Best Practices*, IGDA White Paper, www.igda.org/sites/default/.../IGDA_QualityOfLife_WhitePaper.pdf.

Krotoski, A. (2009) EA spouse grumbles on: working conditions no better in games industry 5 years later, London: *The Guardian*, http://www.guardian.co.uk/technology/gamesblog/2009/apr/09/ea-spouse-controversy-working-conditions-games-game-rant-epic.

Lastowka, F.G. and Hunter, D. (2004) Laws of the virtual worlds, *California Law Review*, 92 (1): 1–72.

Lawson, B. (2005) *How Designers Think: The Design Process Demystified*, Oxford: Architectural Press (Elsevier).

Lazarus, R.S. (1968) Emotions and adaptation: conceptual and empirical relations, in W.J. Arnold (ed.), *Nebraska Symposium on Motivation*, Lincoln: University of Nebraska Press, pp. 175–266.

Lazarus, R.S. (1991) *Emotion and Adaptation*, New York: Oxford University Press.

Miles, M.B. and Huberman, A.M. (1994) *Qualitative Data Analysis: An Expanded Sourcebook*, Thousand Oaks, CA: Sage Publications.

Myers, D.G. (1999) Close relationships and quality of life, in D. Kahneman, E. Diener and N. Schwarz (eds), *Well-Being: The Foundation of Hedonic Psychology*, New York: Russell Sage Foundation Press, pp. 374–91.

Nandhakumar, J. and Jones, M. (1997) Designing in the dark: the changing user-developer relationship in information systems development, in K. Kumar and J.I. DeGross (eds) *Proceedings of the International Conference on Information Systems (18th), 15–17 December 1997, Atlanta, Georgia, USA*, Madison, WI: Omnipress, pp. 75–8.

Nutt, D. and Railton, D. (2003) The Sims: real life as a genre, *Information Communication and Society*, 6: 577–92.

Oakley, K., Sperry, B. and Pratt, A. and Bakhshi, H. (eds) (2008) *The Art of Innovation: How Fine Arts Graduates Contribute to Innovation*, London: NESTA.

Ollerenshaw, A. and McDonald, J. (2006) Dimensions of pastoral care: student wellbeing in rural catholic schools, *Australian Journal of Primary Health*, 12: 137–45.

Olson, C.K. (2010) Children's motivations for video game play in the context of normal development, *Review of General Psychology*, 14: 180–7.

Orlikowski, W.J. and Baroudi, J.J. (1991) Studying information technology in organizations: research approaches and assumptions, *Information Systems Research*, 2: 1–28.

Oshry, D. (2012) Bodycount developer details 'unlawful' working conditions, Codemasters responds, http://kotaku.com/5876174/.

Oswald, A., Tella, R.D. and MacCulloch, R. (2003) The macroeconomics of happiness, *Review of Economics and Statistics*, 85: 809–27.

Palmer, M. (2012) Video games sector pleads for tax breaks, *Financial Times*, 15 February, http://on.ft.com/QFTSvE.

Parkinson, B. and Fischer, A.H. (2005) *Emotions and Social Relations: Cultural, Group, and Interpersonal Processes*, New York: Psychology Press.

Polkinghorne, D.E. (1988) *Narrative Knowing and the Human Sciences*, Albany: State University of New York.

164   *Changing the Rules of the Game*

Ranson, S., Hinings, B. and Greenwood, R. (1980) The structuring of organizational structures, *Administrative Science Quarterly*, 24: 1–14.

Rehak, B. (2003) Mapping the bit girl, *Information, Communication and Society*, 6: 477–96.

Ryan, R.M. and Deci, E. (2001) Self determination theory and the facilitation of intrinsic motivation, social development and well-being, *American Psychologist*, 55: 68–78.

Sainsbury of Turville, Lord D. (1998) Sci/Tech license to thrill, http://news.bbc.co.uk/1/hi/sci/tech/225615.stm.

Scherer, K.R. (2005) Appraisal theory, in T. Dalgleish and M.J. Power (eds), *Handbook of Cognition and Emotion*, Chichester: Wiley & Sons, pp. 637–63.

Selai, C. and Trimble, M.R. (1999) Accessing quality of life in dementia, *Aging & Mental Health*, 3: 101–11.

Shweder, R.A. and Haidt, J. (2000) The cultural psychology of the emotions: ancient and new, in M. Lewis and J.M. Haviland-Jones (eds) *Handbook of Emotions*, 2nd ed., New York: Guildford Press, pp. 397–414.

Siegel, S. (1956) *Nonparametric Statistics for the Behavioral Sciences*, New York: McGraw-Hill Book Company.

Stacey, P. (2009) The inner life of design: responding to wellbeing challenges in game design, Paper delivered at British Academy of Management Conference, Brighton.

Stacey, P. (2010) Emotional prototyping for service system design, Paper delivered at Academy of Management Annual Meeting, Montreal, Canada.

Stacey, P., Tether, B. and Bascavusoglu-Moreau E. (2011) Empathic service systems: 'designing' emotion in a cancer care service system, *System Sciences (HICSS), 44th Hawaii International Conference Proceedings*: 1–10.

Strauss, A.L. and Corbin, J.M. (1998) *Basics of Qualitative Research: Techniques and Procedures for Developing Grounded Theory*, Thousand Oaks, CA: Sage Publications.

Subrahmanyam, K., Kraut, R.E., Greenfield, P.M. and Gross, E.F. (2000) The impact of home computer use on children's activities and development, *Children and Computer Technology*, 10: 123–44.

Taylor, S.E. and Brown, J.D. (1988) Illusion and well-being: a social psychological perspective on mental health, *Psychological Bulletin*, 103(2): 193–210.

Tester, S., Hubbard, G., Downs, M., MacDonald, C. and Murphy, J. (2004) Frailty and institutional life, in A. Walker and C. Hagan (eds) *Growing Older: Quality of Life in Old Age*, Berkshire: Open University Press, pp. 209–24.

TIGA (2012) UK video games sector afflicted by brain drain of skilled staff, http://bit.ly/TpB9Td.

Tschang, F.T. (2005) Videogames as interactive experiential products and their manner of development, *International Journal of Innovation Management*, 9: 103–31.

Walsham, G. (1993) *Interpreting IS in Organizations*, Chichester: John Wiley.

Walsham, G. (1995) Interpretive case studies in IS research: nature and method, *European Journal of Information Systems*, 4(2): 74–81.

Walsham, G. (2003) *Research Methodologies for Information Systems in the Development Context: A Tutorial*, Aldershot: Ashgate Publishing.

Weick, K.E. (1995) *Sensemaking in Organizations*, Thousand Oaks, CA: Sage Publications.

Weick, K.E., Sutcliffe, K. and Obstfeld, D. (2005) Organizing and the process of sensemaking, *Organization Science*, 16: 409–21.

Williams, R.B. and Clippinger, C.A. (2002) Aggression, competition and computer games: computer and human opponents, *Computers in Human Behavior*, 18: 495–506.

9
Critical Perspectives on the Games Industry: Constructs and Collusion

Wallace McNeish

Introduction: imagining the games industry

> Spent two hours in the morning trapped in a room with the Pol
> Pots from marketing ... like we don't have anything better to do
> eight days before shipping ... I think everyone hates and dreads
> Marketing's meetings because of how these meetings alter your per-
> sonality. At meetings you have to explain what you've accomplished.
> You end up becoming this perky, gung-ho version of yourself that
> you know is just revolting. I have noticed that everybody looks
> down on the gung-ho type people at Microsoft, but nobody consid-
> ers themselves gung-ho ... Fortunately gung-ho-ishness seems to be
> confined exclusively to marketing meetings. Otherwise I think the
> Campus is utterly casual. (Daniel in Coupland, 1996: 25)

Douglas Coupland's satirical novel *Microserfs* (1996) explores the lives
of a group of technology geeks who work as low-level programmers
and testers at Microsoft's headquarters in Redmond near Seattle in the
mid-1990s. Through Daniel's blog style diary entries their motivations,
hopes and dreams are revealed as they are gradually tempted to relocate
to Silicon Valley in California by the lure of being in at the start of a new
and exciting games software project. Coupland draws upon months
of observational research in both of the novel's dramatic locations to
capture the optimistic zeitgeist of the time in the American software
industry, and anticipates the technology boom and dot.com bubble
of the late 1990s. The novel is laced with ironic knowingness which
reveals much about the difference between the projected self-image of
the software industry, the realities of the business and the everyday lives
of its workforce. The self-image of the software developers is that they

are creative cultural entrepreneurs working in a cooperative, casual, flexible and open campus-style white space environment, where motivations to work long hours are derived less from financial reward than from artistic, technical and personal developmental compensations. In sociological terms, the developers are ideal typical members of Florida's creative class who share a common identity through adherence to a creative ethos which is inseparable from their economic function, and determines similar social, cultural and leisure choices (Florida, 2004).

The reality of the software workers' lives is, however, significantly different from their self-image as revealed in Daniel's diary. They are microserfs, working in a feudally structured business organization that is driven by tight deadlines with the requirement to generate profits for its shareholders through the mass sale of knowledge-based commodities. Coupland shows how every aspect of the workers' personality must unquestioningly be given over to the company, how stretching individual objectives are set by management, how rivalries and jealousy over bonuses and company share reward schemes are rife, and how, as a result, there is constant personal anxiety and a high level of burnout amongst a young staff after only a few years of service. Diary entries insightfully illustrate the collusive self-denial that the software developers perpetuate amongst themselves in order to keep working. Their resentment of the marketing department is not simply because of the constant task-related self-justification that is required, but because the marketers stand as a constant reminder that they are in the business of creating commodities – a reality which jars with their constructed self-image as creative cultural bohemians.

It is precisely this gap between image and reality which lies at the heart of the critical analysis of the computer games industry that will be developed in this chapter. Such gaps are central to the stimulation of the sociological imagination which aims to penetrate the opacity of the social constructs that shape social reality, and thereby generate critical social scientific knowledge (Mills, 2000). This chapter begins by setting out the key discursive claims that the computer games industry uses to construct itself in economic, cultural and socio-political terms. These rhetorical claims are animated by what Bourdieu has defined as 'the charismatic ideology of creativity' (Bourdieu, 1993: 76). Such claims are derived from, and furthered by, the growing economic power that the games industry possesses. The chapter then proceeds to deconstruct those claims by making use of a multiperspectival critical sociological approach that draws on insights from political economy, social theory and cultural studies. The fact that computer games are first and foremost commodities will be central to this critique. In conclusion, it will be argued that the reality of the computer games industry is much closer to the classic critical formulation of the culture industry as detailed by Horkheimer and Adorno (2000 [1944]), than to the creative industry discourse which dominates contemporary representations.

Games industry hyperbole?

Since Coupland's time of writing, in what Dovey and Kennedy (2006) call the post-Playstation era, computer games production has emerged to become a significant player in the global information economy and a ubiquitous aspect of cultural consumption in the network society (Castells, 2000). The games industry has mushroomed exponentially into a global enterprise that was expected to be worth upwards of $68 billion per year by the end of 2012 (McGonigal, 2011). Across the world, hundreds of millions of games are sold annually to hundreds of millions of gamers, and although most play on average for an hour or two per day there are at least six million hardcore gamers in China who play for more than 20 hours per week, and ten million in the United Kingdom, France and Germany. In the United States there are approximately five million extreme gamers who play for more than 45 hours per week (McGonigal, 2011). In the United States, the games industry employs approximately 250,000 workers (de Jong, 2007), while the latest report from National Endowment for Science, Technology and the Arts (NESTA) estimates British employment in the industry at 10,000, with a £2 billion annual turnover, and a net contribution of £1 billion to GDP (Livingstone and Hope, 2011).

A complex global multi-media and multi-medium matrix of games production and consumption has developed over the past two decades. This matrix links together console manufacture, graphic, video and sound card development, artistic creation, software engineering, code writing, marketing, advertising and retail, Internet services, newsgroups, gaming communities, fanzines, blogs, novels, strategy guides, critics, journalism, education and training programmes and academic research. To this, by no means exhaustive, list should also be added a variety of military-related projects and applications (Herbst, 2008; Rentfrow, 2008). It is a rhizomic techno-cultural matrix that is geographically uneven, but which, despite current macroeconomic instability, appears to be constantly expanding to colonize previously game resistant aspects of contemporary economy and culture. There is strong market-driven convergence in terms of ownership and production between the games industry and the film industry (Brookey, 2010); and there is strong technology-driven convergence through digitization across all forms of new and old media, communications and computing (Miller, 2011). Given the economic power and cultural ubiquity of the computer games industry, it is hardly surprising that hyperbolic claims are made by its purveyors across the matrix of production and consumption. Such claims are made at the level of the economy, art and culture, and even at the level of politics and social well-being. They are linked together by a charismatic ideology of creativity (Bourdieu, 1996), which emphasizes the innovative power of the artist (such as designer, developer, software engineer, hi-tech entrepreneur) over the economic imperatives which drive the industry, and thereby detracts attention from the economic power which enables such claims to be made so powerfully in the first place. For example, in relation to the economy, the UK games industry wraps itself in the Union Jack to present itself as a creative national treasure that should be nurtured as the latest incarnation of the great British tradition of artistic and technological excellence:

> The UK has long been a world leader in technological innovation. Britain had the world's first industrial revolution. Its code breakers at Bletchley Park helped win the Second World War and created the first computer. Their inventiveness is echoed in the multitude of innovative high-tech start-ups peppering the country today. This technological ingenuity is matched only by our creative flair [...] we shouldn't be surprised to find the UK at the global forefront of video games and visual effects [...]. In these industries, research and development meets content development, and scientists and software engineers work hand in hand with artists and designers to produce interactive and audio-visual content that is consumed the world over. (Livingstone and Hope, 2011: 12)

The UK games industry makes this type of claim, almost inevitably, to ask the government for more investment in education and training, research and development, and tax breaks so that it can remain competitive in the global marketplace. It also does so as a creative industry whose adaptable, flexible and risk-taking workers, it is claimed, possess the requisite human capital to innovate the advanced economies out of their current economic downturn (Florida, 2011). To its potential recruits (who are increasingly graduates from proliferating higher education computer arts programmes), as developers, graphic designers, creative entrepreneurs and concept-driven intrapreneurs, the games industry offers the promise of stimulating and fulfilling work in a cutting edge technological environment. It is especially attractive as a career to game enthusiasts who often view the work undertaken as an extension of their own hobby time (Lee and Lin, 2011), with the added bonus of the opportunity to earn relatively high salaries that in 2012 averaged £33,000 across the UK industry (MCV Survey, 2012).

In relation to art and culture, computer games are increasingly taken seriously as cultural artefacts, at least at the level of the middlebrow, by the arbiters of public taste like broadsheet newspapers, academies of film and television arts and cultural critics. Game designers like Gabe Newell (*Half-Life*), Will Wright (*The Sims*), John Cormack (*Doom, Castle Wolfenstein, Quake*) and the Howser brothers (*Grand Theft Auto*) are feted as creative geniuses who are akin to the auteur directors of the film industry. Computer games have become a staple of mass culture with characters such as Lara Croft, Sonic the Hedgehog, Pac-Man, Mario, Duke Nukem and John 'Soap' McTavish having a strong resonance across popular media genres, while films of games and games of films have become industry norms (McAllister, 2004). Academic commentators have joined this chorus of cultural celebration with journals like *Game Studies, Eludamos* and *Games and Culture* analyzing far beyond the merely technical, to apply new media theories to tease out the cultural meanings and aesthetic qualities that are encoded into computer games and decoded by their players. Computer games clearly constitute a new semi-autonomous field of cultural production which operates its own internal structuring logic, systems of symbolic exchange, forms of cultural capital and rules of recognition and reward (Bourdieu, 1993).

Positive claims made for the cultural creative aspects of the computer games industry extend further than the economic and cultural, to the realm of progressive politics and the formulation of policy to enhance social well-being. For example, in a development of Mulgan's notion of 'Connexity' (Mulgan, 1998), Leadbeater (2008) argues that games industry-pioneered innovations in digital interactivity, modularity and online community building are models for we-think, a new conception of mass innovation in democratic practice and social problem solving. Games, it is claimed, are educative instruments about social and political issues because their creative interactivity enables the player to role-play, make choices involving different variables and see how those choices affect outcomes. Chatfield (2011) cites the online game *Darfur is Dying*, which has been played by over three million people, as a prime example of a serious game that explores the ethics of war and social displacement from the inside. According to Chatfield, 'there is tremendous enthusiasm for politically and ethically engaged gaming within much of the industry' (Chatfield, 2011: 187). McGonigal (2011) epitomizes this discourse about the progressive socio-political significance of gaming and its relationship to progressive creativities when she argues:

> The truth is this: in today's society, computer and video games are fulfilling genuine human needs that the real world is unable to satisfy. Games are providing rewards that reality is not. They are teaching and inspiring and engaging us in ways that reality is not. They are bringing us together in ways that reality is not. (McGonigal, 2011: 5)

Each type of claim made for the computer games industry, at the level of the creative economy, at the level of art and at the level of progressive politics brings different agents together to manufacture this new cultural field. What Bourdieu calls an 'illusio' (1996: 172) is collectively produced by the different stakeholders who have interests that are furthered in and through the field. This 'illusio' is constituted by a shared belief in the rules of the game of artistic creation and validation that is played out in modern societies. How can the reality which such 'illusio' obfuscates in relation to the games industry be revealed? How can the rhetoric and hyperbole concerning the games industry be cut through? To begin the process of separating image from reality it is necessary to start with the product itself. Stripped back to their base level, computer games are commodities, a fact that has profound implications for the way in which they are produced and for their potentials as a form of cultural practice.

Computer games as phantasmagoric commodities

> A commodity appears at first sight an extremely obvious trivial thing. But its analysis brings out that it is a very strange thing, abounding in metaphysical subtleties and theological niceties. (Marx, 1990 [1868]: 163)

If the words 'computer game' are inserted before the word commodity in the first line of this famous quotation from Marx's *Capital* then his words give an indication of the critical approach that will be developed here, while also pointing to the complexity of the subject matter. Marx argues that any product of human labour which is sold in the marketplace becomes a commodity defined by monetary exchange value that is acquired through relationships to other commodities. Commodification is far from straightforward, rather it is a profoundly alienating process whereby exchange value obscures the original use value of the product and abstracts it from the social relations of production which underpinned the conditions of its creation. Multiple illusions are generated, and Marx finds it necessary to turn to allegories of religious and mystical experience to illustrate their ideological power. The metaphor of the tribal fetish, an inanimate object of veneration that is imbued with supernatural power, is used by Marx to show how commodities have what Derrida describes as a 'ghost effect' (Derrida, 1994: 148) which makes them appear disembodied, free-floating and spectral. Commodity fetishism generates a false perception of social and economic reality because the products of human labour relationships appear to take on lives of their own, something which Marx pointedly describes in terms of 'the phantasmagoric form of a relation between things' (Marx, in Gunning, 2004: 9).[1]

The metaphor of phantasmagoria is a very deliberate choice on Marx's part as it enables both explanation and demystification (Gunning, 2004). During the eighteenth and nineteenth centuries phantasmagoria exhibitions and public shows involving the use of concealed magic lanterns to project ghostly and hallucinatory images onto screens in darkened settings became a popular form of entertainment across the cities of Europe. Combining an array of occult and arcane practices with displays of galvanism (the newly discovered force of electricity), with varieties of aural stimulation (for instance the glass harmonica) and optical illusion (such as the *camera obscura* or distorting mirrors), the phantasmagoria aimed to confuse, confound and discombobulate audience senses (Warner, 2006). Marx's metaphor works to draw the reader's attention to the special effects created by the hidden technologies employed to create the phantasmagoric experience. In the same way that sensory overload causes the audience to forget the magic lantern and its operator, the commodity fetish casts an ideological spell to make consumers focus on the dazzling 'social hieroglyph' (Marx, 1990 [1868]: 167), of exchange value, and thereby forget the real social nature of the commodity product. At the heart of Marx's social theory is an exhaustive analysis of the commodity form within the general framework of capital which aims to decipher and reveal the mystery that it contains so as to bring real human relationships rooted in concrete social, economic and political relations into high relief.

The phantasmagoria was devised and popularized in a period when Enlightenment reason had begun to make significant progress in disenchanting the world towards the secular modern condition. Science was in the ascendancy but strong vestiges of premodern superstition still remained and the phantasmagoria took advantage of this tension by exploiting the gap between the rational beliefs of the audience and their sense perception, to create an immersive form of modern entertainment that was the forerunner of cinema and television (Gunning, 2004). Over time, science and the aural and visual cultural technologies it has spawned have gathered pace to offer audiences who can no longer really believe in the supernatural fleeting experiences of phanstasmagoric simulacra where time and space are compressed, and distinctions between the real and unreal are blurred. Computer games are the latest and most sophisticated descendant of the magic lantern hokum of the early industrial period.

Translated into Baudrillard's history of the development of simulation (Baudrillard, 2007), a progressive deepening and broadening out of simulacra has taken place from the counterfeit phase that operated in early modernity between the Renaissance and the Industrial Revolution, the production phase that operated during the fully modern industrial period and the code-governed simulation phase that operates during the contemporary postmodern juncture. In passages that are strongly suggestive of the computer games industry, Baudrillard argues that 'present day simulators try to make the real, all the real, coincide with their simulation models' (Baudrillard, 1998: 170). This attempt is not about achieving mimetic coextensivity with the real; rather the aim is simulated hyperreality whereby 'the real is produced from miniaturized units, from matrices, memory banks and command units – and with these it can be reproduced an indefinite number of times' (Baudrillard, 1998: 170). For Baudrillard, simulation is a process that goes beyond simple feigning or pretending; rather it occurs where there is a reproduction, at least on the surface, of some aspects of the condition that is not actually possessed – it is an immersive process that blurs distinctions between the real and the unreal.

Computer games are arguably the most phantasmagoric of all contemporary cultural technologies because they take immersion and simulation to new levels through carefully designed forms of interactivity. The depth that this immersion is presently able to reach, and what this immersion might mean in socio-political terms, is a moot point (Lockwood and Richards, 2008). It would appear, however, that each advance in digital technology brings the possibility of total immersion in virtual environments ever closer. What has been a long-standing staple of science fiction may become science fact as computer games technologies are developed to further refine the immersive aspects of phantasmagoria. Currently there are limitations because the cybernetic interface between human body and machine technology has not been perfected. Game design is therefore extremely important as it is necessary to draw the player into the simulacra by stimulating the imagination to gain the player's active collusion in the simulation. The most popular console and PC games involve role playing of one form or another in a consistent fictional game space. Narrative devices, game conventions, goal achievements and interactive choices facilitate character development, and with such customization comes character identification. If this is done well, then immersion is deepened and the game experience heightened (Berger, 2008).

Behind the gaming experience stands the hardware of the platform console or the PC that the computer game is played upon. The very names of some of the leading games consoles, for example Microsoft's bestselling X-box, Sega's Dreamcaster and the gaming PC manufacturer Alienware connote an air of the mysterious and the fantastical. What might be conceptualized as a form of technological fetishism is engendered as the consoles are expressly marketed as technologies of wonder that will magically transport users to other realms – Sony's Playstation is particularly suggestive of these transportive properties. Indeed, the very design of consoles and gaming computers as sleek enclosed plastic and metal boxes which entirely conceal the electronic gadgetry within, alongside wireless game controllers and related mobile technologies, combine to reproduce the hauntological power of the original experience of phantasmagoria for the information age.

Games consoles and game software are first and foremost commodities; they are mass produced, mass marketed and mass consumed cultural products; hence like all other commodities they have a fetishizing effect. Arguably with computer game technologies, this fetishizing effect is intensified because they are specifically designed to induce phantasmagoric experiences amongst players. Few, if any, Western consumers of beautifully packaged and technologically advanced consoles will have any conception of the labour process which was involved in their manufacture, or of the complex division of labour which is integral to the development of the carefully constructed interactive games which operate upon them. Nor are they likely to have any conception of the way in which the technology works to give them their immersive gaming experience. Clearly computer games are far from obvious trivial things, rather they abound in 'metaphysical subtleties and theological niceties' (Marx, 1868 [1990]: 163), which operate to obscure both their nature as industry produced mass commodities, and to generate phantasmagoric experiences amongst their players. In order to reveal more of their mystery it is necessary to look more closely at how the industry is organized, and at the labour process which is integral to the manufacture of the commodities which it produces.

From Fordist manufacture to post-Fordist development

Computer games are the product of a powerful industry that is organized on a multinational basis with centres of design creation, manufacturing and distribution that span the globe. As Kerr comments, 'digital games appear to epitomize an ideal type of global post-industrial neo-liberal cultural product' (Kerr, 2010: 1). They epitomize neo-liberalism in terms of both hardware platform manufacture and software development because the games industry is organized like any other contemporary global business enterprise with an international division of labour, whose aim is to minimize regulation and thereby maximize profits. Where Kerr's definition is perhaps contentious is in relation to the use of the term postindustrial because it appears to forget that the games industry does not live by software alone.

Software developing and publishing may indeed be conceptualized as operating in a postindustrial manner, with its key centres located in core developed world states, most notably the United States, Japan, France and the United Kingdom, where the post-Fordist mode of flexible accumulation has developed across some of the key sectors associated with the postmaterial, knowledge or information economy (Harvey, 1989). It is of course the post-Fordist mode of flexible labour organization combined with wider post-industrial socio-economic trends towards the aestheticization of commodities and the commodification of aesthetics (Amin, 1997), which enables the computer games industry to project an image of being at the forefront of contemporary forms of cultural economic endeavour. However, what remains largely unacknowledged in the celebrations of creative economic and cultural creativity that surround the industry, is that the platform operating systems (whose manufacture is dominated by three powerful multinational companies, Sony, Microsoft and Nintendo), are currently produced in the newly industrialized countries like Mexico and China where the cost of labour is cheap and labour regulation is minimal. Vast factory complexes are organized along primitive Taylorist and Fordist lines, where labour discipline is strictly enforced by rigid hierarchical management systems, and all autonomy and creativity is removed as thousands of workers perform repetitive short-cycle routinized tasks over long shifts to produce standardized mass products.

A recent European Union funded research report entitled *Game Console and Music Player Production in China* (Poyhonen and Wan, 2011) found evidence of widespread abuse of basic labour rights in four major factories studied in Guangdong province. Findings include: full-time wage levels that are difficult for workers to live on (an average of €124–142 per month, regular use of unpaid interns between the ages of 16 and 18); excessive working hours as workers attempted to raise their wage levels (60–100 hours overtime is a norm during peak season with the requirement for alternative day and night shifts usually lasting one month); significant negative effects upon workers' health (from chemical hazards, standing for long hours, sleep deprivation, exhaustion due to lack of time off); punitive labour discipline (toilet break monitoring, fines for slow work or other breaches of factory regulations) and a general disrespect for trade union rights amongst management (Poyhonen and Wan, 2011: 4–5). It is unlikely that any of the workers concerned could ever afford to buy one of the consoles which they manufacture, let alone possess the necessary leisure time to enjoy playing the games which operate upon them. One of the factories at the centre of this report, Foxconn, is particularly notorious because in May 2010 it set nets up around its high buildings after there had been a spate of eleven suicides by jumping in less than a year, and a total of seventeen over the past decade (Johnson, 2011). In early 2012, there were reports across the Western media that 300 X-box workers had taken to one of the roofs at Foxconn and were threatening suicide in a dispute about pay and conditions (Rundle, 2012).

Games software is designed, developed and published under very different conditions from the way in which the platform operating systems are manufactured. At the heart of this production matrix are the game development studios which are either independent, semi- or entirely owned by publishers, or semi- or partly owned by the hardware platform manufacturers. Because of the high costs and high risks involved in game development full independence for games developers is increasingly a rarity. *Grand Theft Auto IV*, which grossed $500 million in its first week on the market in 2008, cost an estimated $100 million to produce with a production team of approximately 550 (Chatfield, 2011). Only a large publishing company like Take-Two, which owns the games developer Rockstar, could possibly make this type of initial investment and withstand the potential risk that it entails. Ownership structures are complex and opaque with consolidation and vertical integration across developing, publishing and platform manufacturing constituting a key industry trend. For example, Bungie Studios was acquired by Microsoft in 2000 so that its new X-box operating system could be promoted with the title *Halo* which was exclusive to the platform, while Maxis, the developer of *The Sims*, was bought by Electronic Arts in 1997 (Dovey and Kennedy, 2006: 48–9). Outside the major platform manufacturers, a handful of multinational publishers currently dominate the world games market: Electronic Arts (USA), Activision (France), Ubisoft (France), Take-Two (USA), Bethesda (USA), Konami (Japan) and Eidos (UK).

It is in the games development studios, and amongst their design and code writing teams in particular, that the myth of creativity which the wider industry propagates for itself is most apparent. Team sizes vary from 10 to 20, up to a few hundred depending upon the particular title being developed, but whatever the size, detailed negotiations and decisions must constantly be made between members about narrative, aesthetics and gameplay across a range of different specialisms that include designers, writers, graphic artists, sound technicians, video engineers and programmers. The sheer complexity of the processes involved requires a fundamentally different approach to organizing the labour process than the rigid Fordist systems under which the hardware platforms are manufactured. Post-Fordist innovations in teamwork, flexible scheduling, outsourcing, freelancing, flat management hierarchies, participative work cultures, open plan working environments and stock option incentives have been pioneered by the games industry and related cultural sectors such as television, magazine journalism, recording, fashion, advertising, marketing and visual effects (Kline *et al.*, 2003).

Post-Fordist flexibility may appear attractive on the surface, but its casual free-to-work-in-the-way-that-one-wants image hides a reality whereby the onus is firmly placed upon the individual game development worker to exploit himself to the maximum, a tendency which is strong across the cultural industries in general (Hesmondhalgh and Baker, 2010). And it usually is a 'himself' because games development is firmly segregated according to gender. A 2004 survey of the UK games industry found only 8 per cent women in its workforce, with many of those employed in marketing, PR and administration (Kerr, 2010: 92). The games industry is a high-risk industry where the financial rewards from achieving a big hit are significant, but where failure rates amongst games development companies are notably above the average for small and medium-sized enterprises. Commercial success hinges on a combination of producing the right commercial product at the right time, marketing it properly and minimizing costs, and above all labour costs – hence an imperative towards self-exploitation is built into the fabric of the way in which the industry operates. Self-exploitation may take a variety of different forms, from working extremely long hours when crunch time deadlines for game publication are close, engaging in precarious unpaid labour as a graduate intern so as to gain the experience necessary to secure a fulltime position, or low-paid individuals freely giving imaginative ideas for improvement to the project team. Unlike Fordist modes of organizing the labour process, in the post-Fordist economy it is not simply the body that is exploited in order to generate profits, but the worker's whole being.

At the heart of the process of self-exploitation is an emphasis upon creativity. Success or failure is attributed to either possession or non-possession of this personal characteristic. This would seem to be a natural extension of the way in which positioning within the wider labour market has become increasingly individualized. Dominant neo-liberal discourses which inform welfare, training and labour market policy ascribe success to having the correct mixture of hard and soft skills, personal competencies and educational attainment, and failure to deficiencies for which the individual is personally responsible (Annetts *et al.*, 2009). Young designers, programmers and engineers working in the games software industry have internalized these discourses and therefore carry a heavy weight of personal responsibility for their own success. Such responsibility operates at a subjective level to enforce self-discipline and hard work, but it may also generate deep personal anxieties and psychological disorders because the pressure to be creative is so intense. If such creativity is not manifest to the degree that is required, then there are queues of young hopefuls willing to take the place of those individuals who fail to make a creative impact (McRobbie, 2011a).

McRobbie's extensive research into the development of cultural entrepreneurship in the UK economy over the past few decades reveals the way in which government's social and economic policies have progressively dovetailed with, and been influenced by, its cultural policy (2011b). This shift is epitomized by the Blair government's DCMS (Department for Culture, Media and Sport) *Green Paper on Government and the Value of Culture* (2004) which opened with the bold assertion that everyone is creative. This assumption implies that individuals simply need to find their inner creative self to be successful. For McRobbie, the instrumentalization of culture has been markedly intensified during the early years of the twenty-first century as the notion of artistic creativity has been appropriated by the state to be used as a model for working life and for wider economic and social policy. This can be seen in the rebranding of national identity through the constant recycling of the UK's cultural heritage across all economic spheres (see for example the quote from Livingstone and Hope [2011] regarding the importance of the UK games industry in the above section on games industry hyperbole). It can also been seen in interventions into education whether it be at secondary level, through the introduction of creative partnerships and the emphasis upon personal development, or in higher education where there have been transformations of the curriculum in the arts, media and social sciences towards project-based work and the development of pedagogical styles centred on active enquiry (McRobbie, 2011b: 120–21).

The UK computer game industry and related cultural industries have been at the epicentre of this creative cultural economic wave. It has been mirrored across the core developed economies as part of the shift towards the post-Fordist mode of flexible accumulation in the economic sectors which provide cultural commodities. Florida's theorization of a creative class (2004, 2011), which has been hugely influential in the fields of regional development, city planning and business studies, owes much to the way in which it has tapped into the general unfolding of this shift. Arguably, this influence also stems from the way in which his theorization reinforces the liberal urban educated elites' view of themselves as winners in the creative age. Florida claims that up to 38 million Americans, up to a third of the total workforce, belong to this class, so in the United States alone there are a lot of winners (Peck, 2005).

But again all is not quite what it seems in the cultural sectors of the economy of which the games development industry is a paradigmatic example. Young computer arts graduates, software engineers and games designers have been schooled in creative project work throughout their education, and expect to replicate that experience in their working lives. They may also expect to experience a degree of precariousness, self-exploitation and non-linearity in their transition to the labour market. Willingness to self-exploit and engage in precarious work arises from a combination of sources. Through self-designation and educational positioning as artists, such individuals may have a strong sense of a creative calling which justifies high-risk self-exploitative enterprise; or they may simply not have recognized that their enterprise is a risky or exploitative one; or the potentials for non-monetary reward in terms of self-actualization, status recognition or even celebrity outweighs the risk and exploitation that is experienced (Hesmondhalgh and Baker, 2010). However, the image that the industry projects of casual, informal and exciting work belies a level of precariousness and an imperative to self-exploit for which few are prepared. Industry insiders themselves consistently point to the lack of preparedness amongst young interns in terms of core skill attributes, flexibility and the requirement to spend long hours on routinized tasks (Cecil and Wright, 2010).

The ubiquity of the creativity paradigm has significant implications which extend far beyond the precarious nature of the work done by young entrants into one cultural industry or another. The sociocultural significance attached to creativity means that all forms of seemingly non-creative routinized work have been downgraded and devalued in the eyes of a whole generation of young people. Intellectual labour, the lifeblood of universities, is suffering a similar fate as it comes to be viewed as unfashionable while its place is usurped by its creative and seemingly more economically important counterpart. As McRobbie says, 'in such a context this championing of new forms of creative education (for example, the live project, the links with industry, internships, the role of creative partnerships) also occludes the place of theory, and the space of critical pedagogy' (McRobbie, 2011b: 130).

Conclusion: the games industry as a culture industry

> Today Alistair told us our new mandate for BoardX: 'Its new title is SpriteQuest. SpriteQuest is a warm, heartfelt journey into magical and fantastic lands, where our hero Prince Amulon allows children to rediscover life's joys as he teaches us all to laugh and dream again'. Something died inside us as we heard this proclamation. Senior management, though, interpreted the ensuing silence as tacit agreement. (Ethan Jarlewski, in *Coupland* 2007: 241)

In *J-Pod* (2007), Douglas Coupland brings the satirical eye which he first cast upon the games software industry in *Microserfs* up-to-date for the wired generation. The novel centres upon a group of six young games developers whose last names all happen to begin with the letter 'J' and who are based in an American company called Neotronic Arts (a gloss on Electronic Arts). They have been commissioned to develop a skate-board game called *BoardX* and work long hours in a shared work station cubicle to bring the project to fruition. Coupland traces the twists and turns of the game's development as it morphs from one incarnation to the next as management constantly interferes in the design process in order to try to ensure commercial success. Eventually, the skateboard concept is abandoned altogether in favour of a new market-driven family-friendly game called *SpriteQuest*, which is subsequently sabotaged by the disgruntled J-Podders who insert an unhinged Ronald McDonald character into a secret game level to create mayhem. Like *Microserfs*, the novel is illustrative of the ongoing tensions within the games industry between business imperatives and artistic/cultural considerations, and the multiple constructs and collusions which abound therein.

During the 1940s, the Frankfurt School developed a powerful critique of what it designated as the culture industry, which comprises interdependent monopolies of mass media, leisure and entertainment. The culture industry churns out standardized mass products that are encoded with conformist liberal ideology, and sold to consumers whose desires have been moulded by advertising, and further stimulated by the cultural products which they consume. Workers' leisure time is no longer their own as it increasingly colonized by the culture industry which demands that all areas of life be given over to either producing or consuming mass commodities; hence leisure comes to resemble work. All previous cultural styles and artistic creations are pillaged and recycled to create an endless stream of manipulative advertising, and derivative variations of cultural commodities which pose as art, and drive out any possibility for more authentic forms of culture which might be critical of or negative about the entrenched unequal socio-political structure. Adorno inverts the dominant liberal conception of the consumer/producer relationship when he argues that 'the consumer is not king, as the culture industry would have us believe, not its subject but its object' (1991: 99). As such, the culture industry operates as a primary agent of ideological domination and control in what Horkheimer and Adorno refer to as the totally administered society (Horkheimer and Adorno, 2000 [1944]).

Horkheimer and Adorno's theorization has been much criticized by contemporary cultural sociologists as being overly negative, too one-sided and elitist (Best and Kellner, 2001). Despite these criticisms, the culture industry perspective remains a powerful indictment of the way in which contemporary mass culture is produced, marketed and consumed. In this chapter, the way that the computer games industry constructs itself as a creative industry has been subjected to critical scrutiny. Its self-designated creative status has led it to claim special status at economic, cultural and socio-political levels. It is perhaps hardly surprising that an industry which explicitly deals in phantasmagoric illusions should create so many illusions about its own status. At the heart of the critical perspective that has been developed here is the separation of the reality of the games industry from its image. The games industry is far from special, rather it is an industry that like any other is concerned with manufacturing and selling commodities with the aim of generating profits. An analysis of the way in which games operating hardware is produced under intensive Taylorist and Fordist conditions in the newly industrialized countries illustrates a reality that stands sorely at odds with the glossy image of creative flexibility and human capital development generated by the games industry in the west. It is in relation to games development inside Western studios that the charismatic ideology of creativity is strongest, but analysis of the post-Fordist labour process reveals a precariousness and a self-exploitative system that is often far from the promise of fulfilling artistic endeavour that the industry promotes to its young recruits.

Game commodities are the product of a complex interaction between labour, technology and culture but just how creative are they in reality? From the perspective of the Frankfurt School, the consumption or playing of games is inextricably bound up with an ideology of individualization, choice and competition which serves to reproduce the dominant global ideology of liberal consumer capitalism. This ideology is encoded through the very process of interactivity and seemingly creative gameplay, while the game narratives reproduce all the conventions of derivative genres. To paraphrase the title of Benjamin's famous essay of 1936 on art in the age of mechanical reproduction, computer games represent the work of art in the age of digital reproduction, and like all such mass-reproduced art it is bereft of aura and authenticity. There is no denying the artistry which goes into making all aspects of a computer game, but their novelty and innovation in terms of art, narrative and gameplay is strongly open to question. A casual look at the top 20 games on the website of the UK high street retailer Game at any time will reveal a proliferation of sequels, derivative sports games, war games and fantasy games. This may or may not be what consumers want, but it is hardly a shining example of vibrant artistic creativity.

Kerr asserts that only 3 per cent of games are commercially successful (Kerr, 2010: 45). Even if this figure is an underestimate, the high risk and high reward stakes that are played for demand an attention to the financial bottom line which curtails experimentation and requires close attention to market trends. The extract from Coupland's novel with which this section opened pointedly makes these commercial imperatives clear. Developments toward oligopoly in terms of games industry ownership and control magnify financial pressures which necessarily detract from any pretensions to artistic autonomy. In many ways the games industry resembles the contemporary Hollywood film industry which is dominated by a handful of studios that are owned and controlled by multi-media multinational companies who churn out derivative, safe, market-driven consumer products. The Hollywood film industry went through something of a renaissance in the late 1960s and 1970s when, for a short period, it was energized by young radical directors and producers who emerged from the sixties counter-culture milieu to make challenging films which questioned the dominant social mores and political norms of the period. The games industry desperately needs just such an injection of real creativity, but are games really a cultural medium where this can happen? And where would be the source of such creativity in today's world?[2]

Notes

1. The usual English translation of the German phrase 'diese phantasmagorische Form' is 'fantastic form'. As Gunning (2004) points out, this is a mistranslation which misses the specificity of Marx's metaphor.
2. My thanks to Andrew Panay and Hazel Work in the Sociology Division at the University of Abertay for stimulating conversations regarding the subject matter of this chapter.

References

Adorno, T.W. (1991) Culture industry reconsidered, in T.W. Adorno, *The Culture Industry*, London: Routledge, pp. 98–106.

Amin, A. (1997) *Post-Fordism: A Reader*, Oxford: Blackwell.

Annetts, J., Law, A., McNeish, W. and Mooney, G. (2009) *Understanding Social Welfare Movements*, Bristol: Policy Press.

Baudrillard, J. (1998) Simulacra and simulations, in J. Baudrillard (ed.), *Selected Writings*, Cambridge: Polity Press, pp. 169–86.

Baudrillard, J. (2007) *Symbolic Exchange and Death*, London: Sage.

Benjamin, W. (1999 [1936]) The work of art in the age of mechanical reproduction, in W. Benjamin (ed.), *Illuminations*, London: Pimlico, pp. 217–53.

Berger, P. (2008) There and back again: reuse, signifiers and consistency in created game spaces, in Jahn-Sudmann and Stockmann (eds), *Computer Games as a Sociocultural Phenomenon*, pp. 47–55.

Best, S. and Kellner, D. (2001) *The Postmodern Adventure: Science, Technology and Cultural Studies at the Third Millennium*, London: Routledge.

Bourdieu, P. (1993) *The Field of Cultural Production*, New York: Columbia University Press.

Bourdieu, P. (1996) *The Rules of Art*, Stanford: Stanford University Press.

Brookey, R.A. (2010) *Hollywood Gamers: Digital Convergence in the Film and Video Game Industries*, Bloomington, IN: Indiana University Press.

Castells, M. (2000) *The Rise of the Network Society: The Information Age, Economy, Society and Culture*, vol. 1, Oxford: Blackwell.

Cecil, C. and Wright, C. (eds) (2010) *Playing the Game: Insider Views on Video Game Development*, London: NESTA, http://www.nesta.org.uk/publications/reports/assets/features/playing_the_game_insider_views on_video_game_development.

Chatfield, T. (2011) *Fun Inc: Why Games Are the 21st Century's Most Serious Business*, London: Virgin Books.

Coupland, D. (1996) *Microserfs*, London: Flamingo/HarperCollins.

Coupland, D. (2007) *J-Pod*, London: Bloomsbury.

Department for Culture, Media and Sport (2004) *Government and the Value of Culture*, London: DCMS.

Derrida, J. (1994) *Spectres of Marx: The State of the Debt, the Work of Mourning, and the New International*, London: Routledge.

De Jong, S. (2007) *The Hows and Whys of the Games Industry*, place of publication unknown: Hourences.

Dovey, J. and Kennedy, H. W. (2006) *Game Cultures: Computer Games as New Media*, Maidenhead: Open University Press.

Florida, R. (2004) *The Rise of the Creative Class*, Cambridge, MA: Basic Books.

Florida, R. (2011) *The Great Reset: How the Post-Crash Economy Will Change the Way We Live and Work*, London: Harper Paperbacks.

Gunning, T. (2004) Phantasmagoria and the manufacturing of illusions and wonder: towards a cultural optics of the cinematic apparatus, in A. Gaudreault, C. Russell and P. Véronneau (eds) *The Cinema: A New Technology for the 20th Century*, Lausanne: Editions Payot, pp. 31–44.

Harvey, D. (1989) *The Condition of Postmodernity*, Oxford: Blackwell.

Herbst, C. (2008) Programming violence: language and the making of interactive media, in Jahn-Sudmann and Stockmann (eds), *Computer Games as a Sociocultural Phenomenon*, pp. 69–77.

Hesmondhalgh, D. and Baker, S. (2010) A very complicated version of freedom: conditions and experiences of creative labour in three cultural industries, *Poetics*, 38: 4–20.

Horkheimer, M. and Adorno, T. W. (2000 [1944]) *Dialectic of Enlightenment*, New York: Continuum Publishing.

Jahn-Sudmann, A. and Stockmann, R. (eds) (2008) *Computer Games as a Sociocultural Phenomenon*, Basingstoke: Palgrave Macmillan.

Johnson, J. (2011) 1 Million Workers, 90 Million, i-phones, 17 suicides. Who's to blame? *Wired Magazine*, http://www.wired.com/magazine/2011/02/ff_joelinchina/all/1.

Kerr, A. (2010) *The Business and Culture of Digital Games*, London: Sage.

Kline, S., Dyer-Witheford, N. and de Peuter, G. (2003) *Digital Play: The Interaction of Technology, Culture and Marketing*, Montreal: McGill Quarry University Press.

Leadbeater, C. (2008) *We-Think: The Power of Mass Creativity*, London: Profile Books.

Lee, Y.H. and Lin, H. (2011) 'Gaming is my work': identity work in internet-hobbyist game workers, *Work, Employment and Society*, 25(3): 451–67.

Livingstone, I. and Hope, A. (2011) *Next Gen. Transforming the UK into the World's Leading Talent Hub for the Video Games and Visual Effects Industries*, London: NESTA.
Lockwood, D. and Richards, T. (2008) Presence-play: the hauntology of the computer game, in Jahn-Sudmann and Stockmann (eds), *Computer Games as a Sociocultural Phenomenon*, pp. 175–85.
Marx, K. (1990 [1868]) *Capital*, Vol. 1, London: Penguin.
McAllister, K.S. (2004) *Game Work: Language, Power and Computer Game Culture*, Tucaloosa: University of Alabama Press.
McGonigal, J. (2011) *Reality Is Broken: Why Games Make Us Better and How They Can Change the World*, London: Jonathan Cape.
McRobbie, A. (2011a) Rethinking the creative economy as radical social enterprise, *Variant*, 41(1): 32–3.
McRobbie, A. (2011b) The Los Angelisation of London: three short-waves of young people's micro-economies of culture and creativity in the UK, in G. Raunig, G. Ray and U. Wuggenig (eds) *Critique of Creativity: Precarity, Subjectivity and Resistance in the 'Creative Industries'*, London: Mayfly Books, pp. 119–31.
MCV Survey (2012) Market for Computer and Video Games Salary Survey 2012, http://www.mcvuk.com/news/read/mcv-s-2012-uk-games-industry-salary-survey-the-results/089686.
Miller, V. (2011) *Understanding Digital Culture*, London: Sage.
Mills, C. W. (2000) *The Sociological Imagination*, Oxford: Oxford University Press.
Mulgan, G. (1998) *Connexity: How to Live in a Connected World*, Harvard: Harvard Business Review Press.
Peck, J. (2005) Struggling with the creative class, *International Journal of Urban and Regional Research*, 29(4): 740–70.
Poyhonen, P. and Wan, D.C.S. (2011) *Game Console and Music Production in China*, Finnwatch: SACOM & SOMO, http://www.makeitfair.org/en/.../game-console-and-music-production-in-china.
Rentfrow, D. (2008) S(t)imulating war: from early films to military games, in Jahn-Sudmann and Stockmann (eds), *Computer Games as a Sociocultural Phenomenon*, pp. 87–96.
Rundle, M. (2012) 300 Chinese Foxconn workers 'threaten mass suicide' at Xbox Plant, reports claim, *Huffpost Tech*, http://www.huffingtonpost.co.uk/2012/01/10/300-chinese-foxconn-workers-threaten-mass-suicide_n_1196345.html.
Warner, M. (2006) *Phantasmagoria*, Oxford: Oxford University Press.

10
The Brief History, Tumultuous Present and Uncertain Future of Virtual Worlds (*Terrae Fabricatae*)

Jordi Comas and Feichin (Ted) Tschang

Introduction

One fact dominates the brief history of virtual worlds (VWs) and the explosion in numbers of worlds, their users and possible activities. VWs owe their existence to the uneasy admixture of video games and emerging social media (Damer, 2008). The overlap of these two phenomena in VWs forms a watershed for cyberspaces, which are computer-mediated spaces of human socio-economic activity. On one side are the cyberspaces of the web: two-dimensional spaces organized by text or image and user with a hyperlink geography. On the other side are VWs, described by Lessig (2006) as spaces that pull you in, in part because of their three-dimensional spatial nature. Bell (2008: 2) fleshes out the feeling of being there, suggesting that virtual worlds are 'a synchronous, persistent network of people, represented as avatars, facilitated by networked computers'. We agree with the focus on the network as the seed of a feeling of presence for multiple users. Without a more complete definition of these networks as worlds, Bell's definition of a network of avatars describes many other kinds of cyberspaces and is too broad to capture the particular qualities of VWs. We therefore extend his definition: a virtual world is the network of avatars, creating co-presence, along with the virtually spatial and concrete qualities of a world. VWs are about people, but also about objects, places, and organizations. They are synthetic and fabricated and one day we will perhaps refer to them as *terrae fabricatae* alongside, and on equal terms with, *terra firma*.[1] A cyberspace without this materiality of place and object is a different kind of cyberspace, one whose interactivity has fewer dimensions.

VWs are growing in numbers, type and in the level of activity afforded in them. In 2007, Gartner Industries predicted that

186

80 per cent of Internet users would have an avatar (Gartner, 2007). This suggests an explosive growth, and the rate and range of users and uses is important to track. Like many newer digital technologies, venture capital cultivated a base of programming experts and entrepreneurs. According to an industry source (virtualworldnews.com, now defunct), a total of $184 million was invested in 23 VW-related companies in the first quarter of 2008, $425 million invested in 15 companies in the fourth quarter of 2007 and $1 billion invested in 35 companies from October 2006 to October 2007. In addition to this investment activity, there were, according to Spence (2008), more than 120 worlds, of which he classified 41 as true VWs and another 50 as non-game applications with VW-like elements (for instance, IMVU or Instant Messaging Virtual Universe, which is a socializing application but without the full 3D spatial immersion afforded by most other applications). By 2011, this growth had accelerated, reaching 300 VWs in 2010, with an estimate of 500 for 2011 (KZero, 2011).

Apart from the overall number of VWs, it is useful to look at the intensity and range of uses. One rough measure is the number of registered users. Spence (2008) found around 300 million users in the 90 worlds he recorded in 2008. A recent industry report estimated 650 million users over 15 years old in game and open-use worlds and an almost equal number in worlds targeting younger children. Registered accounts provide a rough measure. Intensity may be better seen in user inputs or contributions, although these are harder metrics to build reliably. In 2008 *Second Life*, an early pioneer, had approximately one million active users spending 90 million hours and $84 million in user to user transactions per month. Although Linden Lab (*Virtual Worlds*, 2012) reports 30 million registered avatars as of 2011, early interviews with CEO Philip Rosedale provided a rule of thumb that 10 per cent of users came back after one month, leading to reports of 250,000 users in 2007. Still, in 2008, there were between 50,000 and 100,000 concurrent users at any given time. The overall VW economy had grown to $2 billion by 2010 and could grow to $6 billion including subscriptions, virtual goods, and related services such as server usage and third party content or service providers (KZero, 2011). The growth of VWs can be attributed to newer platforms such as mobile or tablet devices as well as to integration into existing digital infrastructures. *YoVille*, for example, which was launched in 2010, and is only accessible through the social networking utility Facebook, grew faster than even the fastest growing youth-oriented VWs. Meanwhile, many firms, after initial experimentation with open worlds (worlds that are open to the public of the general Internet), have begun to experiment with worlds in a box, that is to say, a VW that they operate and that is sectioned off from the larger network.

VWs are worlds because they rely on the graphics and perception of geography, object and person. Moreover, all these worlds are distinct from other cyberspaces because they exhibit both the asynchronous persistence of the world with the synchronous co-presence of users. However, not all worlds are the same. VWs include both massively multiplayer online games (MMOG) as well as open worlds. Game and open (or sandbox) worlds are related but distinct phenomena. In order to understand their relationship, we look to three dimensions: their technological features, the intention of their design and the evolution of their usage. Game and open worlds share the most commonalities in this order: technology, usage and design intent. Technologically they are nearly indistinguishable. Their usage similarity varies and is partially determined by how they are adapted to over time by users and communities of users (Taylor, 1999). They are most distinct in design intent. Game worlds are designed to be formal games. *World of Warcraft* is an archetype. Open-use worlds are designed for multiple possible purposes. *Second Life* is an archetype. While this difference matters, overall game and open worlds are similar and are linked in many dynamic ways. We therefore argue that they should all be considered as virtual worlds when compared to other cyberspaces, information and communication technologies (ICTs), and the broader mediascape.

With the growth and distinctiveness of VWs established, this chapter addresses a range of questions to map out the short history, tumultuous present and uncertain future of VWs. More specifically we will delineate the origin of virtual worlds, their emergence from existing technologies and how they might be defined in terms of technology and usage. We will then discuss the current state of VWs and present a model of the creation (genesis) and sustenance (cultivation) of VWs in terms of five inter-related factors, namely: platform, policies, individuals, communities of people and the places and objects of the world. Finally, we will discuss future directions of VWs. The future of VWs will be shaped by their peculiar institutional status. We will argue that the field of VWs is shaped by three different logics. These logics point to several possible outcomes for the field including a greater metaverse of linked worlds, a balkanization of separate worlds, or a collapse of these worlds.

A brief history of virtual worlds

What is a virtual world?

VWs are not un-real worlds. Rather, their reality is one that is the result of computing technologies and their co-evolution with usage by people individually or in aggregate. If a VW is not simply an application or a piece of software, how are we to define it? One place to begin is with the familiar idea of the magic circle which separates playful spaces from everyday life (Huizinga, 1950 [1938]). VWs have always been built with all types of bridges and portals to the real world. Hence, we find a theoretical definition that depends on their stark separation from the real world inaccurate. At the same time, the sense of experienced place is very real and relevant (Boellstorff, 2008). However, it derives from what happens in the virtual world as opposed to the permeability of the border or boundary of this world as one kind of social space from all the other natural or fabricated ones that abound across human societies.

However, while there is a sense of place one experiences when using an avatar to navigate a VW, there are, we argue, three interlocking dimensions that define virtual worlds while also distinguishing them from other kinds of cyberspaces or virtual communities (Rheingold 1991; 2000). This set of dimensions grows from theories of adaptive structuration that resist technological and social determinism of technology use and instead posit a dualistic approach (Orlikowski, 1992; DeSanctis and Poole, 1994). A bulletin board or a blog may be virtual communities, but they are not virtual worlds unless we dilute the meaning of the term virtual world to the point where it is no longer useful. The three dimensions (3Is) are immersion, identity and interaction.

Immersion. This relates to feeling aware of the world as an interactive space other than the one the user is in. Immersion is created through the combination of a sense of place, of body and of others (Lanier, 2001). The degree of immersion has been an increasingly important factor in the evolution of games and now VWs, due to enhanced graphical abilities and photo-realism. Graphical richness is associated with immersion. In computer games, this traces back to products like *Wing Commander* in the mid-1990s, when cinematics and 3D were argued to have transformed the use of the medium.

Identity. The personification of users as avatars online leads to the issue of identity and the associated question of whether the user is representing his or her real self, a facsimile or a fabrication. The notion that avatars are a real or artificial projection of some durable, essential self is a false choice. An individual's identity is socially constructed, and is variably coupled to other identities including real-world identities. Further, the very essence of the social basis of the virtual world leads to the conclusion that any world that seems real to users is one populated with identities (Boellstorff, 2008). Ondrejka terms this pseudonymity in order to capture both the identity's realness as well as its dis-articulation from real-world identity (Ondrejka, 2007). While identity exists in VWs as it does in real worlds, and is just as socially constructed, users have much more direct control over the parameters of this construction (Berger and Luckman, 1967). They can also control the coupling or overlap between real world and VW identities. In other words, in a VW you can choose your appearance, even if you cannot choose exactly how your appearance will shape other users' perception of you. You can also choose whether or not to allow others to know your other identities in the real world. We would not argue against the idea that real world identities may be loosely coupled (who I am at work and at church may be different), rather we argue that it is much easier to maintain a distinctly decoupled (self-contained) identity in a virtual world, as well as to maintain a multiplicity of them in the virtual world due to the relatively decoupled nature of these identities. People may indeed have alternative avatars to distinguish work and leisure. The virtual world consultancy KZero (2011) reports that average accounts per user climbed to almost two before falling from 2003 to 2008, suggesting that many users had two or more avatars.

Interaction.   VWs are always on, meaning that their persistent (if not for all practical purposes perpetual) existence is a rich platform for many types of interaction. We have modified Bartle's (1996) typology of roles to account for how interactions are played out within and across VWs and the real world. Interacting takes many forms, including playing, socializing, collaborating and transacting. More types may yet emerge given the open-endedness of VWs. In general, as the bridges and portals between virtual and real worlds increase and are easier to traverse, the range of interactions and the possible importance of them in terms of consequences will increase. In short, rather than seeing a fusion of real and virtual worlds, the boundary will increase in importance because of its porosity. We suspect that real and virtual worlds will both be more distinct, or in the case of virtual worlds, immersive which will in turn make the interactions richer and fuller along many dimensions including economic ones.

The three dimensions work together to make a virtual world come to life in the sense of crossing a fuzzy threshold from possibility to a tangibly real space that matters to users and that has dynamics similar in complexity to any other human society or community. As we illustrate in Figure 10.1, the three dimensions are necessary and sufficient for a VW to come into being as a world, but not necessarily to be sustainable over time. Immersion promotes identity construction and immersion facilitates interactivity. Meanwhile, identity mediates any type of in-world interactions. Hence, the degree of immersion directly affects interactivity and indirectly affects interactivity through promoting identity. It should be noted that while other frameworks also focus on identities and presence (via avatars), they do not include interactivity (Schultze and Orlikowski, 2010). This may be because they were formed in order to explain change in VWs, as opposed to our intent which is to explain use and usability of the VW and variation across VWs.

To demonstrate how the 3Is can be used, we will compare them to two of the most visible cyberspaces which are not worlds according to the framework. Twitter and Facebook are certainly interactive cyberspaces that are deeply social. However, they are not virtual worlds. These two leaders in social media do not provide any sense of physical immersion, are less interactive than VWs (Twitter is typically a one-way communication, Facebook is typically asynchronous or synchronized), and typically reinforce a tight coupling of the identity in the virtual space with

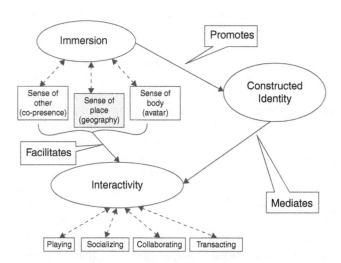

Figure 10.1 The 3Is – three dimensions that make a virtual world come to life

the user's real-world identity. Their greatest value to users comes from linking cyberspaces to the real world as opposed to VWs whose value comes in their protection or walling off from the real world.

With this definition of what a VW is, we can turn to a brief overview of how they came to be and their tumultuous present.

Virtual reality as a dream

Virtual reality has long been a topic of keen interest to many, including engineers, programmers, artists and cultural critics. One of the first significant cultural instances of an avatar-based virtual reality is Neal Stephenson's *Snow Crash* (1992), although this was predated by other works of cyberpunk, including William Gibson's *Neuromancer* (1984). This deeper-rooted and older history of fascination and even obsession with a virtual reality matters because the cultural ideas and viewpoints with which we perceive and respond to virtual worlds (and by which they were developed) are coloured and shaped by these more diffuse and broader ideas of the dream (and possible nightmare) of a virtual reality. In this instance, reality does imitate art. A case in point is the observation often made by the developers of *Second Life* that they were inspired, and indeed working towards, a metaverse described in the early cyberspace novel *Snow Crash* (Au, 2008).

While these developments were underway, researchers in universities and elsewhere were attempting to create virtual realities through other means. Castronova (2005) provides an overview of the attempts to create a sensory virtual reality using sensory input hardware in the 1980s and 1990s. These often lab-based academic efforts focused on recreating the sensory inputs of the real world for virtual environments via virtual reality means – for instance through a motley crew of helmets, gloves and goggles meant to fool our senses into creating a sense of immersion.

While those technologies certainly provide excitement and even entertainment value, there is a simpler, more human way to create immersion in virtual worlds. Game developers and then the virtual world creators and innovators discovered for themselves that the sociability inherent in sharing virtual spaces with others was by itself enough to spark off a feeling of immersion (Castronova, 2005). Again, the first of these efforts was university-based and leading these efforts was the first multi-user domain (MUD) or dungeon, created by Roy Trubshaw in 1978 and further developed by Richard Bartle in 1980, both computing students at the University of Essex. This was the forerunner of most modern online spaces, where users would inhabit spaces defined by linguistic information, such as rooms, and interact within them.

Morningstar and Farmer (1991: 273), reflecting on the early 2D social world, *Habitat*, found that 'the essential lesson we have abstracted from our experiences with *Habitat* is that a cyberspace is defined more by the interactions among the actors within it than by the technology with which it is implemented'. Turkle's (1995) groundbreaking ethnographic work on MUDs established that identity and community were formed via the simplest of interfaces: text on a screen. Hence, as discussed below, the genesis of the world as a real, lived-in, space is due not to technology but to the context for interaction the technology affords or enables.

This early work documenting the role of interaction in early VWs indicates that the VWs we find today stem from a set of parallel and overlapping technological spaces. We can view these applications as each contributing a type of cyberspace to the toolkit that would eventually be available for the creation of VWs. Four types of applications, each associated with a type of cyberspace, developed in particular and partially overlapping ways.

First were the applications creating information spaces, involving communication, informating as well as the storage and retrieval of information. These applications are the foundation of the other spaces because without the ability to store and retrieve information across networks, the other spaces would not exist. Information spaces do support play and socializing types of interaction, for instance via chat, discussion forums, and in the case of virtual worlds, informing avatars via note cards. Perhaps least recognized is that these information spaces have been essential to collaboration on the Web. For instance, knowledge management systems all involve some information creation, codification, storage and transfer.

Second, exchange spaces allowed for economies to emerge. While virtual goods economies were probably first extensively studied in MMO worlds such as *Everquest* by scholars including Castronova (2001), most open virtual worlds that had to be commercially viable have had to incorporate some kind of storage facility. Almost universally, virtual worlds now have an economy that runs the generation and consumption of content – what we term transactive types of interaction. However, the forms of commerce found in VWs include a broader range of exchange activities than just e-commerce, namely users' exchange of digital objects, expertise, emotion and status. This richer set of exchanges blurs the public and private arenas of exchange interaction in VWs. In all, we see the same range of exchanges across economic and social activities as we see in real worlds.

The third set of applications, those of social or networked spaces, started with early bulletin boards, followed by the Usenet groups (Castells, 2001). These were really communities of practice (Wenger, 1998) oriented around topics rather than projects. As the Internet-based applications matured, general users gravitated to social interactive means such as chat (for instance MSN), social networking sites (first Friendster, then Facebook), while the hyperlinked Web itself remained primarily as an information space.

The fourth set of applications, interactive spaces, specifically involves play (in the case of MMOs) and collaboration (in the case of open-use VWs). These applications initially involved the influence of MUDs in creating imagined spaces that were actively used for (largely avatar-based or token-based) playing and other forms of interaction. In addition, there were early open-use worlds establishing many of the practices of avatars and cyber-sociality we see today, such as *Alphaville*, later *Active Worlds* (Damer, 2008). The advent of 3D games also provided an impetus to early online games such as *Ultima*, Asheron's *Call* and *Everquest* (predated by the earlier online games). The dominant forms of application were top-down, centrally controlled systems. The present incarnation of these spaces in VWs like *Second Life* are more emergent and based on bottom-up rule-making. For example, a 3D game provides all the rules of play and content to users for a price. However, there is also a subaltern history of gamer response and community formation to games. This degree of interactivity around the rules of the games and content took the form of modding – or game modifications – that were shared and discussed on websites of varying degrees of formality and official sanctioning (Scacchi, 2010). VWs mark a new moment in the balance of top-down versus bottom-up design and control of interactive applications. Many MMOs have explicitly adopted modding and other user-generated content (UGC) practices that have always been commonplace in games production, if typically viewed with unease by gaming companies. Likewise, selected VWs like *Second Life* fully embrace the bottom-up nature of UGC. These patterns have been reinforced by the broader creation and elaboration of social media (Levine *et al.*, 2000; Bruns, 2008; Shirky, 2008).

Tumultuous present: genesis and cultivation of VWs

The four kinds of cyberspaces discussed in the previous section of this chapter are necessary for VWs to contain the technological affordances of the 3Is: immersion, interaction, and identity. They are prerequisites for, but not determinants of the creation and sustainability of VWs. The elements still have to come together in a design or a platform, usually by a for-profit company, or, in some cases an open source community or other collaborative form. We suggest that since we are discussing worlds, we can think of the birth and growth of VWs as two stages: genesis and cultivation. The companies or organizations that build the worlds, and the users who populate them, play their roles singly and in concert in these stages.

In this section, we discuss a stylized model of genesis and cultivation. This is based on on-going qualitative research in the field of VWs and more in-depth participant-observer research in *Second Life, Habbo Hotel, Guild Wars, Entropia Online, Metaplace, Vastpark* and *Tirnua*. The model has five factors, among them technological, social and managerial factors that are essential to the genesis and cultivation of VWs. It differs from the model discussed by Messinger *et al.* (2008) by adding the factors that are under more direct control of designers or managers or, in the case of individuals and populations, the objects of their interest. More specifically, the factors are the policies of the VW; the platform of the VW; the particular individuals (be they users or players); the population of the VW, organized into various types of communities and groups and the objects and places of the world, its virtual materiality.

The model is depicted in Figure 10.2 and in Figure 10.3 in the next section. In Figure 10.2, we see policies and platform, the two factors most clearly under the control of world builders (such as designers and owners). However, the policies and platforms will not create a world. The interesting feature of VWs is that their actual genesis as recognizable worlds depends on the dense interactions among the other three factors. These create the economic and social systems rich enough to foster the ongoing dynamic between interaction, immersion and constructed identity. Beyond genesis, the cultivation of a robust and growing world will continue to depend on the platform and the policy.

Worlds are only partially malleable by designers, a term that covers the individuals, companies or other collectivities that create and manage a VW. The intent of designers is evident in the platform and the policies. However, the actual realization of a given VW is the result of complex trade-offs and adaptations between the designer, the user and the capabilities of the technology itself. Platform, for example, includes the balancing between design intent and user-defined experience that keeps users engaged. Meanwhile, policies include a variety of ways to implement and enforce rules and other constraints on the individual users and the user population as a whole. Policies may be

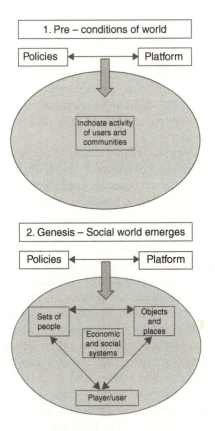

Figure 10.2   Genesis of worlds

regulatory or institutional, and refer to designation or self-designation of community managers to monitor communities, garner feedback, or even enforce.

Genesis of worlds

How do worlds appear? First, the policies and platform must create a context for the interactions among people, individuals and objects. Contrary to what one might expect, the user-created virtual world does not start as a blank canvas. Linden Lab's experience and recent VW designs both indicate the importance attached to the design features and policies, especially at early stages, as these have a powerful influence in determining the experience of the world. World building starts with both the designed elements of the worlds as well as the policies that signal to potential or early world users what to do with the world. Platform design issues include deciding whether and how the VW platform's architecture supports community formation, such as the group management and communication modes amongst group members that *Second Life* provides. A contrasting example to this was Google's attempt to develop a virtual world with *Lively* – there was little content, no sense of a (virtual) world to explore, and few features to promote interaction, leaving users with very little to do beyond socializing with strangers (possibly because the community had not yet formed). Generally, the more mature VWs have been quite successful at creating, then sustaining a play community, often through the beta phase when early residents of the world begin creating a web of relationships, or take on leadership roles (for discussion of an earlier world, *Activeworld*, see Schroeder *et al.*, 2001).

Social interaction is also designed into the platform. For example, the use of persistent and visible avatar names in VWs fosters a greater sense of pseudonymous identity in a VW than in the cyberspaces that allow more anonymity. *Second Life* features in its platform tools to build profiles, much like the profiles used in various social media applications, tools to manage groups and various communication channels for dyadic or group real time or delayed communication.

Design features can also include the regulatory policies that the programme's designers put in place to ensure or deny certain forms of play or interaction, both between players (as a community) and between players and the world. These rules could be as detailed as the nature of a currency's means of exchange with other currencies or goods, the nature of transactions of goods, the types of challenge offered, the choices allowed to users and so on (Bartle, 1996). For example, without policy changes *Second Life* would not have created the positive incentive for would-be creators to create content (Au, 2008). The specific policies that Linden Lab put in place in its redesign of *Second Life* were the following: it ended monthly subscriptions and using monthly land use fees for virtual land; it allowed for exchange between the official in-world currency and real money; and it recognized residents' intellectual property rights over the content they created.

These features greatly increased *Second Life's* appeal to would-be content creators and their consumers alike: they 'spurred the growth of a substantial mercantile class (e.g. artisans, entertainers, shopkeepers, weaponsmiths)' (Rymaszewski *et al.*, 2007: 316). The resulting range and richness of types of places and other content was quite dramatic.

That these rules can matter so much to the type of world to be created, or that a community would find them so influential, in either an enabling or regulating and intrusive way, offers food for thought and leaves much to do for virtual world designers. *The Sims Online*, the MMO variation of Maxis's highly popular PC game *The Sims*, seemed to have several advantages on its side, including a very well-known brand and a studio backing it. *The Sims Online*, despite having the huge advantage of a widely regarded brand identity, folded in part due to its corporate owner, Maxis, resisting the native uses of the world its residents developed (Ludlow and Wallace, 2007). The game world *Uru* also folded, but as Pearce (2006, 2009) has documented, the diaspora of its users influenced other worlds like *There.com* and *Second Life*. This suggests that the notion that virtual worlds are user-created is partly a myth. To this end, VWs have to operate like computer games, whose designs embody many of the same considerations (Salen and Zimmerman, 2003). Platforms and policies need to enable users to activate rules or to operate by norms and regulations, in order to have pleasant experiences. Any examples of users exhibiting socially negative behaviours indicate a need for social regulation.

Once the context has been created by platform and policies, the interactions amongst the other three factors come into play. This is depicted in the second step in Figure 10.2. Players, people and the world can now interact autochthonously, that is within the world itself. The emergence of economies within VWs illustrates the autochthonous nature of the interactions. In, arguably, the first visually oriented 2D open-use virtual world (predating most online games), Lucas Art's *Habitat* (1986–88) possessed a content economy of sorts, where users could purchase items for adorning their avatars and homes, and where a strongly interactive, social world was offered, albeit one that was highly emergent (Morningstar and Farmer, 1991). Castronova's (2001) initial study of VWs was grounded in his experience with the game world *Everquest*. His focus on the economics of virtual worlds brought much needed academic attention to the topic. As it turns out, real economies are necessary for the internal dynamics of a virtual world to work; worlds without economies do not fare well (Castronova, 2005).

Economies are even more important for the open-use worlds, whether they are purely user-generated or not. Gaming VWs are designed by the development team, and the only creative dimensions that users are allowed to play with are those of personalization (of an avatar or one's virtual gear), acquisition (of game world objects that have power and other properties) and organizational formation (such as guilds). Attempts to create worlds without a system of evaluating objects in that world, of aggregating information on the value of them, fail to generate enough activity to form a living, robust world. The economy may be very simple, or may operate differently from real world economies; however, certain key functions such as the assigning of property and currencies must be enabled to create ways to value and mutually evaluate objects in the VW (Castronova, 2005). Even more importantly, designers discovered that a means for enabling the generation and propagation of content is essential (Tschang and Comas 2010). The economy may or may not be formally linked to the real world economy. In fact, it seems to be the case that bridges between virtual and real world economies will occur, whether the controllers of a VW want it or not (Taylor, 2009). Most gaming VWs invest resources in trying to protect their internal economies, often unsuccessfully (Dibbell, 2006). Other gaming VWs such as *Entropia* and *Metaverse* (prior to its closure) embraced or sought to embrace the conversion of currencies; playing those games is often a matter of purchasing virtual currency directly with real world currency.

The advancement of virtual worlds to include avatars and other forms of content spawned a desire for forms of interaction or well-being in the synthetic materiality of the world. This seems the basis for the emergence of parallel social systems centered on status and identity instead of exchange value. As with any human society, the psychological, social and economic are deeply entwined. A good point to start describing this social system is the individual user or player.

All virtual worlds, including the user-created and massively multiplayer online role playing games (MMORPG) varieties, have been predicated on social forms of play. The individual players and the relationships between players and types of players are the fundamental building blocks of the community. The individual players may be content creators, sellers or buyers, but they all play some roles. In this fashion, individual play is contextualized by the social setting of the VW. This social interaction includes activities like participation in communities, or the meeting of game-like challenges as a group. Communities can be organized by interests or subcultures, by functional relationships (buyers and sellers), by activities (a building project) and by relationships (friends or a social network), amongst other dimensions. The *Second Life* community, for instance, is defined as 'the intersection of numerous smaller communities, many of which intersect, but others not at all' and is 'formed primarily around personal interests' (Au, 2008: 174).

Bartle's (1996) earlier work on player types in role-playing games, in which he described socializers, achievers, explorers and dominators, establishes the general point that any world will have an ecosystem of player or user roles. We have seen these types vary across virtual worlds. While residents of *Second Life* engaged in many of the categories of play described by Bartle (1996), additional categories of interaction could be observed in studies of *Second Life*, including those seeking experiences (such as role-playing and alternative lifestyles). Psychological studies by Yee (2009) suggest that slight variations of this typology better fit MMORPGs. The first variation relates to creating where creating is a broader category than achieving, which has a game-like connotation. Players are interested in creating or building content, activities (for instance games), communities and organizations and even identities and avatars. In creating content, for example, these creators contextualize a playing space for others who wish to explore, socialize, transact (content) and otherwise interact. For instance, fashionistas buy, wear and collect content related to clothing or avatar appearance. Generally, these virtual objects provide players with the power to make an impression on the world, as well as to get a feel for the world. A second type is living – quite literally, simply passing time. Linden Lab itself calls this 'inhabiting' while the players call themselves 'residents' – as a keen observer noted of the first *Second Life* users: 'they immediately started building – homes!' (Au, 2008: 57).

As VWs and their users have evolved, a newer form of play may be emerging. This is one seen, for example, in *Second Life*, where many players delighted in becoming something other than what they were in real life: dressing as animal avatars, they turned themselves into 'furries', or they dressed differently to shock, or adopted an avatar from the opposite sex. This may be a kind of role-play or identity play, to add to the other archetypes Bartle (1996) discovered. Identity play is marked by the interest in developing and crafting a particular differentiated identity. Again, businesses arose to service the needs of these subcultures. In contrast to identity play, traditional MMORPGs' overriding focus has been on role-playing (activities like socializing and achieving are subsumed to role playing), while in other user-created VWs such as *There* and *Habbo.com*, the play is more about socializing. In identity play, the identity is the focus of play, and not simply a context for other playful activity. Nevertheless, the general point is that, regardless of the world, players are engaged in interacting with one another in an ecosystem of player types.

While games like MMORPGs organize players into pre-set social structures such as groups and guilds, social structure in user-created worlds is even more emergent. Open-use worlds, from the early *Alphaville* to the *OpenSim* worlds to *Second Life*, appear to have generated a wide variety of playing communities due to the design features used. One can set up an island to engage players in literally any form of play. While the founding members of the community can have an initial undue influence, later members can also change the island's makeup.

While it is commonly considered by developers and observers alike that communities are at the heart of VWs, in reality, both the player as individual and the people as community are core to the sustainability of a VW (Morningstar and Farmer, 1991). Communities aggregate players and their relationships. In a mutually dependent fashion, the player engages in the type of play as defined by the community, namely a role. While players can play in a vacuum, much as in a single-person computer game, in social play, the social experience – bonding, status seeking and recognition – is the core of the experience. Thus, the community cannot really be disentangled from the player, and indeed, is mutually dependent on the player.

Cultivating the world: platform and policies *redux*

Once a world has had a genesis moment the sustainability of the VW as a vital and viable cyberspace depends on the design parameters of policies and platform once again (noting that policies can also be enacted by people, namely, responsible community members). This stage and the return to the importance of policies and platform are shown in Figure 10.3. The key difference now is that policies and platforms co-evolve with the dynamics within the world.

The initial stage of the world, genesis, creates value of some kind. In other words, the dynamics of the world become valuable to users and communities of users. This value creation is evident in the rise of various indigenous, or dig-indigenous (a neologism we use to mean originating in the digital realm) success stories in VWs. These are stories of some value being realized, whether or not it is a monetized value. For example, *Tringo* is a game originally designed within *Second Life*. Highly popular for its playability and among land owners for bringing foot traffic, the game was later licensed to a real world gaming company and has been available since 2007. Another high-profile success story is that of the first real world millionaire in *Second Life*, Anshe Chung, who featured on the cover of *Businessweek* and who made her

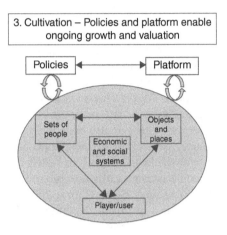

Figure 10.3   Cultivation of a VW

money as a virtual land developer (Hof, 2006). Meanwhile, less visible, but perhaps as significant, has been the deep engagement of academics and librarians with *Second Life*, evident for example in the activity of many virtual campuses as well as consortia such as the New Media Consortium (see http://sl.nmc.org/) or the *Second Life* Educator's Wiki (see http://wiki.secondlife.com/wiki/SLED).

Can these successes be cultivated into on-going value creation and revenue generation? This is an open question for specific VWs and for the field as a whole. Some initial evidence from these success stories and the corporate pioneers they inspired provide insight into the complexities of cultivating VWs.

VW operators have learnt that even sustaining a community requires fine-tuning the interactions of different types of players. This is more complex than a first glance may suggest and hence policies have to protect different types of users without turning off others. Faced with individual, social and economic activities such as Ponzi banking schemes and gambling that were socially abhorrent to players or potential players, *Linden Lab* had to step in to regulate or even impose bans (Riley, no date; Konrad, 2007). On the other hand, in regulating the play of so-called griefers, Electronic Arts reportedly imposed more management constraints on *The Sims Online* than was deemed necessary by some players (Ludlow and Wallace, 2007).

An illustration of the on-going co-evolution of the world and policies and platform comes from the practice of building or creating in UGC worlds like *Second Life* and the now defunct *Metaplace*. Malaby (2009), in an ethnography of *Linden Lab*, describes how building itself became a kind of playful activity and one mediated and governed by the expectations of the software and of the other users. This matches our own observations of so-called sand boxes in *Second Life*. Sand boxes are areas that certain land owners make open to building by anyone. They are literal and figurative well-springs of creation and creativity. In the ones we observed, norms and other formal rules governed the social system. For example, the land owner had volunteer moderators to enforce rules about how much one could build and other cleaning up issues. Users self-regulated in two ways. First, there was a very positive, encouraging atmosphere of helping and sharing building tips as well as simple objects. Second, users would observe from an avatar's position and graphics if he or she were in the midst of building and would be less likely to interrupt in those times. Hence the overall feel of a busy workshop was maintained by this mix of formal and normative rules.

In general, many VWs rely substantially on their community practice, engaging community managers early on, at times even in the beta testing stage, and into the operational phase, where such managers also gather feedback in addition to enforcing rules. Some of the newer VW companies like Metaplace and Tirnua are even more proactive in using communities to help gather feedback on the development of micro level design parameters for their worlds. Communities also play a big part in shaping and governing the world as it unfolds in its operational phase. This is undertaken through codes of conduct and rules of play (often created by so-called community leaders) to regulate players' play and other interactions. For instance, island owners often take it upon themselves to ban users or to enforce their actions (Comas and Tschang, 2010). Some *Second Life* island owners face a continual arms race to ban griefers or restrict their actions (for instance by disabling the use of scripts). In all, this helps players to detach from, return to and re-engage with the community, and it helps to create a persistent world.

The role of all five factors in VWs matters. For designers or pioneers in these new worlds, this can be an important lesson. For example, many of the corporations that arrived in VWs between 2008 and 2010 were attracted to the interaction possibilities, to marketing or other new ways to engage with customers. As projections of 80 per cent of internet users soon having their avatar were published (Gartner, 2007), the *terrae fabricatae* were deluged with new users and entrants to their spaces. Many companies flooded VWs, especially *Second Life*, seeking to establish themselves in what they hoped might be the next big thing. One side effect was that the growth of an ancillary industry of VW designers and builders was spurred. However, many of these efforts disappointed their owners and sponsors. By 2012, many had pulled out of VWs or scaled back their activities.

One of the reasons why these corporate pioneers failed to realize their goals is the failure to understand the interactive, transactive nature of the worlds. They tended to see the VW as a unidirectional media channel. This lack of understanding led to further problems such as poor design of virtual spaces or ignoring the local perspectives or attitudes towards the importance of the sharing, making and authenticity of content and experiences. There is a tension between the play orientation of users and the commercial objectives of corporations that may be coming online to exploit profit opportunities. Given that the trajectory for VWs, as we have described in this chapter, is towards more portals and bridges across the magic circle dividing the real world and virtual worlds, we still recognize that real-world businesses worry in general about only a few major issues, including value creation, value capture and cost reductions; the impact of engagement with a VW on the brand; and security, whether their internal information may be hurt by leakage or other means.

There is still the problem of generating revenue to support and sustain the VW. Worlds like *The Sims Online* and *There.com* suffered limitations in their own way, and even *Second Life* has seen growth plateau. Generally, VWs such as MMORPGs can be measured by the number of active users who actually pay and/or log in regularly to do play and thus pay in some other way. However, user-created VWs are a more open environment, and many users also engage in casual (light), non-paying but nonetheless valid play, such as socializing. Despite enabling user creation to the highest level yet seen, *Second Life* has had good but still not great success at securing revenue from players, and Linden Lab has had to change its business model at least three times, while most of the time seeking to tap the interests of real-world businesses. The lack of success of earlier worlds like *Active Worlds* and even of more recent ones like *There* and *The Sims Online* has been due not only to their limited ability to engage users, but also their operators' inability to develop a sufficient base of paying players or find a viable alternative revenue source to attract enough paying players.

Furthermore, there is a wide diversity of work and play activity (and especially that of identity play) that a virtual world can encompass. VWs, as with computer and video games more generally, suffer from the sort of uncertainty that play causes, since the outcomes of play are highly performative (Malaby, 2006) and experiential in nature, that is to say we do not know what the variations of play or its outcomes are until we are playing or after we have played. Identity play also creates a problem for corporations who generally need to know the true identities and intentions of players, a concern brought up in our interviews with world owners. Businesses expecting to identify, count and otherwise measure users' actions in a quick and easy manner (like eyeballs on websites) have suffered disappointment. The inherent uncertainty of play creates tensions between different users and ultimately leads to community fragmentation. Each community engages in deep play within its own borders; this fragmentation may ultimately affect the appeal of this medium to a mass market of consumers. This will then be the antithesis of the borderless world the Web has become.

A last, major problem that dogs open-use VWs like *Second Life* is the emergence of socially unacceptable forms of play: the potential for extreme user behaviours such as griefing, taboo behaviours or individuals letting their virtual world activity harm real world relationships like an addiction.

The uncertain future: metaverse, cyberfeudalism or cataclysm?

Aside from the sheer novelty of VWs, the sense of uncertainty and turbulence around them can be explained as the result of being an institutional field with multiple logics (DiMaggio and Powell, 1991a, 1991b). With the creation of hundreds of new VWs, both game and open-use ones, with a variety of technological, operating and business models, we argue that we are observing the emergence of a new institutional field. Institutional theory states that field formation will move from a period of flux to one of greater stability where fewer organizational forms will come to be accepted as legitimate (Scott, 1995). The patterning of fields, when studied historically, is often explained as the result of institutional logics that reflect so-called master organizing principles of society (Thornton and Ocasio, 2008); as social constructions, they are perceived as externally legitimized by individuals even as they operate more directly at the level of people and interactions which shape and define appropriate or legitimate choices (Friedland and Alford, 1991).

The flux or turbulence in the field is observable in many ways. A few indicators include the lack of agreement on a term to describe the same phenomenon (virtual worlds, MMOs, synthetic worlds), the emergence of multiple professional associations jockeying to represent the industry, high numbers of start-ups as well as closures and the attention and engagement of actors from other fields including government, other industries and civil society.

The flux in the field is due to the influence of three institutional logics. Where there are multiple logics, there is more flux or turbulence as actors perpetually create and recreate the field. In this field, three logics that generate turbulence are a logic of profit, a logic of play and a logic of sharing. By analysing the mechanisms or processes that structure interactions in the field, we found that each was the unique reflection or expression of three distinct intuitional logics. In their most ideal-type form, each logic defines legitimate ends: a logic of profit is about instrumental, measurable ends; a logic of play is about enabling unmediated culture, intrinsic joy in activities, and engagement as its own end; a logic of sharing is about creating and maintaining common goods. The field is still too young to determine whether the multiple logics will persist or whether one will come to be dominant. However, based on prior research and theoretical logic (Thornton *et al.*, 2012), several outcomes are possible and merit the attention of institutional researchers as well as scholars of VWs. They include dominance of one logic over the others, co-optation of one logic by the others, persistence of multiple logics and partition of fields into new fields according to institutional logics. These trajectories, based on the differing institutional logics shaping the field, combined with changes in the technology, the business models and the governing mechanisms of VWs, set the stage for three possible outcomes. We think it is too early to ascertain the most likely outcome, but at least we can sketch out each one.

First is the metaverse, after the talismanic term coined by Stephenson (1992). This future would have multiple cyberspaces stitching together with each other as well as with the broader Internet. This would lead to a potentially seamless set of cyberspaces where users and organizations would connect, communicate, collaborate and compete in a common cyberspace. Clearly, such an outcome would depend on technological protocols and the political rule-setting to enable such a metaverse.

The opposite outcome would be a walling off or isolation of virtual worlds from each other. We call this cyberfeudalism, to capture the sense of isolation from unlinked and un-traversable worlds. This may accelerate a trend already underway of walling off the Internet's initial open architecture. Cyberfeudalism would create a set of virtual worlds closed to each other. While this may increase monetization opportunities for some companies, it would also possibly suppress the innovation possibility or open knowledge sharing that has been the basis of much IT innovation.

A third option is the collapse of virtual worlds as a distinct and viable type of cyberspace. In institutional theory this would be field collapse. For the creators and users of VWs, field collapse would be the cataclysm. It would be a fascinating outcome to observe and analyse, as collapsed institutional worlds are difficult to capture data on. In fact, one of us has already observed the collapse of one such world, *Metaplace*, as a participant-observer. On the day of the (virtual) world's end, it was not unlike a party commemorating an organizational collapse, combined with a sci-fi trope of a world collapsing and a mad dash of would-be survivors deciding what to do, where to go (the next world) and what to keep (taking photos of precious content and memories). While the world may end, its echo may not. Historical examples of strong effects after apparent failures suggest that we may find that the ideas, technologies or uses of VWs diffuse out of a collapsed field and affect other aspects of cyberspace or our networked era. Thus, even if the VWs as we have described them cease to be meaningful cyberspaces, the experiences they created for users and world designers will be the seeds for future creations of cyberspace.

In another case, the brief history of virtual worlds already offers one exemplar for the diffusion of VWs. Pearce (2009), in her study of a diaspora from the game world *Uru*, documents how those refugees from a world closed by its operators carried and germinated the seeds of engaging VWs into *There.com* and then *Second Life*. Likewise, the end of VWs may also be the beginning of new cyberspaces built from the debris of the old.

Note

1   While we are sympathetic to Castronova's term of 'synthetic worlds' because it avoids a suggestion of un-reality and emphasizes the fabricated nature of virtual worlds, we will use the more common term virtual worlds. *Terrae fabricatae* is the Latin translation of fabricated or synthetic worlds.

References

Au, W.J. (2008) *The Making of Second Life*, New York: HarperCollins.
Bartle, R.A. (1996) Players who suit MUDs, http://www.mud.co.uk/richard/hcds. htm. Bell, M.W. (2008) Toward a definition of 'virtual worlds', *Journal of Virtual Worlds Research*, 1(1), http://journals.tdl.org/jvwr/article/view/285.
Berger, P.L. and Luckman, T. (1967) *The Social Construction of Reality: A Treatise in the Sociology of Knowledge*, New York: Doubleday.
Boellstorff, T. (2008) *Coming of Age in Second Life: An Anthropologist Explores the Virtually Human*, Princeton: Princeton University Press.

208   *Changing the Rules of the Game*

Bruns, A. (2008) *Blogs, Wikipedia, Second Life, and Beyond: From Production to Produsage*, New York: Peter Lang.

Castells, M. (2001) *The Internet Galaxy: Reflections on the Internet, Business, and Society*, New York: Oxford University Press.

Castronova, E. (2001) *Virtual Worlds: A First-Hand Account of Market and Society on the Cyberian Frontier*, CESifo Working Paper Series No. 618 SSRN eLibrary, http://papers.ssrn.com/sol3/papers.cfm?abstract_id=294828.

Castronova, E. (2005) *Synthetic Worlds: The Business and Culture of Online Games*, Chicago: University of Chicago Press.

Castronova, E. (2007) *Exodus to the Virtual World: How Online Fun Is Changing Reality*, New York: Palgrave Macmillan.

Comas, J. and Tschang, F.T. (2010) Code rules: how multiple logics of playing, profiting, and sharing shape the field of virtual worlds, Paper presented at EGOS Conference 2010, Lisbon.

Damer, B. (2008) Meeting in the ether: a brief history of virtual worlds as a medium for user-created events, *Journal of Virtual Worlds Research*, 1(1), http://journals.tdl.org/jvwr/article/view/285.

DeSanctis, G. and Poole, M. S. (1994) Capturing the complexity in advanced technology use: adaptive structuration theory, *Organization Science*, 5(2): 121–47.

Dibbell, J. (2006) *Play Money, or How I Quit My Day Job and Made Millions Trading Virtual Loot*, New York: Basic Books.

DiMaggio, P. and Powell, W. (eds) (1991a) *The New Institutionalism in Organizational Analysis*, Chicago: University of Chicago Press.

DiMaggio, P. and Powell, W. (1991b) Introduction, in DiMaggio and Powell (eds), *The New Institutionalism*, pp. 1–38.

Friedland, R., and Alford, R.A. (1991) Bringing society back, in DiMaggio, P. and Powell, W. (eds), *The New Institutionalism*, pp. 232–63.

Gartner, Inc. (2007) Gartner says 80 per cent of active internet users will have a 'Second Life' in the virtual world by the end of 2011, http://www.gartner.com/it/page.jsp?id=503861.

Gibson, W. (1984) *Neuromancer*, New York: Ace Books.

Hof, R. (2006) *Second Life's* first millionaire, *Businessweek*, http://www.businessweek.com/the_thread/techbeat/archives/2006/11/second_lifes_fi.html.

Huizinga, J. (1950 [1938]) *Homo Ludens: A Study of the Play Element of Culture*, Boston, MA: Beacon Press.

Konrad, R. (2007) Second Life gambling ban angers virtual world, http://www.msnbc.msn.com/id/20077727/ns/technology_and_science-internet/t/second-life-gambling-ban-angers-virtual-world/.

KZero (2011) 2011 and beyond: key industry trends and market developments, www.kzero.com.

Lanier, J. (2001) Virtually there, *Scientific American*, 284(4): 52–61.

Lessig, L. (2006) *Code*, 2nd edition, New York: Basic Books.

Levine, R., Locke, C., Searls, D. and Weinberger, D. (2000) *The Cluetrain Manifesto: The End of Business as Usual*, Cambridge, MA: Perseus Books.

Ludlow, P. and Wallace, M. (2007) *Second Life Herald: The Virtual Tabloid that Witnessed the Dawn of the Metaverse*, Cambridge, MA: MIT Press.

Malaby, T. (2006) Coding control: governance and contingency in the production of online worlds, *First Monday*: Special Issue 7, http://firstmonday.org/issues/special11_9/malaby/index.html.

Malaby, T.M. (2009) *Making Virtual Worlds: Linden Lab and Second Life*, Ithaca: Cornell University Press.

Messinger, P.R., Stroulia, E. and Lyons, K. (2008) A typology of virtual worlds: historical overview and future directions, *Journal of Virtual Worlds Research* 1(1), http://journals.tdl.org/jvwr/article/view/285.

Morningstar, C. and Farmer, F.R. (1991) The lessons of Lucasfilms' habitat, in M. Benedikt (ed.), *Cyberspace: FirstSteps*, Cambridge, MA: MIT Press, pp. 273–301.

Ondrejka, C. (2007) Collapsing geography (second life, innovation, and the future of national power), *Innovations: Technology, Governance, Globalization*, 2(3): 27–54.

Orlikowski, W.J. (1992) The duality of technology: rethinking the concept of technology in organizations, *Organization Science*, 3(3): 398–427.

Pearce, C. (2006) Productive play: game culture from the bottom up, *Games and Culture*, 1: 17–24.

Pearce, C. (2009) *Communities of Play: Emergent Cultures in Multiplayer Games and Virtual Worlds*, Cambridge, MA: MIT Press.

Rheingold, H. (1992; 1991) *Virtual Reality*, New York: Touchstone (Simon & Schuster).

Rheingold, H. (2000) *The Virtual Community: Homesteading on the Electronic Frontier*, revised edition, Cambridge, MA: MIT Press.

Riley, D. (no date) Virtual banking banned in *SecondLife*, *TechCrunch*, http://techcrunch.com/2008/01/08/virtual-banking-banned-in-second-life/.

Rymaszewski, M., Au, J.W., Wallace, M., Winters, C., Ondrejka, C., Batstone-Cunningham, B. and Rosendale, P. (2007) *Second Life: The Official Guide*, Hoboken, NJ: John Wiley.

Salen, K. and Zimmerman, E. (2003) *Rules of Play: Game Design Fundamentals*, Cambridge, MA: MIT Press.

Scacchi, W. (2010) Computer game mods, modders, modding, and the mod scene, *First Monday*, 15(5), http://firstmonday.org/htbin/cgiwrap/bin/ojs/index.php/fm/article/view/2965.

Schroeder, R., Huxor, A., and Smith, A. (2001) Activeworlds: geography and social interaction in virtual reality, *Futures*, 33(7): 569–87.

Schultze, U. and Orlikowski, W.J. (2010) Virtual worlds: a performative perspective on globally distributed, immersive work, *Information Systems Research*, 21(4): 810–21.

Scott, R.W. (1995) *Institutions and Organizations*, Thousand Oaks, CA: Sage Publications.

Shirky, C. (2008) *Here Comes Everybody: How Change Happens when People Come Together*, London: Allen Lane.

Spence, J. (2008) Demographics of virtual worlds, *Journal of Virtual Worlds Research*, 1(2), http://journals.tdl.org/jvwr/index.php/jvwr/article/viewArticle/360.

Stephenson, N. (1992) *Snow Crash*, New York: Bantam Books.

Taylor, T.L. (1999) Life in virtual worlds: plural existence, multimodalities, and other online research challenges, *American Behavioral Scientist*, 43(3): 436–49.

Taylor, T.L. (2009) The assemblage of play, *Games and Culture* 4(4): 331–9.

Thornton, P. H., and Ocasio, W. (2008) Institutional logics, in R. Greenwood, C. Oliver, K. Sahlin and R. Suddaby (eds), *Sage Handbook of Organizational Institutionalism*, London, Sage Publications: pp. 99–129.

Thornton, P. H., Ocasio, W. and Lounsbury, M. (2012) *The Institutional Logics Perspective: A New Approach to Culture, Structure, and Process*, Oxford: Oxford University Press.

Tschang, F.T. (2007) Balancing the tensions between rationalization and creativity in the video games industry, *Organization Science*, 18(6): 989–1005.

Tschang, F.T. and Comas, J. (2010) Developing virtual worlds: the interplay of design, communities and rationalities, *First Monday*, 15(5), http://firstmonday.org/htbin/cgiwrap/bin/ojs/index.php/fm/article/view/2957/2525.

Turkle, S. (1995) *Life on the Screen: Identity in the Age of the Internet*, New York: Simon & Schuster.

Virtual Worlds. Second Life (2012), http://www.spacetoday.org/VirtualWorlds/SecondLife.html.

Wenger, E. (1998) *Communities of Practice*, Cambridge: Cambridge University Press.

Yee, N. (2009) Changing the rules: social architectures in virtual worlds, in W. Bainbridge (ed.), *Online Worlds: Convergence of the Real and Virtual*, London: Springer, pp. 213–23.

Index

GPSR Compliance
The European Union's (EU) General Product Safety Regulation (GPSR) is a set
of rules that requires consumer products to be safe and our obligations to
ensure this.

If you have any concerns about our products, you can contact us on

ProductSafety@springernature.com

In case Publisher is established outside the EU, the EU authorized
representative is:

Springer Nature Customer Service Center GmbH
Europaplatz 3
69115 Heidelberg, Germany